CW01573038

Claire

Solving the Management Case

The Marketing Series is one of the most comprehensive collections of books in marketing and sales available from the UK today.

Published by Butterworth-Heinemann on behalf of the Chartered Institute of Marketing, the series is divided into three distinct groups: *Student* (fulfilling the needs of those taking the Institute's certificate and diploma qualifications); *Professional Development* (for those on formal or self-study vocational training programmes); and *Practitioner* (presented in a more informal, motivating and highly practical manner for the busy marketer).

Formed in 1911, the Chartered Institute of Marketing is now the largest professional marketing management body in Europe with over 22,000 members and 25,000 students located worldwide. Its primary objectives are focused on the development of awareness and understanding of marketing throughout UK industry and commerce and on the raising of standards of professionalism in the education, training and practice of this key business discipline.

Books in the series

Solving the Management Case

**Angela Hatton, Paul Roberts
and Mike Worsam**

*Published in association with
the Chartered Institute of Marketing*

BUTTERWORTH
HEINEMANN

Butterworth-Heinemann Ltd
Linacre House, Jordan Hill, Oxford OX2 8DP

 PART OF REED INTERNATIONAL BOOKS

OXFORD   LONDON   BOSTON
MUNICH   NEW DELHI   SINGAPORE   SYDNEY
TOKYO   TORONTO   WELLINGTON

First published 1992
Reprinted 1993

© Angela Hatton, Paul Roberts and Mike Worsam 1992

All rights reserved. No part of this publication
may be reproduced in any material form (including
photocopying or storing in any medium by electronic
means and whether or not transiently or incidentally
to some other use of this publication) without the
written permission of the copyright holder except
in accordance with the provisions of the Copyright,
Designs and Patents Act 1988 or under the terms of a
licence issued by the Copyright Licensing Agency Ltd,
90 Tottenham Court Road, London, England W1P 9HE.
Applications for the copyright holder's written permission
to reproduce any part of this publication should be addressed
to the publishers.

British Library Cataloguing in Publication Data
Hatton, Angela
    Solving the management case. – (The marketing
series)
    I. Title   II. Roberts, Paul   III. Worsam, Mike
    IV. Series
    658.4

ISBN 0 7506 0196 5

Photoset in Great Britain by Redwood Press Limited, Melksham, Wiltshire
Printed in Great Britain by M & A Thomson Litho Ltd, East Kilbride, Scotland

CONTENTS

PREFACE

Do you want to improve your management skills? Know more about the process of management? 'Crack' a case study?

You may be new to general management, studying management as part of a professional or academic qualification, or simply interested in learning more about the business of management. Whatever your background or experience, the practical and down-to-earth approach in this book will help you in your business and everyday life where planning, decisions and control are just as important.

Compiled as a practical guide for working managers, Parts One and Two offer a 'user's guide' and overview of the key *management tools*. Part One includes practical hints and tips to help in the effective use of the manager's toolbox. From techniques for analysis through strategy development and decision-making to report writing and presentation, this guide is supported by examples and exercises developed to improve the skills of management. Part Two offers summaries and reviews of key techniques, activities and tools from across the business spectrum. It is not intended to be an exhaustive glossary of management and marketing terminology; simply an *aide-mémoire*, which will be of value as a quick reference guide.

Part Three demonstrates a systematic approach to the development of a management problem, a systematic approach that is based upon a proven sequence which moves smoothly through the processes of analysis and decision, planning and control. The approach is easy to understand, the tools are explained in careful detail; the technique is easy to learn and invaluable.

For the management student the book provides a valuable ongoing reference but, in particular, shows how to 'crack' a case study. The case study is a well-proven method of teaching and examining management, since it mirrors very closely the problems faced by managers in the world outside the classroom. Many students have problems when faced with a case study, but quite needlessly. Pass rates of the highest order have been achieved by students of the Chartered Institute of Marketing when using the sequential method that is worked through in detail in Part Three. It is effective on all case studies, whether they be at MBA level or 'mini cases' used as part of an examination paper.

The same 'case study' sequence provides the working manager with a practical and systematic methodology for effectively tackling management problems. Together, the three sections provide a practical handbook and an invaluable reference guide for management.

The book is positioned so that it can be used for self-study by individuals and as a class text for those studying management – in which case we recommend that the material be covered early in the course.

A.H.
P.R.
M.W.

ACKNOWLEDGEMENTS

Target Group Index data is used with the kind permission of the British Marketing Research Bureau (BMRB). We would also like to thank Center Parcs for kindly allowing us to quote material from their brochure and NOP Market Research for kindly allowing us to reproduce material from their British Tourism Survey.

Part One

The Tools of Management

1 *The toolbox*

Most books on management fall into one of three categories:

- How I became successful – hints and tips to follow.
- Themes of the moment to adopt – excellence, quality etc.
- Texts – thorough analyses of aspects of management through the perception of an academic.

This book is in a fourth category; it works only with key underlying principles upon which success is founded. It shows how you can use those principles. It is pragmatic; you will not be distracted by unnecessary theory (although you will find references to the theory should you care to explore).

Few attempts are made to examine alternative methods of achieving the same end. We do not really care whether we drive a Ford, a Peugeot or a Rover – we *are* concerned with our car's function. Will it do the job? Neither are we concerned with deep knowledge. Thus what goes on under the bonnet of our car is something better left to the specialists. All we really need to know, as drivers, is whether the car takes leaded or unleaded petrol (or diesel) – and where to put it in. We need to know about oil, water and about tyre pressures. We must have a guided tour of the controls, and some practice in driving under the various conditions we are likely to meet. As a driver we are unlikely to need to know how the car works. Nor how to fix it. We will, of course, have an emergency call-out service on 24-hour availability.

Similarly, as managers we are unlikely to need to know how a specialist function works. We need to know what it can do, and what budget is reasonable to achieve a given objective – but to know the detail is as redundant as a driver knowing how to set the timing or how to adjust the carburettor.

We have to be careful too, because we will have come to management from a specialist area. We may have a financial background, come from marketing, production, or from any of the specialist areas. As a manager *even within a specialism* we must be careful not to let that specialism blind us to the abilities and potentials of others.

Management is a craft skill – although it is not often thought of as such. The secret for success in any craft (or business) lies in the individual's knowledge of the subject and in the skilled use of the tools of the trade. Plumbers, electricians and joiners all have their own toolbox and are expert in the use of the tools within it. They have a detailed understanding of their specialist area, they do not need a detailed understanding of other areas.

General foremen, however, do need a general understanding of all areas. In whatever craft or trade they originally trained they now must be able to manage specialists from other crafts and trades, to blend the whole team so that a contract is completed effectively. It is not important to be able to do the job of the specialists – but it is vital to know *what to expect* from the specialists; to know what to expect (and demand) in terms of quality against time, in what order to call for specialist input, and to know the key indicators that show how well a job is progressing (figure 1.1).

The business world also has its tools, the tools of the functional specialists. Accounts, marketing, production, administration, distribution, personnel have many and varied

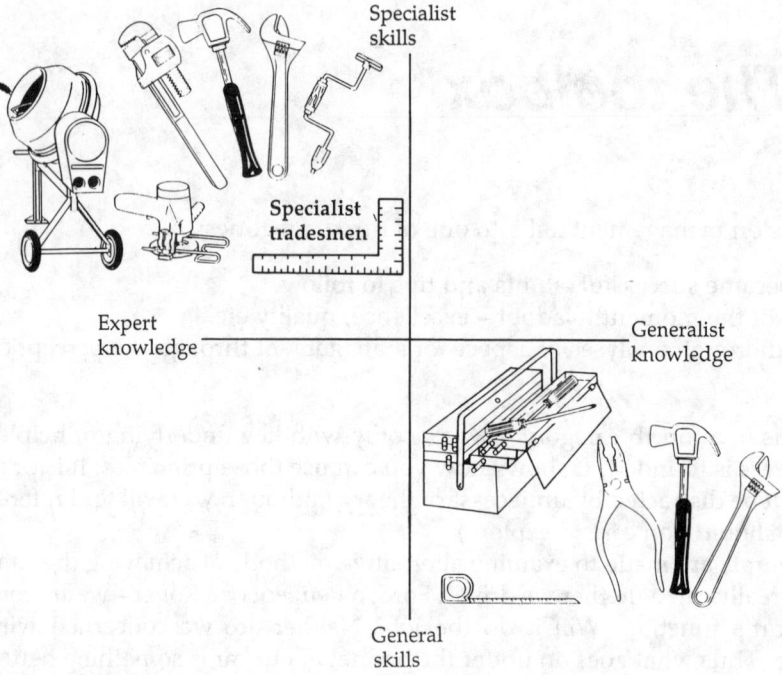

Figure 1.1

specialist skills – and each attracts people with a certain type of personality and motivation. Each of the main areas of specialism is subdivided in just the same way as 'wood workers' are divided into *joiners* who make and *carpenters* who fix. Joiners are supported by wood machinists and carpenters subdivide into form workers, first and second fixers, finishers and maintainers.

The training required to perform competently in these business areas takes as many years as an apprenticeship for a craft. A manager needs training to know the tools of the trade and to develop skills in their use. The manager's toolbox is a briefcase; the tools are creative, analytical and evaluative (figure 1.2). As with the foreman, the manager needs to identify and achieve tasks, to know when and how to call in specialists, to generate positive motivation.

Managers do not usually think in terms of tools, but the various creative techniques, SWOT analyses, report writing and presentations are everyday tools that the most successful managers are very skilled at using. In fact they are used so routinely that they come to be regarded as 'simple common sense'. They appear so, of course, once they have been learned. Their habitual use ensures that they are often not recognized as skills that can be identified, and learned. So they are not skills that a manager thinks necessary to break down into components and learn. 'Managers are born, not made...', 'I came up the hard way...' – such comments reveal the true level of misunderstanding that underlie the abysmally low level of management training in the UK.

This book will help you to shop around the specialist management areas selecting the various tools that the general manager needs in his or her briefcase. We will show you how and when they can and/or should be used and provide you with opportunities to

What tools do you find when you unpack the manager's briefcase?

Figure 1.2 *The manager's toolbox*

gain practical skill in their application. Like any craft expert, use will only come with practice – so the book provides opportunities for you to develop both your knowledge and your skills.

How to use this book

Part One is subdivided into the four main areas of management work – analysis, strategy development, decision-making and control, persuasion. Different chapters examine the key management tools and give guidance as to how and when they should be used. Each chapter is self-contained, but you cannot afford to be selective. The good manager needs a basic competence across a width of specialist areas. The tools described in Part One are needed when tackling a management problem or cracking a case study.

Think of yourself as a gifted do-it-yourself builder with a need for general knowledge across a wide range of skills. You need to be able to lay bricks, but not dig foundations; to replace a tap, but not run a new water main; to add a power socket to a supply, but not to re-wire a house. Concentrate simply on getting enough knowledge and skills to do your job effectively. Then open up to the additional knowledge and skills you will need to advance your career (figure 1.3).

Throughout Part One you will find terms in bold type (e.g. **budgeting**). This indicates that further information about the term can be found in Part Two, which is arranged alphabetically. Part Two enables you quickly to refresh your memory and to review the management implications of key topics.

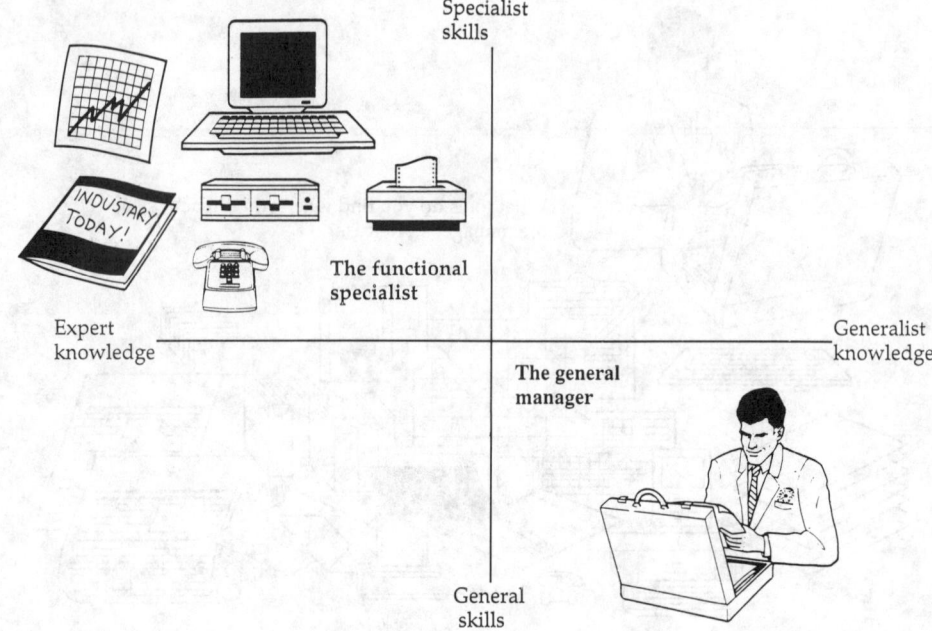

Figure 1.3

Part Three addresses a management problem in the form of a case study. It provides you with a process, a systematic method of work which can be universally applied in management – we call it the Sequence. A process is needed as a basis for the management discipline that will ensure quality work. Without a framework the approach is likely to be *ad hoc* and unreliable. Serious errors and omissions will occur and the end result will be in doubt.

Managers work into the future. They are very much concerned with taking their entities forward. Of course they have a great deal of interest in current results, and some concern for history; but their prime interest is in planning and organizing for the future. It follows that they are constantly working to forecast the future – and the future is notoriously fickle. It is therefore necessary to anticipate as many contingencies as reasonable, and to provide for them when setting up management plans.

What is a case study?

A management training case study is simply a chunk of real life that has been extracted from its context and written up as a series of documents. The technique is widely used, and is effective, simply because good case studies have a ring of truth – they come from reality, and it shows.

Why are there case study examinations?

How can a manager's abilities be tested? Obviously not through theoretical answers in an examination room. These test knowledge recall, not skill. Yet there has to be a test, otherwise how can a qualification be awarded? The answer is an examination based upon a real life situation, an exam where each candidate is presented with the facts about an entity, given a role within it and up to a month to become thoroughly familiar with the material. A case study, in fact. By such means it is possible to test practical ability to make reasoned, and reasonable, management decisions; and to test the candidate's ability to communicate in a management report.

A typical example is the Analysis and Decision (Case Study) paper set by the Chartered Institute of Marketing. They say:

> The aim of this paper is to extend the practice of candidates in the qualitative and quantitative analysis of marketing situations, both to develop their powers of diagnosis and as a contribution to the creation of firm bases for decision-making. Candidates should be able to:
>
> 1 Identify, define and rank the problem(s) contained in marketing case studies.
> 2 Formulate working hypotheses regarding the solution(s) to problems identified in marketing case studies.
> 3 Assemble, order, analyse and interpret both qualitative and quantitative data relating to a marketing case, using appropriate analytical procedures and models.
> 4 Describe and substantiate all working assumptions made regarding the case problem(s) working hypotheses and data.
> 5 Generate and evaluate the expected outcomes of alternate solutions to case problem(s).
> 6 Formulate recommendations for action and feedback on case problem(s).
> 7 Prepare and present appropriate marketing case reports.

All managers are concerned with every one of the seven CIM requirements, whatever their functional responsibility. Probably marketing is more immediately concerned with the future than other functional specialists, although the financial managers may well argue a strong case. Concern for the future tends to grow with seniority rather than function.

All managers should be concerned more with planning for the future than with supervising the present. If the planning has been done thoroughly, the present should take care of itself. Operational staff exist, in the main, to take care of the present and the immediate future, to free their seniors to take a more strategic view.

It is difficult to find one term that encompasses all the forms of organization in which managers work. Management is a universal skill that adjusts to the particular needs of a situation. Managers are found in HM Forces, in charity work, in public service, in commerce, everywhere in fact where results have to be achieved. To prevent the range of terminology becoming confusing, and to avoid wearisome explanations, we have chosen to use the term that sits most conveniently within each context that we cover. Please read from the viewpoint of your own requirement and background, adjusting 'business', 'company', 'concern', 'entity', 'firm', 'organization' etc. to the term with which you are comfortable.

Maximize your learning

Management is not just a body of knowledge, it is a skilled craft. An individual manager will be judged by how he or she applies management expertise. Developing skills takes time and effort. To maximize your benefit from this book it should not be read from cover to cover in a short burst of activity. Take time to be guided and do undertake the activities – this is a working manual, not a text book.

Practice develops skills
and reinforces knowledge

2 *Management information – the raw material*

The manager needs an understanding of the quality and quantity of information available in the same way that a joiner needs an appreciation of the nature and characteristics of wood. Information is the raw material used by managers.

Management involves decision-making, in a wide variety of contexts, and information is fundamental to the process of decision-making. Without information managers are forced to work blind, relying only on guesswork and 'gut feel'. In such circumstances the **risk** of getting it wrong is high and success becomes a matter of chance and luck rather than skill and judgement. Calculated risks and objective decisions are dependent on reliable and relevant information.

Having the right information available at the right time is therefore an essential prerequisite for effective management. **Information** is found in **data** and the terms should not be confused. Data needs refining and sorting to turn it into reliable and usable information.

Management Information Systems often exist within organizations to provide a flow of relevant information to management. To get the most from the information available, managers need a thorough appreciation of the sources, the costs, limitations and uses of the information. Unfortunately the information resource is frequently misunderstood and mis-used. It is an aid to decision-making *not* a replacement for it.

Good managers do not take important decisions lightly nor accept more risk than necessary. They have control and feedback information which allow them to know when corrective measures are needed. Decision-making will always entail risks, and managers do not achieve a 100 per cent success rate. They will 'get it wrong' as much as 40 per cent of the time. Good managers understand and accept this, and demand information so that risk is reduced to an acceptable level. They will also move very fast when control information indicates that corrective action is needed.

Information users – the stereotypes

The 'gut feel' manager

This manager fears that using information may in some way devalue his or her reputation as a decision-maker. Additional information is shunned in favour of reliance on experience and hunch.

Such managers make the job unnecessarily difficult by reducing their options. Working in blinkers is guaranteed to give tunnel vision!

The procrastinating manager

A lack of information is used by this manager as an excuse for not making a decision. He or she is constantly asking for additional data (not information). Collecting data takes time and money, so this manager wastes resources *and* is in danger both of missing opportunities and of gaining a reputation as indecisive.

The 'can't decide' manager

Information is not handled well by this manager. Instead of throwing light onto the situation it confuses rather than clarifies; it provides apparently conflicting evidence which hinders rather than helps decision-making.

Such managers allow themselves to be manipulated by information. Frequently they are faced with masses of information and data, which are impossible to assimilate. A failure to critically assess data and information, coupled with inadequate research briefings, are common faults in the 'can't decide' manager.

Note: In any situation where there genuinely is nothing between two options, toss a coin to decide. Further time spent on the decision will be a waste of resources. But be sure to monitor the results very closely, and be prepared to take remedial action if needed.

The information balance

None of these stereotypes represents a professional management approach to information – the key lies in finding the information balance. Information aids decision-making, because reliable and relevant information reduces the risk of making the wrong decision. Theoretically if you could be perfectly informed you would be bound to make the right judgement. The problem is that information takes time to acquire and, like all other resources, it bears a financial cost. Pre-thinking the information that is going to be needed can ensure that it is available when required – and that costs are minimized.

An organization that uses its available information resources effectively can gain a competitive advantage:

- by reducing the number of 'wrong' decisions;
- by having an advanced early warning system of market changes and so being able to respond rapidly to opportunities and to threats;
- by providing managers with a system to monitor organizational health.

Investment in the information resource can maximize the use of existing information, improve both the quality and quantity of available information and bring forward new information. Management training, computerization and an increase in the external **secondary data** available have helped to improve the sophistication of the management information potentially available.

The price of information

Although better information is desirable, it does not come cheap. More information = more cost.

The price tag for information comes not only in pounds or dollars, but also in the time taken to collect it. Waiting for information can delay decisions. Collecting information can sometimes give the competitors clues about proposed strategy. The cost in loss of competitive edge and missed market opportunities can be high, far higher than the price of pre-thinking need. Managers have to take all costs into account when weighing up the need for more information. These management considerations are sometimes referred to using the mnemonic CATS – cost, accuracy, timing and security (see **marketing research**).

Assessing the need for information

- Evaluate the significance of the decision.
- Evaluate the risk involved in the decision.
- Assess the reliability and relevance of available information.
- Calculate the information gap.
- Consider the information balance.

Evaluating the significance and risk

Calculating the significance of a decision is subjective. A useful starting point is to consider the consequences. What will happen if I get it wrong?

A large scale investment or a long term commitment is a more important decision than one involving small sums or limited commitment. Therefore a decision to build a new factory requires more information and thought than a decision to redecorate an office.

- Management can fall into the trap of treating all decisions as of the same importance.
- Assessing the significance of decisions and treating them accordingly is an essential management discipline.

The degree of risk is related to the significance of the decision, the uncertainty involved and the familiarity of the situation. Crossing the road is a significant decision, the consequences of getting it wrong can be serious, but it is a decision we make routinely so our familiarity with the situation reduces the risk involved. Actuaries and bookmakers are recognized as professional risk evaluators, but quantifying risk is an equally important element in the work of a manager.

Having considered the significance of the decision, the risk involved in taking it can be quantified. Techniques are available for use, but there is no over-riding simple formula which can be applied. It is very much a matter for the practising manager, often in consultation, to take a considered view on the element of risk involved. Thinking objectively through the decision process as part of the process of risk calculation is an excellent management discipline that has the added benefit of throwing up inconsistencies and omissions – especially if one is presenting the case to one or more colleagues.

ACTIVITY

Choose a scale against which you feel you can grade the risk factor of all the decisions you make. A simple 1–10 scale is fine. By consciously calculating the risk involved in each decision, and relating results to your initial thinking, you will become better and better at assessing risk. You will also be able to measure your own performance.

Assessing existing information

Information will almost certainly be already available. This needs to be identified and carefully assessed. Existing information needs to be checked for:

- reliability – can the source and collection method be identified?
    - is the information trustworthy *for your purpose*?
- relevance – is the information up to date?
    - does it use definitions and parameters which are relevant?

It is always good to organize information into schematics and diagrams to make it easier to use, but be sure you take decisions on the numbers rather than on their pictorial representation (see **gee wiz statistics**).

Only if it passes the tests of reliability and relevance should the information be used. It is possible that this existing information will be adequate to allow the decision to be made, but if it is not the collection of **primary data** will have to be considered.

Note the word 'adequate'. All a manager needs is adequate information – sufficient for the actual need. It is tempting to call for complete information, but unless this is really needed it is not justified.

Calculating the information gap

Identify what information is needed to get the decision right, or at least to reduce the risk to an acceptable level. Identify the information that is available. If it falls short of need you have an information gap.

Draw up a list of additional information requirements. These should then be carefully reviewed. Is this information essential to the decision? Is it *need to know*, or *nice to know* information? Do not be afraid to ask the questions Why? and How?

- Why do we want it?
- How will we use it?

Too much information

- No time to make decisions
- Managers are confused, distracted by the amount of information
- Information gets missed!

Figure 2.1   *The information balance – too much*

Once a list of needed additional information is available it is possible to assess the cost of obtaining it. By comparing the costs against the benefits the manager is in a position to decide on the correct information balance.

Considering the information balance

Too much (figure 2.1)
This is typical of the 'can't decide' manager.

Too little (figure 2.2)
Getting the balance right means weighing up the costs of more information against the risks involved. This represents the balance of the 'gut feel' manager.

Just right (figure 2.3)
The skill of achieving an information balance lies in being able to identify when you have enough information to make a sufficiently informed decision. This represents the risk-evaluating manager.

In many cases decisions have to be made without sufficient information. Either the facts required are not available, can only be obtained after the deadline for the decision, or at prohibitive cost. Management is a pragmatic art, and if the information is not available the decision still has to be made. As with a 50:50 decision one should monitor the results of this kind of decision especially closely.

Not enough information

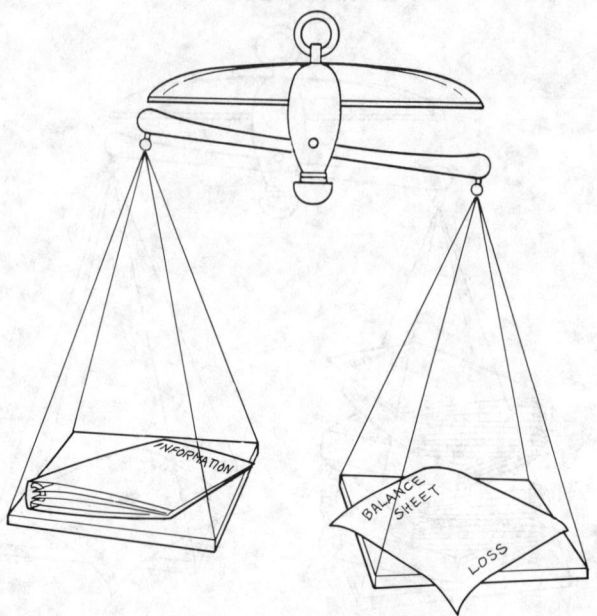

- Business success depends on luck!
- Decisions are uninformed
- Risk of getting it wrong is high

Figure 2.2 *The information balance – too little*

The information balance

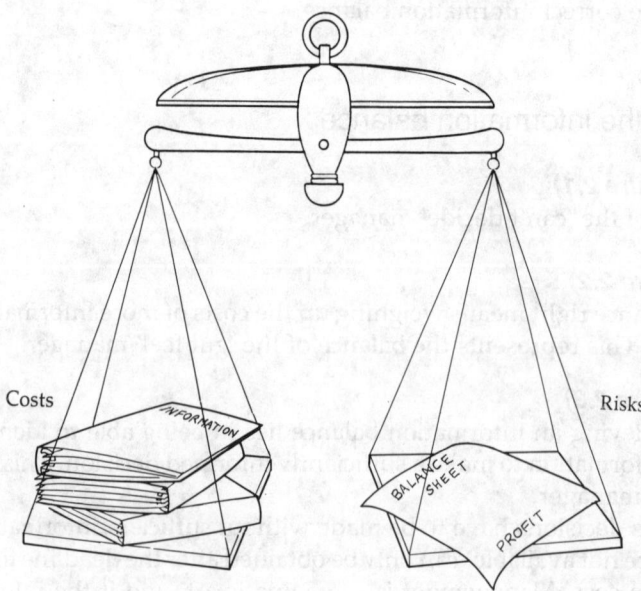

Costs   Risks

Figure 2.3 *The information balance – in balance*

Mistakes

Every manager makes mistakes. It cannot be helped. In the practical working environment there is pressure to make a constant stream of decisions, some large, some small. In almost every case there is insufficient information available *at the time the decision must be made*. Thus the manager has to use his or her best judgement. It is not possible to be right every time.

You can rate your decisions in much the same way that sportsmen and women maintain records of performance. Yardsticks of achievement are:

	Percentage of correct decisions
Reasonable	55
Good	60–65
Excellent	65–70
Superb	70–80
Untruthful	80+

The safeguard that makes a reasonable decision-maker into a valuable manager is his or her ability to take corrective action, quickly. This applies to all managers; it is essential to have **control** on decisions. This ensures that the results of the actions that follow the decision are reported back in time for corrective action. Thus a good manager is constantly making decisions, monitoring the results and making amendments.

The information gap and case studies

Management students working on case studies constantly request more information. Case studies are not absolute replicas of the real world and there are some limitations with their use, including this information restriction. Information gaps exist, but there is little opportunity to fill them – you may in fact be prohibited from seeking additional information from that given in the case.

There is no point in getting frustrated by this, the rules are the same for all. It will help to think of yourself as a management consultant receiving a first briefing by post, without recourse to any further information. In many cases you will, in fact, be given the role of a consultant and in reality information is often withheld from consultants, at least until they have won the trust of the client company.

So how do you handle the information gap?

- Identify clearly what information you want and have not got. Are you sure you need it? Remember to make the distinction between need to know, and nice to know information.
- Assess the cost/benefit of collecting this information.
- Remember that marketing research (MR) is an investment in the information resource and should be approached with the same care as any other investment decision.

- Consider the process for providing the missing information to the organization and be able to make clear recommendations for filling the information gap.

Unless the manager is going to undertake the research personally, there will be another party involved in the process of filling the information gap. This may be a member of an internal research department, or an external agency.

Success is dependent on developing a close working relationship from the outset. The nature of the problem has to be clearly thought through and the type, accuracy and speed with which information is needed clearly identified in order that the researcher can produce a realistic proposal (figure 2.4).

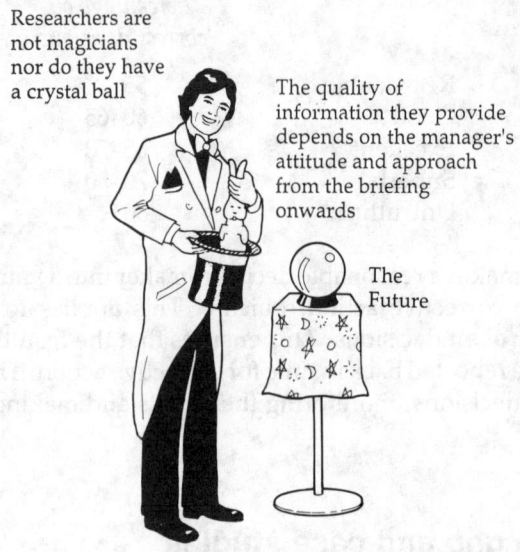

Researchers are not magicians nor do they have a crystal ball

The quality of information they provide depends on the manager's attitude and approach from the briefing onwards

The Future

Figure 2.4

The research process is not like a tap which can be switched on and off to provide instant responses whenever they are required. Both manager and researcher have their role to play in the marketing research process (figures 2.5, 2.6). If the channels of communication are kept open and each party understands the other's role, the research process should successfully provide a valuable information infill.

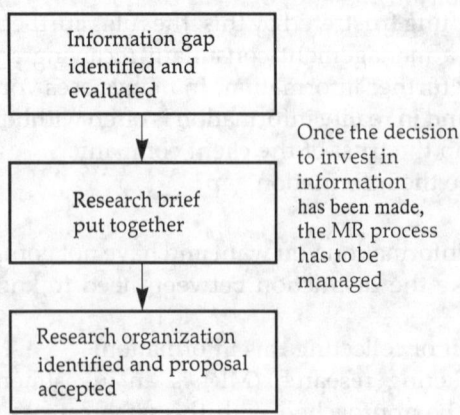

Information gap identified and evaluated

Research brief put together

Research organization identified and proposal accepted

Once the decision to invest in information has been made, the MR process has to be managed

Figure 2.5   *The manager's role in research*

The research brief

One of the key elements of the research process is the quality of the research brief. Preparing a brief for an external agency is an essential skill for the manager.

Checklist for a research brief

1 Clear definition of the problem being examined.
2 Background to the problem and any information currently available.
3 Objectives of the research – as a basis for discussion and agreement with the researcher.
4 Constraints: costs; accuracy; time; security.

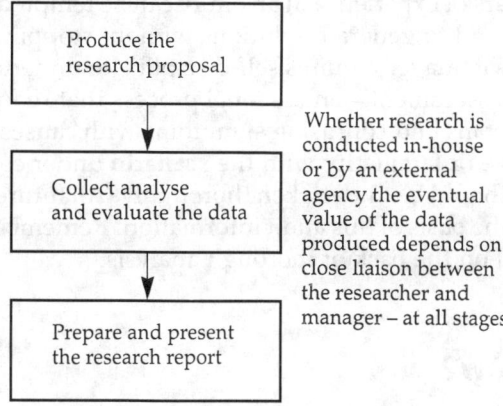

Whether research is conducted in-house or by an external agency the eventual value of the data produced depends on close liaison between the researcher and manager – at all stages

Figure 2.6 *The researcher's role*

ACTIVITIES

1 Keep a log this month of the information which is made available to you – reports, printouts, cuttings and journals. How many do you read? How many do you use?

Is your information balance correct?

List five ways in which the quality or quantity of information available to you could be improved. Do your best to make the changes that are needed.

2 Select two major personal purchase decisions you have made recently. Quantify the risks involved at the time of decision, and assess the size of your information gaps at the time of decision.

Determine how effective your decisions were, and whether the time and cost of obtaining further information would have been justified.

To take decisions in conditions of uncertainty
requires confidence – and an effective
system of monitoring and control

(see chapter 8)

3   *Taking stock*

The first step on any journey is the most difficult. Knowing where and how to get started is often the most daunting aspect of any task. Management consultants meeting a new client and students faced with a new case study scenario have some advantage over the practising manager. For them, faced with the unfamiliar, the first step is obvious – they have to take stock of the current situation and familiarize themselves with the salient details.

A manager with years of experience in an entity can be tempted to take short cuts, to jump to conclusions, and to generate solutions without stopping to analyse the situation objectively. This manager requires self-discipline to undertake the process of an audit. An **audit** is an assessment – an essential process that reduces the possibility of overlooking crucial details and confusing symptoms with causes.

Whatever the degree of familiarity with the **scenario** under consideration, the first step of 'taking stock' should be undertaken thoroughly. All future strategies and plans will be developed on the basis of this audit information. Remember that effective plans can only be generated on the back of thorough analysis.

Where are we now?

A management audit is carried out in order to clarify the present position. It is conducted to provide an answer to the question 'Where are we now?' The first point in this process is agreeing who 'we' are.

Are 'we' the entity, or a department or function within the entity? It is equally valid to audit the position of a brand or of an individual, or to consider the merits of alternative strategies. There are no constraints in using the technique, only a necessity to be clear about the focus. Thus audits can be carried out for the business as a whole, or for any part of it. In such cases it is usual to refer to them as 'marketing audits' 'distribution audits', and so on.

Once the scope of the audit has been confirmed, undertaking the process involves collecting and interpreting all the relevant **information** available to you.

- With a case study this information is likely to be contained in the text or video provided. Sometimes one can research additional material, often not. It is important to read and understand the briefing notes that accompany the case.
- The consultant or manager will need to seek out relevant information, to build his or her own case study as it were, from both internal and external sources. The aim should be to build up a clear picture based on current knowledge and available information.

Collecting information is one thing, making sense of it another. A systematic approach is required to help you sort the available information so that you grasp the relative importance of a variety of factors and can assess their relevance to the situation you are considering. One popular and flexible technique, the SWOT analysis, is so useful in helping to assess a situation and to compare alternatives that it is recommended as the prime tool of analysis.

SWOT analysis

SWOT is the acronym for Strengths, Weaknesses, Opportunities and Threats. A SWOT analysis helps managers to identify key issues to provide:

- A working summary of key facts, a snapshot of the scenario under investigation.
- A focus on what needs to be tackled.
- An awareness of the relevant opportunities and possible threats.

A SWOT framework is a **matrix** that allows all factors to be categorized under the four headings. Strengths and Weaknesses are always paired, as are Opportunities and Threats (figure 3.1).

A commonly used approach for creating a SWOT analysis is to divide a page into four quadrants and to note key factors under the appropriate sections. These should be brief summaries or notes which then become points of reference.

Strengths and weaknesses
These will be internal factors which are controllable and things which management can do something about, e.g. the available capacity of the operation, the staff turnover or the reputation/image of the organization.

Opportunities and threats
These are external factors which cannot be changed by management. These uncontrollable factors make up the external environment in which the organization operates. Changes in this environment have to be responded to if long term survival and success is to be ensured.

In order to avoid overlooking possibly important issues when undertaking an analysis it is advisable to produce personal checklists of factors that need to be considered in a

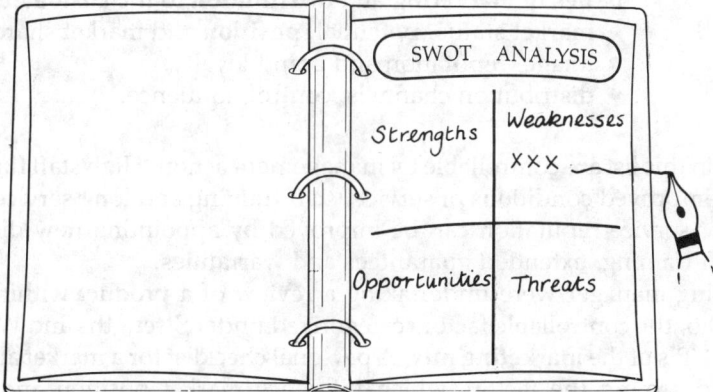

Figure 3.1 *SWOT schematic*

SWOT. These references will be an invaluable addition to your personal toolbox. They are personal because they reflect your predisposition to approach a task in a certain way. In management we are dealing more with an art than a science, and the personality of each manager is unique and therefore rather special.

Beware of allowing your preference to approach a problem in a certain way to colour your reaction to it. Personal bias must be guarded against at all times. You have to be objective in every analysis.

Strengths and weaknesses: internal analysis

Note that the factors which are relevant will vary according to the standpoint from which the analysis is conducted. At corporate level the controllable factors are related to the elements that make up the business as a whole. These can easily be remembered by using the 5 Ms:

Men:
All factors related to human resources:
- staff expertise, numbers, levels, turnover;
- management, style, skills, expertise;
- industrial relations, morale, **motivation**;
- organization, **structure**, internal communications.

Money:
All factors relevant to the financial health of the organization;
- **cash flow**, profitability, **forecasts**;
- credit rating, assets, image with shareholders and financiers;
- financial backing, support, available funding.

Machinery:
Operational factors:
- operational capacity and efficiency;
- **quality** control;
- technological position, **research and development**.

Materials:
Purchasing and suppliers factors:
- suppliers' reliability, flexibility, exclusivity, **value**;
- stock levels and logistics of distribution;
- **costs**, internal and external sources.

Markets:
Issues of **marketing** and **distribution** to the **customers**:
- market status, potential, **position** and market share;
- image, reputation and brand loyalty;
- distribution channels, control, influence.

The factors in this list are controllable by management action. High staff turnover can be tackled by improved conditions of service, staff training and long service incentive schemes. Poor service reputation can be improved by appointing new distributors, improved staff training, extended guarantees and warranties.

If a marketing manager were undertaking a review of a product within the company's portfolio, the controllable factors categorized under Strengths and Weaknesses would be the 4 'P's of the **marketing mix**. A personal checklist for a market audit would be constructed around the factors which influence market position and customer demand:

- Product
- Place
- Price
- Promotion

As with the 5 Ms of the corporate review these 4 Ps cover the variables which can be changed by management action.

It is often difficult to decide whether a characteristic is actually a Strength or a Weakness. This may seem odd, but as you work with examples you will find that many obvious strengths actually have compensating weaknesses. To deal with this situation, firstly ensure that all the information available is considered in the context of the situation under analysis. If that does not clarify the position note the aspect of that characteristic which is a Strength and the counterbalancing aspect that is a Weakness.

Exclusive distribution can be a:

- Strength – it contributes to a prestige image;
- Weakness – limited availability limits sales potential.

Classification is often a subjective matter, not one to be concerned about provided a consistency of approach has been adopted and all relevant factors have been considered.

Good management requires plans which capitalize on strengths and tackle significant weaknesses – a clear grasp of the key issues *in context* is essential. The purpose of the analysis is to get the issues down on paper; judgements about their relative significance in the context of proposed strategies should be made later.

Opportunities and threats: external analysis

Organizations are part of the wider environment in which they operate. Decisions must take account of current and predicted changes in that environment. The 'opportunities and threats' classification of a SWOT analysis focuses management's attention on the variables which are *external* to the organization and therefore uncontrollable by management action.

The uncontrollable variables which require monitoring are sometimes referred to as the *macro-environmental factors*.

- Demographics: Changes in population: numbers, location and age/sex breakdowns. Affects the size of market segments.
- Law and politics: All changes in legislation relating to operations or customers. Political changes, e.g. Europe 1992, wars, political trade embargoes.
- Economics: Factors affecting the income levels of any market segment (including the public sector). Rates of interest, inflation, employment levels, availability of credit, etc.
- Technology: As it influences goods demanded and production methods.
- Culture: Influences customer behaviour and attitudes. Fashion, religion and social factors are all influencers, e.g. the green movement and the changing attitudes to work and leisure.

Competitors' activity must be added to this list, as their actions can also represent both opportunities and threats to the organization and cannot be controlled by management.

Changes can and should be viewed as *both* Opportunities and Threats. Higher interest rates and higher inflation may be threats in terms of their impact on costs and aggregate consumer demand, but they also provide the opportunity to offer 'value for money' products. Managers need to take a positive attitude to environmental change and make a point of looking for the opportunities associated with any apparent threat.

Sometimes changes in the macro-environment occur suddenly – hurricanes, earthquakes and droughts often hit with little or no warning. Political and economic crises are equally dramatic, and often as hard to predict – the oil crisis in the early 1970s, the dramatic changes in Eastern Europe in 1989/90, the abrupt departure of Margaret Thatcher from the Prime Ministership of the UK. Management has to be alert and flexible to adapt and modify plans in the light of changed circumstances. **Contingency planning** is a necessary part of good management.

Other environmental changes can be predicted. The changes brought about by freeing trade within the EC (1992 and the Single Market), shifts in population, economic developments and legislative changes, are all identifiable in advance. The most successful entities are those whose managers recognize the likely changes and plan for them ahead of time. Those that have *pro-active* management.

Firms who wait 'to see what will happen' are *re-active* in their approach and their entities are less likely to thrive. Developing and implementing strategic responses takes time and market opportunities do not last for long. A risk strategy is a necessary part of every manager's toolbox.

Techniques like scenario planning have been developed to help managers produce alternative strategies and action plans ahead of potential changes. Speedy responses are critical to the success, and often the survival, of organizations working in rapidly changing markets. Failure to adapt to the environment leads to failure and possible extinction.

Undertaking a regular situational analysis allows managers to recognize and respond to significant environmental changes. Successful organizations are those which monitor the environment, forecast changes, and are pro-active in their strategic responses.

Undertaking a SWOT analysis

SWOT is a tool for sorting key facts and issues – it allows work to be organized in summary format that suits the needs of the individual manager, is comfortable to work with and can be referred to easily. There is no right or wrong way to do a SWOT, nor is there a right or wrong time to use one.

The technique of dividing a page into four quadrants is useful, quick and simple to carry through. It can be used on a flip chart or board when working with a group, or on a sheet of A4 when alone. Whenever a position needs to be clarified it is appropriate to consider a SWOT. The technique should become second nature to you. When embarking on a new project, getting to grips with a case study, evaluating optional courses of action at work or in private life a SWOT is the best tool we know for helping to clarify relevant factors and provide a structure.

A manager or a case study student will typically use the SWOT tool on a number of occasions while tackling one management scenario. Included in the working papers, they provide valuable personal summaries and references which will help in the development of strategies which are relevant and which address key issues.

However, a SWOT *does not provide solutions*. A SWOT is not a solution in itself. Its role is to help picture a situation, to help identify what information is needed and what decisions are likely to be required, by when.

The following extract provides an outline of a scenario similar to one that would be found as part of a management case study. Read it through and make a note of the key issues in a SWOT framework. Suggested rough and final analyses follow. (Do not necessarily expect your work to duplicate the examples, in management much depends upon the personal perspective(s) of the manager(s) involved.)

THE CASE OF
'THE EATING PLAICE'

In 1965 Mr John Traverse opened his first fish and chip shop in the suburbs of Manchester. In 1973 when his eldest daughter joined him in the family business there was a thriving chain of 15 shops in the Manchester area. Continued expansion in the North of England and Scotland was managed during the 1970s and early 1980s by John Traverse, his daughter Jacky and his two sons – by 1988 there were 89 'Eating Plaice' shops open.

Centralized buying, an emphasis on staff training and a generous profit sharing package for local managers contributed to a reputation for a high quality, value product.

The economic upturn of the 1980s, and increased demand for convenience foods and eating out were by-and-large beneficial to the business. But competition from Indian and Chinese take-aways, new hamburger bars styled on the McDonald's model, a dramatic increase in the usage of restaurants and interest in healthy eating, tended to depress demand for the traditional 'chippy'. Menu changes were tried, with varying degrees of success in different regions, with meat pies proving the most popular new line so far.

By 1990 forecasts for the business were looking gloomy. Planned new shop openings were cancelled. Average store profits were down for the third year running, costs were increasing and it was more difficult to recruit and retain good, reliable local shop managers.

The case is now repeated, but annotated to indicate the thinking processes that underlie the SWOT matrix that follows.

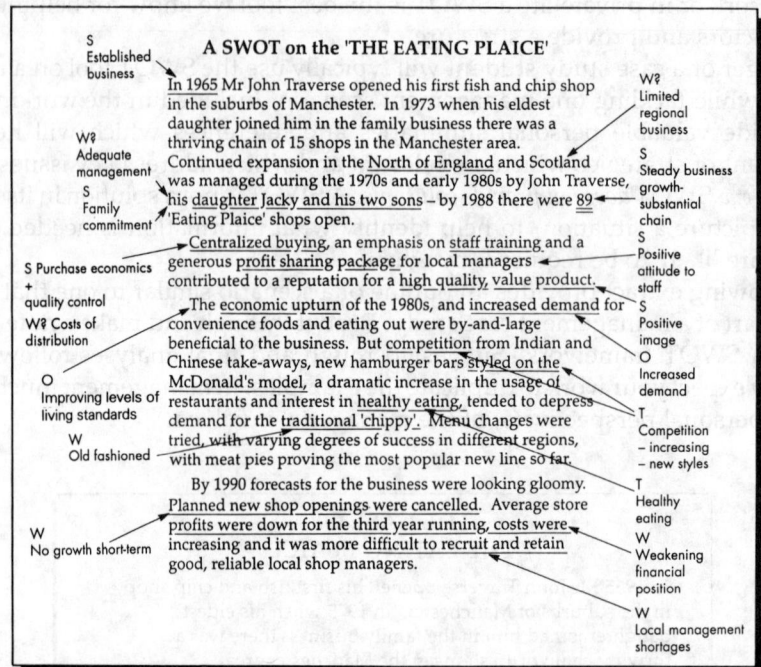

A SWOT on the 'THE EATING PLAICE'

S Established business

W? Adequate management

S Family commitment

S Purchase economics + quality control

W? Costs of distribution

O Improving levels of living standards

W Old fashioned

W No growth short-term

In 1965 Mr John Traverse opened his first fish and chip shop in the suburbs of Manchester. In 1973 when his eldest daughter joined him in the family business there was a thriving chain of 15 shops in the Manchester area. Continued expansion in the North of England and Scotland was managed during the 1970s and early 1980s by John Traverse, his daughter Jacky and his two sons – by 1988 there were 89 'Eating Plaice' shops open.

Centralized buying, an emphasis on staff training and a generous profit sharing package for local managers contributed to a reputation for a high quality, value product.

The economic upturn of the 1980s, and increased demand for convenience foods and eating out were by-and-large beneficial to the business. But competition from Indian and Chinese take-aways, new hamburger bars styled on the McDonald's model, a dramatic increase in the usage of restaurants and interest in healthy eating, tended to depress demand for the traditional 'chippy'. Menu changes were tried, with varying degrees of success in different regions, with meat pies proving the most popular new line so far.

By 1990 forecasts for the business were looking gloomy. Planned new shop openings were cancelled. Average store profits were down for the third year running, costs were increasing and it was more difficult to recruit and retain good, reliable local shop managers.

W? Limited regional business

S Steady business growth- substantial chain

S Positive attitude to staff

S Positive image

O Increased demand

T Competition – increasing – new styles

T Healthy eating

W Weakening financial position

W Local management shortages

These factors can now be transferred on to a SWOT matrix for easy reference (*see* below).

SWOT

STRENGTHS	WEAKNESSES
• An established business • Strong family commitment • Steady business growth • Substantial chain of outlets • Purchase economies + quality control • Positive attitude to staff • Incentivized local managers • Positive image for value for money • Willing to make changes – try new products	• ? lack of adequate management skills • No further growth short term • ? limited regional business • Costs of distribution • Recruitment + retention difficult • Traditional product/unhealthy? • Financially weak – falling profits and revenue growth
OPPORTUNITIES	**THREATS**
• Increased demand for 'eating out' and convenience food products • Generally rising living standards	• Trends to healthier eating • Economic recession • Increased competition • New styles of competition

---

ACTIVITIES

With practice you will find SWOT easy to use and a valuable tool. Try using it in the following ways.

1 Carry out a SWOT analysis on your company or organization.

2 Getting to know the competition is important in developing clear business strategies, so 'do a SWOT' on each major competitor – and then compare the results. The differences should give you an indication of actual and potential competitive advantages; of areas where you are exposed; of opportunities that await exploitation.

3 You can usefully repeat the exercise for a social club you are involved with or a business that you use as a customer. A customer's view of a company's strengths and weaknesses are likely to differ from the managements' view. Those external perceptions are so vitally important that pro-active managers will seek out the views of suppliers and of customers. 'Management by walking about' is how Peters and Waterman describe this practice in their famous book *In Search of Excellence*.

In the above exercises the SWOT approach has been used to get a picture of the whole entity – at corporate level. You should also use SWOT to look at aspects of an operation and, in these examples, as a basis for marketing audits.

4 Select a service or product with which you are familiar and undertake a SWOT analysis of it. Strengths and Weaknesses will be in terms of the 4 Ps and Opportunities and Threats in terms of the market – e.g. product modifications and market extensions.

   Do the same exercise for a competitive product and compare the results.

5 Do a personal SWOT analysis. This requires an honest view of your personal characteristics, and should include factors such as loyalty, motivation and creative abilities; abilities like competence in a language, professional qualification(s), (in)ability to drive.

   A personal SWOT is a valuable approach to career planning. You will identify areas of strength, others where you need some personal development. SWOTs are excellent preparation for job search and for interviews.

SWOT guidelines

Do:

- Use SWOT when and how it suits you – it is a management tool that is always available.
- Use SWOT whenever there are a lot of factors to be considered.
- Be clear about the focus of every SWOT.

- Be clear about which factors can be controlled by the entity and which cannot – this distinction has important ramifications for business strategy development.
- Make a point of undertaking SWOTs regularly – situations change!

Do not:

- Present SWOT analyses to clients or examiners. SWOTs represent the essential groundwork, the quality of your analysis/preparation is judged by the quality of your strategies and decision-making.
- Be afraid of doing several SWOTs at various stages in a project or case study.
- Waste time agonizing about whether a factor is a Strength or a Weakness, Opportunity or Threat. There will almost always be a compensating Weakness for a Strength and Threats should be turned into Opportunities.

A SWOT is not an end in itself
it is a tool of analysis not of decision

4 *Interpreting financial information*

The very thought of trying to discuss, let alone understand, the mystifying world of finance often strikes fear into the most competent of managers. And yet understanding the fundamentals of finance is actually relatively simple because it is a discipline which has been structured around a basic series of rules and regulations. By understanding a few straightforward fundamental principles of financial analysis you will be amazed how quickly you can focus attention on the key financial issues and become comfortable using the tools of financial analysis. You may even manage to re-focus the attention of your finance department on matters which require their urgent action because of your ability to keep it simple!

Statutory information

Most financial information about a company will be obtained from its annual report and accounts. In most cases a UK company is required by law to prepare a set of accounts on an annual basis. These accounts are audited by an independent body of professional accountants and included within the annual report. This report will be made up of the following elements:

- the chairman's report;
- a report of each operating unit within the company; } listed companies only
- the directors' report;
- the accounts of the (consolidated) company. } all companies

Much information can be gained from what the chairman says in his report – and indeed what he does not say! The directors' report will include information relating to the directors of the company, dividend policy, corporate policy regarding human resources, donations to political and charitable organizations and events which have a material effect on the financial health of the company but which occurred after the end of the financial year, e.g. military conflict in an area of the world resulting in the closure of a subsidiary.

This chapter will focus on the annual accounts and what information they can provide. A typically laid out profit and loss account, balance sheet and source and application of funds statement is set out and used to help you identify the sort of questions you should be asking and the analysis you can undertake to get the most from the financial information available. This will require an understanding of a few technical terms which are explained in Part Two of this book (see **financial analysis** and **financial ratios**).

The numbers you will be working with in this chapter may appear simplistic. Yet they can represent millions. £3,461,467.23 can be manipulated much more easily (and just as effectively) if it is represented as £3.46. Always simplify large numbers unless you *absolutely must* have totally accurate information. You should re-work the examples of financial ratios from the specimen set of accounts in this chapter to ensure that you fully understand the computations.

Case studies will usually only give summary information from the accounts of the company, but all information of relevance will be included.

Annual accounts

The accounts need to be *treated as a whole* and will usually contain:

- a balance sheet – reporting at a point in time;
- a profit and loss account – for a period of time;
- a source and application of funds statement for a period of time;
- notes to the accounts.

In almost every case comparative data for both current and immediate past years will be given. This is to provide the user with both an understanding of movement in the net worth of a company, and how that movement in net worth has been generated.

Remember that there are many users of the accounts. They have completely different objectives:

- investors (shareholders) need to know how the company has performed in the last year and how the directors have managed the company;
- banks need to know that any loan obligations which the company has to them are safe and that the company has the funds available to meet its commitments;
- suppliers may need to know that any potential major contract can be comfortably paid for;
- stockbrokers will wish to analyse the accounts to determine what action(s) they should recommend to their clients – to buy, hold or sell;
- management needs a measure of its performance over the period concerned.

Providing the necessary level of detail, together with comparative figures, for all parties to gain information on which to base a part of their decision-making means that the accounts can appear daunting.

The first secret in handling financial analysis is to bring it back to basics from which you can do your analysis. A complete balance sheet and profit and loss account can always be summarized as shown opposite.

XYZ plc
Profit and Loss Account for the year 199X

	£'000
Turnover	220
Gross profit	110
Operating profit	45
Profit before tax (PBT)	30
Profit after tax (PAT)	23
Retained profit	16

Note: The summary profit and loss account is not intended to cast down.

XYZ plc
Balance Sheet as at 31 December 199X

	£'000	£'000
Fixed assets		150
Current assets	67	
Current liabilities	(35)	
Net current assets		32
Liabilities over 1 year		(30)
Capital employed and shareholders' funds		152

It is important to remember that numbers on their own mean nothing. It is the trends that are important. The interpretation of those trends results in an understanding of the company's position and performance.

Before any detailed analysis is done it is best to cast a quick critical eye over the figures to identify large movements which may in themselves indicate the need for further investigation. Look at the example on page 30 and identify any major changes.

XYZ plc
Profit and Loss Account for the year ended 31 December 199X

	199X £'000	198X £'000
Turnover	220	150
Costs of sales	(110)	(80)
Gross profit	110	70
Distribution costs	(15)	(14)
Administration costs	(50)	(40)
Operating profit	45	16
Interest payable	(15)	(2)
Profit on ordinary activities before taxation	30	14
Taxation	(7)	(7)
Profit on ordinary activities after taxation	23	7
Extraordinary items	(5)	—
Profit for the financial year	18	7
Dividends	(2)	(2)
Retained profit	16	5

The notes on pages A & B form an integral part of these accounts.
(*Not provided for this example.*)

XYZ plc
Balance Sheet as at 31 December 199X

	199X £'000	198X £'000
Fixed assets	150	121
Current assets		
Stocks	10	7
Debtors	55	24
Cash at bank	2	1
	67	32
Creditors – falling due within 1 year	(35)	(12)
Net current liabilities	32	20
Creditors – falling due after more than one year	(30)	(5)
Capital employed	152	136
Capital and reserves		
Short capital	4	4
Revenue reserves	148	132
Shareholders' funds	152	136

The notes on pages A & B form an integral part of these accounts
(*Not provided for this example.*)

XYZ plc
Source and application of funds for
the year ended 31 December 199X

	199X £'000	198X £'000
Sources of funds		
Profit on ordinary activities before taxation	30	14
Extraordinary items	(5)	–
Items not involving movement of funds:		
Depreciation	16	12
Funds generated from operations	41	26
Other sources		
Sale of fixed assets	–	2
Funds generated	41	28
Application of funds		
Purchase of fixed assets	(45)	–
Tax paid	(7)	(5)
Dividend paid	(2)	(2)
Movements in working capital		
Stocks	(3)	(1)
Debtors	(31)	(3)
Creditors	48	5
Movement in cash balances	1	22

The notes on pages A & B form an integral part of these accounts
(*Not provided for this example.*)

The major changes, and the questions they provoke are:

- Profit before tax (PBT) has risen dramatically from £14,000 to £30,000 and there has been a big increase in turnover.
- What has caused this increase in business activity?
  Has there been investment in new assets or even a company acquisition?
  What about a new product?
- Not all the rise in turnover has been translated into profits. This is not unusual since we would expect the cost base to rise given the dramatic increase in sales activity. Has there been large promotional support?
- Interest costs have also risen – this suggests a large new loan which may have been used to finance the purchase of new assets, perhaps new production equipment.
- What is the extraordinary item? Look at the notes to the accounts, which will always provide an explanation for this item. (Not provided for this example.)
- The fixed assets and creditors have risen by large amounts – this supports the idea of investment in new assets, financed by borrowing.
- Why have debtors risen so much? We would expect them to rise in line with the increase in sales turnover. Have the sale force been securing orders from less credit-worthy clients?

We have not provided notes for this example but the further information contained in notes to accounts should always be studied. In case studies the data may, however, be given as part of the narrative.

Once you have had a preliminary look at the accounts, and have targeted in upon interesting areas about which you need further information, you can use financial ratios to extract further detail. Note that ratios are only valuable if comparisons are available. A liquidity ratio of 1 is meaningful only if we know the average ratio for this type of company. We should be comparing ratios to past experience, and to the achievements and expectations of others operating similarly to ourselves.

Ratio analysis divides into these main types:

- Performance ratios – usually used by management and analysts to assess the underlying performance of the company.
- Financial ratios – these are used mainly by institutions to assess the liquidity of the company. They may also be used by suppliers to assess credit-worthiness.
- Stock market ratios – used by market analysts to assess trends and measure the company against other quoted companies.

ACTIVITY

The most commonly used ratios are calculated below for XYZ plc, based on figures from the above accounts. Double check our work by calculating the ratios for yourself.

Performance ratios

	199X	198X
Net (before tax) profit margin	13.6%	9.3%

This is a ratio to measure how much of the company's turnover (sales) has been translated into profit. It is calculated by dividing profit before tax by turnover and is expressed as a percentage.

	199X	198X
Gross profit margin	50%	45.7%

This represents the gross profit generated from turnover after attributing only the direct costs of production or stock for resale. It will exclude distribution costs, selling and administration costs etc. It helps to determine the basic profitability of the business. It is calculated by dividing gross profit by turnover and is expressed as a percentage.

	199X	198X
Other costs/turnover	29.5%	36%

This is a measure of overheads necessary to generate the turnover. It includes all other costs included as part of operating profit. (i.e. it excludes interest costs). It is calculated by totalling, in this case, distribution and administration costs, dividing by turnover and expressing the result as a percentage.

	199X	198X
Return on capital employed (ROCE)	29.6%	11.8%

This measures the profits generated from the net assets that are owned. The most usual definition is to express the operating profit as a percentage of the capital employed in the business (also known as *net assets* or *net worth*). We would normally expect this ratio, in non-service-based industries, to be higher than the rate of interest at which money can be invested on the High Street – otherwise one might do better to invest in a building society account!

	199X	198X
Debt turnover (days sales outstanding)	91 days	58 days

This is a measure of how long debtors have been owing money. In theory you should only use trade debtors in the calculation; this will be detailed in the notes to the accounts. If no further information is given use the debtors figure stated on the balance sheet. The calculation is trade debtors/turnover × 365 days.

Be careful in using this ratio since it assumes a steady turnover throughout the year and may be misleading in seasonal businesses.

Days of credit, i.e. how quickly bills are paid, cannot be obtained from published accounts, but is a key management ratio. Too often there is discrepancy between days of debt and days of credit, to the disadvantage of the company.

Financial ratios

Key financial ratios are used to calculate the liquidity of the company and will tend to concentrate on the balance sheet. The most useful ratios are:

	199X	198X
Debt ratio (gearing)	42.8%	12.5%

Money can be raised by a company from either its shareholders or by borrowing. The ratio between the funds raised by (or due to) borrowing and those raised from investment by shareholders is known as the debt ratio. Gearing is an adaptation of this and measures the level of debt borrowed from third parties as a percentage of all debt raised (borrowings plus shareholders investment).

Shareholders funds (equity) are always detailed on the balance sheet but long term borrowings may not be immediately clear. You should consult the notes to the accounts for creditors due under and over one year. From this you should add those elements which relate to long term borrowed funds. It is normal practice to exclude any bank overdrafts.

If no notes are detailed then use the total of creditors as an approximation. Divide the long term debt by the total of debt and shareholders' funds. Express the result as a percentage.

A highly geared company is vulnerable in times of high interest rates when it may find that the costs of servicing the debt is beyond its ability. Acceptable gearing limits vary with industry and the prevailing economic climate but, in general, a figure of 50–60 per cent is the highest level usually acceptable. Note that a gearing level of 50% also represents a debt ratio of 100%.

	199X	198X
Current ratio (liquidity ratio)	1.9	2.7

This is a test of whether a company can meet its obligations as they fall due: i.e. does it have enough cash or 'near money' to pay its immediate liabilities. It is calculated by dividing current assets by current liabilities.

Different levels are acceptable in different industries and circumstances although a level in excess of 2.0 is safe across the board.

Interest cover

199X	198X
3.0	8.0

Another ratio used for liquidity assessment – particularly in highly geared companies – is the number of times the interest costs are covered by operating profit. This is particularly used in times of recession and it is the movement in this ratio that is important. It is calculated by dividing operating profit by interest costs.

Dividend cover

199X	198X
11.5	3.5

Another ratio on liquidity, dividend cover, relates the amount of dividend declared to the profit available for distribution, i.e. profit after tax but before any extraordinary items. Normally this ratio would exceed 3.0.

Acid test

199X	198X
1.6	2.1

Sometimes it is necessary to assess the liquidity of a company by excluding stocks from current assets. This is because in many industries stocks cannot be readily sold. The acid test is simply debtors and cash divided by current liabilities. This ratio should exceed 1.0

Stock market ratios

Stock market ratios are used to assess the investor's shareholding in the company. The most common are:

Earnings per share (EPS)
In the notes to the accounts will be given the number of shares in issue over the year. The EPS is calculated as the profit after tax (i.e. the amount of profit available for distribution to the shareholders), divided by the average number of shares. For public companies this figure is quoted on the face of the profit and loss account. It measures the ability of the company to generate profits available for distribution to the shareholders by way of dividend, even though it may not all be paid out in this way.

Price/earnings ratio
This is an assessment of the value of the company on the stock market. Hence the price of a share on the market divided by its EPS will give a ratio which is of value when compared to competitors in the same industry and over time.

This ratio is often used as a starting point in assessing the value of a quoted company for acquisition.

Interpretation of XYZ plc finances

Applying these simple ratios to the XYZ accounts provides us with much useful financial insight. The main points are:

- PBT has more than doubled – mainly by an increase in sales activity.
- There has been investment in new assets (see source and application of funds statement) – purchases of fixed assets financed, it appears, by borrowing.
- Efficiency seems to have improved (gross margin is better and other costs as a

percentage of turnover have fallen). In a price war XYZ may have the ability to match competitors in the short term.

- Return on capital has improved, which will please investors.
- There is scope to increase the dividend.

But

- Gearing has risen and this limits the ability of XYZ plc to borrow in the future. However to get to 60 per cent gearing the company could borrow another £163,000.
- The level of debtors needs to be watched. The more time it takes to collect debts the greater the drain on cash flow. There is also need to consider the effectiveness of credit control.

ACTIVITIES

1 Examine your own company's annual report, and work out the same information as you have in this chapter. Use it to gain insight into the activities of your company. Consider what concerns you would have as a director, and how a competitor would view the firm.

2 Look at the annual reports of companies competing with your own. Evaluate who appears to be doing best, who worst, and why.

3 Read the financial pages of a quality newspaper regularly for at least a month. Assess the judgements of the journalists as they analyse company performance.

4 Using the stock market information that is published daily:
   – compare the results for several companies in competition;
   – compare the ratios achieved by companies of the same size – but in different industries.

Summary

Financial data are produced to provide a variety of users with general information. Like all data, they need to be processed to produce information which is valuable to you. Your task is simply to extract a few of the pieces of information and translate them into a story – numbers on their own mean nothing. It is the trends and their interpretation that are important.

Financial accounts are published information that is presented in standard format. They are limited in their use to operational management since they tend to be historical in nature. For this reason **management accounts** are produced. These are highly confidential, operational documents, whose purpose is to provide management with information upon which to make decisions and from which to monitor progress.

For obvious reasons management accounts are not freely available and we usually have to make do with the limited amount of information contained in the financial accounts.

No manager can afford to be frightened
of numbers –
but there is no need to become a slave to them

5 Creative techniques

Tools of creativity do not belong exclusively in the toolboxes of the designer, novelist or graphic artist. The manager's need for creativity may be less obvious, but it is no less a necessary and fundamental skill.

Creativity in management terms does not refer to an ability with colours, words or shapes, but to an open-minded approach to ideas, facts and problem-solving. In business terms, creativity is more about identifying a new approach. It evidences an essential characteristic of the good manager – a willingness to accept change.

Unfortunately it is all too easy for managers to get bogged down in the systems, traditions and culture of an organization or function: 'we do it this way because we have always done it this way . . .'. It is commonplace for managers to be so overly familiar with a situation that they cannot see the whole picture – they 'cannot see the wood for the trees'. Reactions and responses are learnt over a period of time, so little fresh thought is given to any situation and new opportunities or threats are missed or ignored.

To overcome management's blinkered view of the business it is common practice to seek out new views, by appointing managers from outside the business or by employing consultants. Adding some of the techniques of creativity to your management toolbox represents a third valuable option. These tools will help to generate broader thinking and improve the quality of your thinking and problem-solving.

Before you can set about adding a more creative dimension to your thinking you need to consider how your thought processes actually work. Our brains are incredibly complex, consisting of up to 15,000 million nerve cells and able to make an almost incalculable number of connections. The scientific world is only just beginning to understand the brain's processes, but we do know some of the basics.

- We make very little use of our brain's potential.
- Our senses transmit some 50 million signals to the brain every second. In order to handle this amount of data the brain filters out many of the signals automatically (a natural process of **exception reporting**). One basic set of filters is concerned with our physiological state – we are only conscious of the messages from our senses when it is necessary, i.e. when we are hot, cold, hungry, thirsty or afraid. As we learn, we add our own filters to this system. These learned responses are based upon experience and are designed to make life easier for us. Unfortunately they also tend to make us resistant to change and to new ideas. They can make us narrow-minded in our responses.
- The brain is split into two hemispheres that operate in unison, but with different functions. The left brain deals with logic, language and mathematics, whilst the right handles visual and spatial impressions, the intangible concepts of love, beauty and loyalty. In many adults the creativity of the right brain is suppressed by the logic of the left.

  Left is for Logic, Right for Rhythm. The balance that managers need to develop is between the logical approach that is based totally upon proven facts and the creative rhythm of hunch or feel. It may appear logical – but does it feel right? A manager with a well-developed sense of intuition is a valuable asset.

- The brain likes to work by association. Each thought is surrounded by a number of associations, each with its own little 'hook'. Given a thought, your brain will automatically search out these associations and provide a stream of memories, knowledge and events associated with it. Creativity relies on the ability to recall, to hook, as many of these associations as possible. Some of the associations are bizarre, but must not be stifled – amongst the most apparently frivolous are often found the germ of a concept that can be worked up into a fully formed idea.
- The brain will continue to work on a problem, once its importance has been established, whilst you are doing something else. When it has a solution it will throw it forward into your consciousness. Eureka! Often it really does 'pay to sleep on it'.

To develop your creativity you need to become a skilled user of techniques which help to:

- develop some of the untapped potential of your brain;
- encourage the creative thoughts of your right brain;
- maximize the number of associations made by your brain;
- remove some of your learned filters which narrow thinking.

This is not easy to do at first. It feels odd to suspend logic while thoughts that appear weird come to the surface. Part of the process is to allow this to happen. To encourage it, but not to work at it. The brain will generate ideas automatically, given a stimulus; but if you have been insisting that your brain works through a logic filter you will be uncomfortable for a time when you begin to relax the filter.

As you progress you will find that creativity begins to flow more easily. You will cease to use terms like 'that's silly' and 'I'm an adult – no time for child's games'. Thoughts are only silly if they are used in a silly way, and what is silly depends upon the context, upon the situation.

Introducing the creative techniques

Brainstorming

You have probably already come across brainstorming even if you have not been formally introduced to it as a creative technique. It works on the principle that two heads are better than one.

Faced with a problem or looking to generate fresh ideas there is a synergy in having more than a single mind on the problem. The ideas put forward by three or four people working together will be greater than the total of ideas generated by those same people working alone. This phenomenon is easily explained. One person's ideas will spark off associations, ideas and connections in others in a way which an individual with only one set of experiences cannot match.

Brainstorming is a management approach used to formalize and draw upon this method of unlocking creative thoughts. It is most successful when managed carefully. (There is still a role for the left brain!) It is usually run as a planned exercise with a randomly selected group of contributors, but it can also be used with smaller groups. This usually happens when a manager cannot see a way forward and calls for a quick 'fix' of creative help.

Anybody can help with a brainstorm; the wider the range of age, skills and experiences the better. There is no need to have prior knowledge of the problem – in fact this can be a negative factor. A person is free to relax and generate ideas when coming to a problem fresh, unencumbered by prejudice and without responsibility for the problem or its outcome.

Brainstorming guidelines

1 Assemble a mixed group – ideally five to seven people from a wide variety of backgrounds, functions and experiences. Try not to use people who have been working with the subject; they will have too many preconceived ideas.

2 Give the minimum brief possible. Remember brainstorming's purpose is to provide ideas on which to work, not to come up with formed plans nor to make decisions.

3 Accept and record every idea thrown up. A flip chart or whiteboard is an excellent focus. Use two scribes to record ideas if they are flowing quickly.

4 Never allow discussion or criticism of any suggestions. Discussion delays and criticism kills the creative flow.

5 Run the session for about 20 minutes. Allow nothing to restrict the creative flow. No distractions or hold ups, no development of points. Do not drag a session out. If it has clearly stopped after 12 or 15 minutes formally conclude it then. Equally if it is running happily after 20 minutes allow it to continue. It will run out in its own good time.

6 Once all the ideas are up on the flip chart the process of sifting can begin. You may want to do this with the group, or alone. The idea is to consolidate similar thoughts and to remove those that are obviously impractical and/or illegal.

Be careful what you throw out! One session came up with the idea of distributing samples from a hot air balloon that drifted across Egypt and Tunisia. Not practical. But a method of getting samples to potential customers was devised. Did the idea come from the brainstorm, or would it have been thought of anyway? Who is to tell . . . but the brainstorm was the direct cause of this particular campaign.

7 Thank those who took part and report back in due course on the outcomes.

Brainstorming should be used to extract a large number of creative ideas very quickly. It will not solve problems nor make decisions. It will open your eyes to new possibilities and to angles which you had not seen before.

ACTIVITIES

1 Brainstorm with your family or friends on:
   themes for a party;
   money generating ideas for a favourite charity or social club;
   alternative holidays.
2 Get together a group of colleagues or friends and brainstorm a number of ways you could use brainstorming at work.
3 Set up a brainstorm at work to help generate new ideas on a current project or case study.

Mind mapping

ACTIVITY

Take no more than 10 minutes and prepare a plan for a report on: the Green Movement.

How did you approach this task? Many people will have found it difficult. The unfamiliarity of the subject coupled with the time pressure and the unexpected demand for the activity may have created a mental block . . . your mind may have gone blank.

Did you end up with a list of points something like this?

The green movement, a phenomenon of the 1980s.
Increased environmental awareness – backed by customer purchasing power.
Green consumer products increasingly available.
Environmentally friendly packaging – a positive product benefit.
Benefits of biodegradable plastics.

The problem with lists is that they begin to channel your thoughts automatically, associations taking you in a particular direction. The third item on your list is associated with the second, and perhaps not with the theme. This is an easy way to lose touch with the focus. A common failing amongst report writers and students is wandering from the point. The example above could lead to a report about packaging rather than the Green Movement.

There is another disadvantage with lists. Whatever appears at the top of the list takes on a perceived importance – it is top, Number One. Items at the top of the list will be loaded with 'higher values'. Our report is likely to end up prioritizing not the most important facts, but the ones we thought of first.

Mind mapping is a technique that will help you to break away from the straight-jacket thinking imposed by working in lists. In a mind map there is no dominant theme, only a central focus. A mind map works out from the centre, and is personal and unique. Colour and imagery add vitality and a mind map works as a useful aid to memory and is an excellent method of note making. The technique for creating mind maps is simple, but the skills and confidence needed take time to develop. Persist! It is worth the effort.

The mind map of the Green Movement in figure 5.1 took 10 minutes to create.

Mind mapping guidelines

1 Decide upon the focus of your map. Write this in a small circle in the centre of the page.
2 As each thought comes add a branch that is attached either to the centre or to an existing branch.
3 Reject nothing. Write down every thought and concept.
4 Work out from the centre, following a branch of associated thoughts until a new thought comes.
5 Do not worry if the same thought pops up in several places – this just shows its importance, and you can tidy up your map later.

6 Let the shape evolve. Do not force a logic on to the process.
7 Use key words and *print* on the lines. This forces discipline, and gives time for fresh thoughts to develop.
8 Add colour and images as the mood takes you.

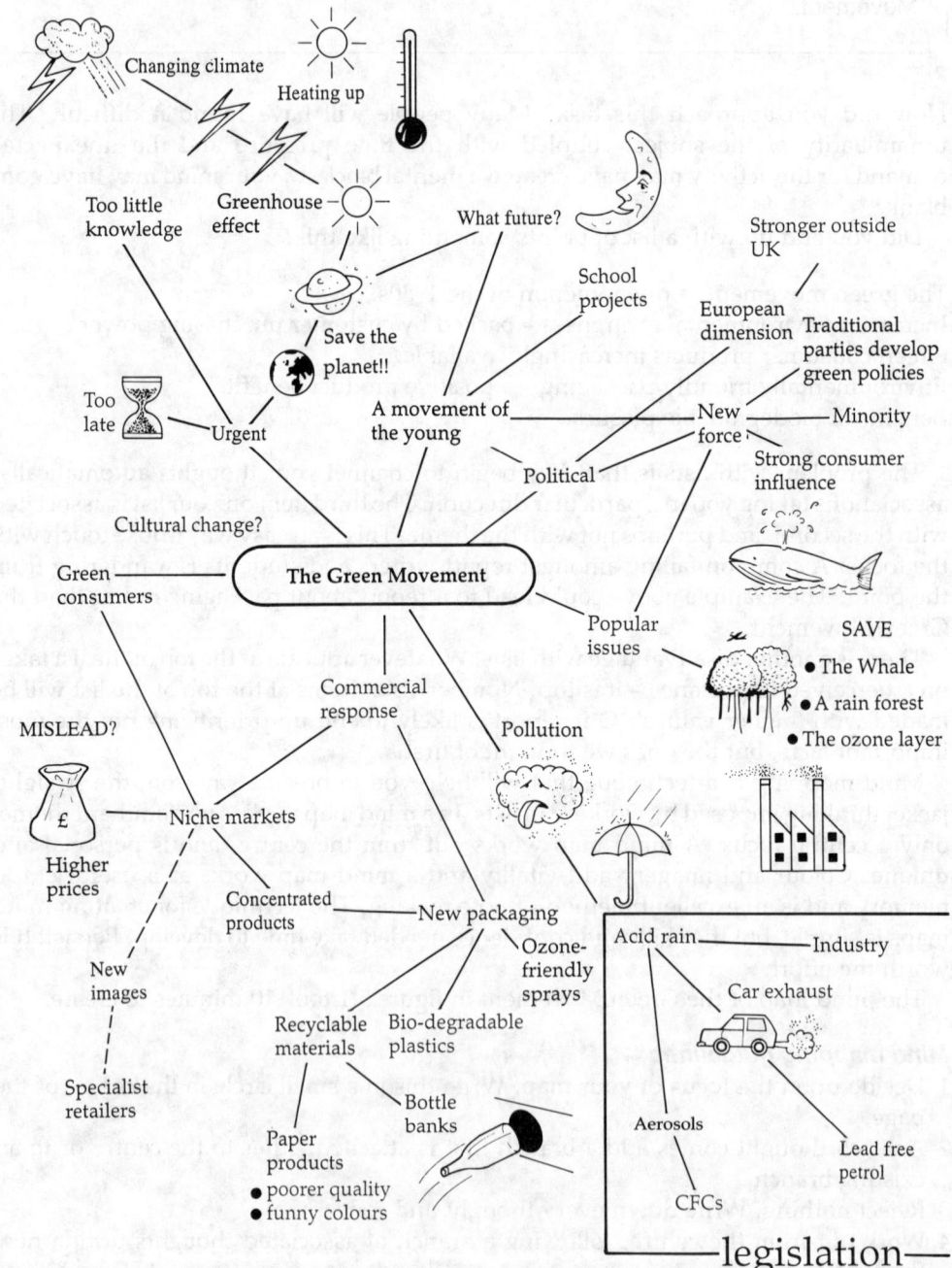

Figure 5.1   *Mind map of the Green Movement*

When the map is developed it is time to check it over for links and for associated aspects. You may want to refine and redraw the map and you certainly will want to add additional thoughts as you gain an overall perspective.

Producing mind maps is fun and will quickly become the most useful creative technique in your toolbox. Take time to develop the skill and persevere with it. Use it as a tool for planning, for idea generation and as a method of note taking.

Learning mind mapping is a little like learning touch typing after you have typed with two fingers for years. You have deliberately to lose speed in the short term because of the greater benefits to be gained.

ACTIVITIES

1 For a *month* use mind mapping to take notes at all meetings you attend. Refine the maps after each meeting to be sure you have included everything and can remember what your abbreviations mean. See what overall picture of the meetings you can deduce, perhaps you are missing some important strategic factor because of your concentration upon tactical matters? It will be interesting to compare your maps with official minutes – which will be the most complete and helpful?
2 Take notes at lectures or conferences in mind map form. Here you are helped by the presenter who will have structured his or her presentation. Using a mind map allows you to concentrate more fully on what is being said, and therefore to remember more.
3 Use a mind map to help you plan your next assignment or project.
4 Produce mind maps to help you write:
   a letter to a friend about your holiday;
   a report to your manager on brainstorming;
   an oral presentation on computers in business.

In mind mapping you are developing confidence in your brain's ability to remember and to provide you with the information that you need. We try to protect ourselves by writing everything down, but then the papers get filed and we often cannot even remember that we wrote about it in the first place!

Lateral thinking

The basic principle is that while we appear to operate in a logical and linear world we, in fact, do no such thing. The route from point A to point B may appear very simple and straightforward, and it is; but only after someone has produced the map!

For the person who embarks on the journey from A to B without help it may prove an impossible task! In fact to get to journey's end a person may have to divert from A to A1 to A2 backwards to A3, to A4, to A5 and finally to B. Looking back from B a simple direct route can be established. Then the diversions through A1/A5 can be eliminated (figure 5.2). That simplification process is exactly what explorers have done in opening new continents, and is the leading contribution of all researchers in the arts and sciences over thousands of years.

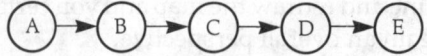

Developed from:

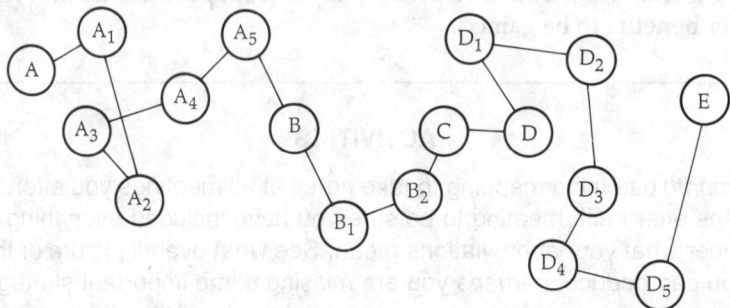

Figure 5.2   *Route diagrams*

Our problem is that we are brought up to expect to move from A to B to C to D, and so on. The reality is that we cannot. We believe that we can because when young we are conditioned by the help of others who are older, wiser and more experienced. When we eventually have to take the decisions ourselves we have to learn what others before us have learned – that there is no mapped route in unexplored country.

So, especially in management, it is usually best to move toward our objective in small steps rather than big leaps. These small steps may appear to be 'off-route'. Off the final, proven route, that is. But we have to go 'off-route' if progress is to be made. A proven technique is to imagine that one has achieved the objective, and to look back to the beginning. Problems taken from a different perspective often are far easier to solve.

Try looking at the problem through the eyes of someone new to the business. An 'amateur', unconditioned by the traditional approach often can see clearly through to the heart of the problem. The perspective of the newly appointed person, or the consultant, should be sought. It is the uninitiated who are likely to ask the difficult questions 'Why? and 'Why not?' Think hard before you answer.

Why?
This is a very powerful question:

- Why are you doing that?
- Why is that the objective?

Often you will find the answer to be confused, unclear. So ask Why? again. Keep asking Why? until the point has been clarified.

Often you will find that the situation is complex, where at first it appeared simple. If that is so then you need to tackle each of the elements of the situation, and not the complete overall scenario.

Why not?

Many people are blocked from actions because they have not thought them through. They follow routine, they follow procedures. But often these procedures were designed for different circumstances, for a situation that is not the same as the one in operation today. 'Why not do it this way . . .?' forces you to reappraise a situation. It should be repeated until all the possible options have been explored.

A mind map is invaluable in this process. Used correctly it will throw up a variety of options. Many, perhaps all, will be wrong at this time – but it is important to identify and consider the options. That way you can be as sure as possible that the best solution has been adopted. Procedure will not have been followed routinely, even if the routine solution is proved valid. Most often, however, a better course of action will be identified, and can be introduced.

> Basic principle: If you are doing something now the same way as three years ago – you are probably wrong!

What if . . .?

This is another question likely to be asked by the novice or learner. It is a *big*, challenging question and it is useful as the basis for a lateral thinking examination of a problem area. It gets you into the unknown, but safely.

- What would happen if we offered the product as a self-assembly kit?
- What would happen if the staff were offered a profit share scheme?

ACTIVITIES

1 Find someone new to a situation – your college, your company or department, your social club. Make a point of asking for their perspective(s) to compare with your own.
2 Choose one of the systems you are responsible for at work – it may be as personal as the filing system or as complex as the planning procedures. Ask yourself the question
   - Why? about each element of the system. Mind map some alternatives and ask yourself
   - Why not? Then choose the most promising options and apply the question
   - What if?

The tools of creativity are well worth the effort of acquisition since they will make a major impact on many aspects of your work and personal life. Skilled and easy use of the three major tools covered in this chapter will come only with practice and application. You have to be determined to acquire them.

Go ahead, managers
have
creative and open minds!

6 *Planning*

Planning is a fundamental activity which helps us to gain some control over an uncertain future. It is an activity with which we are all familiar as we constantly use the process of planning in our everyday lives: what and when to plant in the garden this season; what to buy and where to shop. We plan our journeys and our career moves.

You already have planning experience, your 'life skills' simply need transferring into the context of business and of management. An important first step is to ensure you understand the terminology, the stages and the dimensions of planning.

Planning is the dynamic force of the management process, the framework on which all decision-making should be anchored. It is the activity which harnesses the resources of the organization, and moves it towards predetermined goals.

Planning terminology has come to business management from managers who would probably have found the term unusual. Generals commanding armies have for millennia designed *strategy* to ensure that wars are won. Strategic aims are achieved through the attainment of *tactical* objectives. Reports from the line of battle have kept senior commanders alerted to progress, hopefully in time for corrective action to be taken, i.e. the commitment of reserves at a crucial point. Finally de-briefings analyse the results, identify the lessons learned and enable commanders to be more effective next time.

Planning basics

However and wherever you are using the planning process the principles are always the same.

- Where are we now?   Audit or review stage.
- Where are we going?   Objective-setting stage.
- How do we get there?   Decisions on route, approach etc.
- Are we on the right track? Control stage.

These are the same stages you would use in planning a journey, for example:

> We will start from home, at 8.30 a.m., and expect to arrive at our Birmingham destination by 12.30 p.m. We will take the M25 and the M1 and should be at the Dartford Tunnel by 10.00 a.m. and the first M1 services area by 11.00 a.m.

Given a pre-planned route, and expected times of arrival at staging posts, it is quite easy to measure progress against intention. If you were delayed on the M1 it would be quite easy to make a phone call from the services area to say 'Hold the lunch we are running 35 minutes late.'

Taking these principles into the world of business is easy, and productive. The first section of this chapter follows the stages of planning, reviewing essential tools of management as they would be used in the planning process.

In chapters 2–4 you have considered the tools of analysis – necessary for reviewing 'where we are now'. Here we consider objectives and the development of options for achieving them. Later the process of deciding between these alternatives to select the best approach will be reviewed and issues of control will be examined. It is necessary *at objective-setting stage* to consider how each objective will be measured for success. In due course each manager will need to be able to:

- Check that he or she is on line to achieve the objective(s);
- Be alerted to actions that could improve the implementation of the plans.

These checks and feedbacks are only possible if the original objectives are clearly and correctly formulated. Good objectives are not easy to write, but the effort in acquiring the skill is well spent. Successful managers cannot operate without clarity of purpose. We shall return to objective-setting shortly.

Flexibility

There is an important caveat about plans. They must be flexible if they are to be a valuable management tool. Those brought out annually, dusted off, modified, and not referred to again until next year are of little (if any) value to the manager. Neither are those written in 'tablets of stone', unable to be changed in the light of changing market conditions. The good manager uses the plan as a guide, a series of statements of intention to be referred to regularly, but which can be modified as necessary.

This may sound contradictory, but if so it is because you have been brought up to believe that managers never make mistakes, that a good manager achieves close to a 100 per cent record of success. As we say elsewhere – but it is important enough to bear repeating – a manager has the task of assessing risk within the context of incomplete information and an uncertain future. Obviously any plan must be open to amendment as new information comes to hand and circumstances change. The use of judgement is what distinguishes a good manager. That, plus the ability to react *when necessary* with speed and accuracy.

Terminology

There can be confusion between the different terminology used in business planning. Different sources use different terms for the same process. This is unfortunate, but cannot be avoided. It is necessary for you to clarify the distinctions, establish the levels of planning, and so underpin your confidence in your own planning activities and documents. Managers working in established organizations will find that they already have a well-defined set of parameters for their plans; and that these will follow the levels we cover here, whatever the organization chooses to call them.

There are only four levels to the planning process: Policy, Strategy, Tactics and Control.

The planning process is like a giant four-dimensional jigsaw. The whole picture is determined at corporate level and then each area of the business is responsible for its own part. If everyone achieves their objectives the picture should be completed according to the plan.

It is helpful always to qualify the terms, e.g. corporate policy, financial strategy, sales tactics. This ensures that you identify the level in the organization as well as the stage of the plan to which you are referring.

Policy

Is established at the very top level in any organization. It is expressed in a *mission statement* and in *policy statements*.

Mission statement

A mission statement is a declaration of the business the organization sees itself as being in and in which it wants to be. It provides executives with parameters within which to operate.

Mission statements can be changed, and should on occasion be challenged, but they will not be changed frequently. They should be phrased to provide the business with both the scope to be flexible and yet with tight enough focus to help concentrate energies. A mission statement needs to be rigid enough to provide clarity of purpose, yet loose enough to enable change and business growth. Too broad and the business tends to lose focus; too narrow and it misses opportunities and fails to identify threats.

It is easy for a series of decisions and diversifications to lead an organization to lose sight of its mission – the core of its business. When this happens it often leads to higher costs and lack of competitive edge. Companies like Hanson Trust have made it their business to identify and acquire such operations, stripping them back to their core activity and improving their performance in the process.

The case of BR is often used to illustrate the need for a good mission statement:

For years British Rail saw their mission as 'being in the railway business'. With this tight focus they were clearly positioned as monopolists, with no reason to worry about the competitive activities of others. Had they had a mission statement concerned with being in the transportation business they may have taken different steps to combat the threat of improved motorway networks and executive coach travel. However, a mission which simply placed BR in the transport business would not have given a tight enough focus. With too many options for diversification executives may have been tempted to investigate the feasibility of air routes to the Americas and of petrol stations in Scotland. This diversity would provide little synergy for the corporate activities.

A better mission statement would have been: 'BR is in the business of providing safe, reliable, land based transport for passengers and freight within the United Kingdom.' This statement provides options for development, but a core focus to enable the direction of effort. It would leave the matter of the Channel Tunnel open to interpretation as to where the UK ends and France begins. (A classic case where the mission should be reviewed!)

Policy statements

Policy is expressed in statements made by the senior management of an organization about how it has decided to operate. These statements usually reflect the culture of the organization and could be considered as rules which managers need to follow. Sometimes these policy statements are inspired by legislation . . .

- We apply an equal opportunities policy in all recruitment

. . . or by the need to be seen to police the organization's own activities:

- It is policy not to encourage or allow the sale of our products to children under 16 years of age.

Policy often reflects the organization's concern with wider social issues:

- It is company policy to donate 10 per cent of all net profits to charity.
- It is policy to use only environmentally friendly packaging materials.
- It is policy to ensure that registered disabled persons make up at least 5 per cent of the workforce.

Policy can also refer to more detailed aspects of the operation:

- We have a policy of refunds with no questions asked.
- Our policy is always to prosecute shop-thieves.

These policy statements reflect choices the organization has made and which they wish consistently to enforce. They are statements that relate directly to how the business is conducted and help executives to make decisions which are acceptable to the organization. They, of course, have knock-on effects: the policy statement on use of environmentally friendly materials is likely to increase production and packaging costs, but offer marketing advantages; the refunds policy can open the door to abuse, but offer competitive advantages. In each case the balance between cost and advantage must constantly be weighed, and the effectiveness of the policy evaluated.

Company policy on any issue offers a valuable insight to the culture of the organization, the way it sees itself, and the way it does business.

Strategy

Once policy decisions have been made the necessary strategies can be determined. We need to know, specifically, what each part of the organization has to achieve, and by when. Strategic objectives express, broadly, what should be achieved, and by when. They are *not* concerned with detailed achievement – only with the broad intention. We cover *objectives* in detail later in this chapter.

There will almost always be a number of strategies available to an organization, e.g. profit can be increased by reducing costs and holding sales, or by increasing revenue and holding costs. Within these two extremes there are a number of other options.

Management's job is to examine the situation and identify and consider all the alternative options or strategies. Each one has to be considered in order to identify the course of action, or strategy, which best fits the resources and position of the organization and is most likely to help it achieve the declared policy. SWOT technique provides an excellent framework for considering the options.

This selection of alternatives is very important, because if senior management does not decide upon and communicate the preferred strategy, different parts of the organization will be trying to achieve results in very different ways. This will cause conflict and a waste of effort. With no indication of strategy from senior management, finance could be trying to increase profit by reducing costs and cutting back on budgets, whilst marketing was trying to achieve the same objective by increasing sales through higher promotional spending, more sales staff and overall increases in budget.

The function of a strategic plan is to minimize conflicts and maximize the use of resources, by ensuring the coordination not just of purpose but of approach.

Tactics

Tactical planning is concerned with achievement of strategy. The broad plan is given in strategic objectives, detailed planning is expressed in *tactical objectives*. Tactical plans are often referred to as *action plans* because it is upon them that action is taken. Policy and strategy lead to no external action. It is only tactical planning which works both inside and outside the organization.

A good action plan has key elements. It sets out in detail who is going to do what, by when, and with what resources. It will be concerned with the actions of individual managers, working in unison but each with a set number of objectives to achieve. Obviously, if all tactical plans conform to strategy, and strategy fits within policy, everybody in the organization is moving to achieve common goals.

As managers become more senior many find it difficult to delegate the tactics to juniors and to re-focus their attention at the more strategic level. Unfortunately it is necessary, in time, to leave the 'battlefield' but not all tactical commanders make good strategists.

It is important to ensure that you understand at which level you are working in an organization, and that you concentrate your planning, and your actions, appropriately. You should not attempt to plan tactically outside your area of responsibility, but you can and should plan *with* others.

Control

Monitoring progress against objectives is such an important element of management that we cover it in chapter 8.

Objectives

Objectives are clear statements of intended outcomes or goals. Corporate objectives indicate what the organization wants to achieve, where it wants to go, the direction in which it is heading. Functional objectives achieve the same end for a department or function of the organization.

A plan is a way of coordinating energy and effort towards achieving a common goal. If that goal is not specific it is very easy for people to pull in different directions, wasting both energy and resources. To be of any value, objectives have to have certain characteristics. They *must* be:

- quantified over time;
- realistic, and perceived as achievable;
- communicated to those concerned with their achievement.

The success of a plan ultimately depends on the people who put it into effect. Their commitment and motivation will depend on their understanding of the goal and their belief that it can be achieved.

Objectives expressed in terms of 'we want to make more profit' are useless as they say nothing about scale or time. Equally, an objective to 'double market share' in a mature market is unlikely to be seen as realistic, unless resources for acquisition are available. To be realistic, objectives must be set in the context of the organization's current position, identified during the analysis of 'Where are we now?'

Examples of good objectives would be:

We intend to increase our revenue by 12 per cent in real terms by the end of 199X.
We intend to increase net profit by 3 per cent over the 12 months ending 31.12.199X.

Both these objectives are specific. They are expressed at corporate level and so are *corporate objectives*. Executives will be in no doubt as to what is expected of the organization. From corporate objectives, strategic and tactical objectives can be developed.

At whatever level you are in the organization, you should have objectives to achieve. Hopefully you will understand exactly what is required of you. If you are setting objectives, remember that they need to be set in terms that have a meaning to those trying to achieve them.

A corporate objective of a 4 per cent increase in the return on capital employed has a meaning to senior management and to the shareholders, but it does not spell out what is expected of individual departments. Each needs objectives that are expressed in terms relevant to them:

Increase sales of product A by 10 per cent in year to 31.12.9X.
Reduce costs of distribution by 3 per cent in period to 31.12.9X, etc.

Taken together, and achieved, all objectives combine to achieve the 4 per cent return on capital employed.

Once corporate strategy has been established it is possible for functions – finance, production, marketing, personnel – to audit their positions and come up with their own strategic objectives. When these have all been coordinated and the end results predicted senior management may well require a re-examination of one or more strategy proposals. Until strategy has been agreed for each function it is not possible to proceed with tactical planning. Thus the detailed plans flow from agreed strategy. Each level in the organization determines its objectives in the light of the strategic objectives set at the level above it.

Objectives and a case study examination

All examiners are tough on anyone who does not write clear objectives. Statements such as 'make more money' will be penalized – you must be specific, just as you have to be in business.

Fortunately you do not have to worry overmuch about the detail in a case study. There is no single right answer to a case and so your objectives will be accepted if they are quantified over time, and are not unreasonable and/or unachievable given your review of the company's current position. The examiner is actually concerned that you show that you understand the process – the need to set good objectives – that you know quantification over time is essential, and that you are not afraid to commit your judgements to paper.

Note that there can be wrong or unrealistic answers. Increasing profits by 40 per cent in eight months would be unusual, and unless there were very special circumstances, and convincing justification, neither an examiner nor a line manager will be convinced that this is a reasonable objective. Equally a small concern with a limited range operating in a small part of the UK would not need, nor be able to afford, a national TV campaign. Yet some case study candidates recommend national TV almost automatically. This shows they are not thinking realistically about the case, and they are certainly not providing evidence of managerial competence.

Timing

Time is the remaining dimension in the planning process. Although this is often stated specifically as part of an objective, it does often occur less specifically. The general time horizons of *short*, *medium* and *long term* have no standard yardsticks and their meaning varies from industry to industry. Fast-moving sectors, like pop music and fashion, will tend to have shorter planning horizons than the more slowly moving conglomerates in power and telecommunications.

As a broad rule of thumb:

- Short term — up to three years, but often only refers to the next one-year plan.
- Medium term — usually two to three years; up to five years.
- Long term — more than five years.

When adding the time dimension to your planning remember that over time nothing remains static. The company, its markets and the environment are all likely to change, so your strategy for the long term can only be expressed in general terms.

Using schematics like the Ansoff matrix is an effective way of communicating strategy over time (figure 6.1).

- Short term — consolidation of our current position.
- Medium term — expansion into European market.
- Long term — diversification into electrical powered products.

Planning guidelines

- Be clear about the benefits of planning – why you are doing it.
- Ensure plans are presented clearly in logical stages consistent with each other and with the mission, policy and corporate plans of the company.

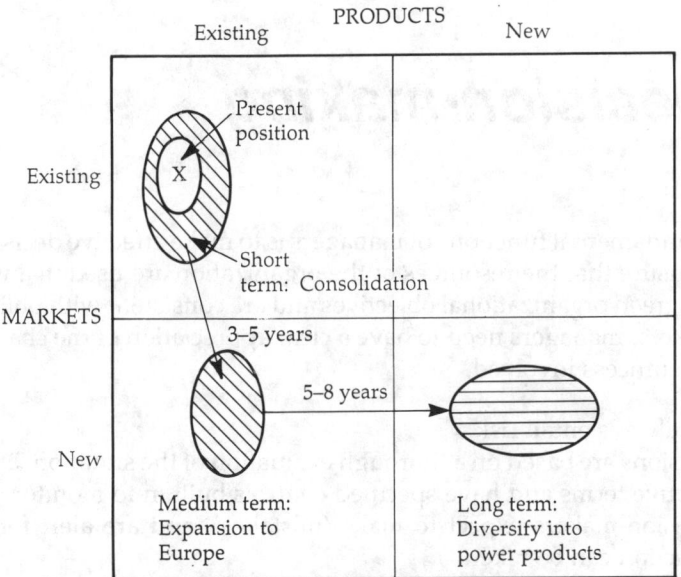

Figure 6.1 *Using the Ansoff matrix to communicate strategy over time*

- Start your plans from your current position and provide a clear focus for the future – a sense of direction and purpose.
- Plans must be quantified, realistic and communicated.
- Plans need to be reviewed and modified when changes occur.

ACTIVITIES

- What is your company's mission statement? Are its activities consistent with its mission? If you cannot find a mission statement use your inductive skills to work back from what you perceive the organization to be doing to what the mission statement ought to be.
- Collect the annual reports from six companies with whose activities you are familiar and try to find out their mission statements. If they are not clearly stated try to work out one for each of them.
- Make a list of four policy statements applicable to your company.
- Review your company and your department's annual plan. Identify three good points and three aspects of each which could be improved. If these documents are not available to you ask why. To be effective plans need to be communicated.
- Identify an activity you are involved with personally at home or in your social life and produce a plan for it, e.g. giving a party; taking a journey; organizing a sports match. Review this plan critically to ensure all the planning stages have been followed through.

Failing to plan is planning to fail

7　Decision-making

One of the fundamental functions of managers is to make effective decisions, decisions which will ensure that the resources of the organization are used in a way which will achieve the agreed organizational objectives and are consistent with policy. To be good decision-makers, managers need to have a clear appreciation of the characteristics and nature of the process involved.

- Decisions always entail risk.
- Good decisions are based on a thorough evaluation of the situation, are expressed in clear objective terms and have specified controls built in to monitor progress.
- Good decision-makers expect to make 'mistakes', and are alert for them so that remedial action can be taken.
- Good decisions can be changed. Up to 40 per cent of decisions will need modification in the light of new information and future developments.

The task of the manager is to develop a system and framework for the decision-making process which allows him or her continually to improve the quality of decision-making, to reduce both risks and costs and to improve the percentage of 'right' decisions. In chapter 2 we considered the raw material of decisions – information – and discussed how it should be used to reduce the risks associated with decision-making. In this chapter we will look at a number of tools and techniques that can be used to improve decision-making.

The decision-making process

The process for good decision-making is:

- Problem(s) are identified.
- Alternative solutions are identified.
- Alternative solutions are evaluated.
- Decision(s) is/are taken on the basis of information available.
- The decisions are acted upon.
- Results of action are monitored and remedial action(s) taken as necessary.

Problem definition

Problems usually become apparent once objectives have been specified – they affect the ability to achieve the target.

The first stage is to examine the situation carefully – check all the available information to ensure that it is precise, complete, valid, reliable, based on fact and plausible.

Managers need to use their experience and judgement throughout the process of decision-making. Next there should be a clear statement of the problem(s) as you perceive them.

Increasing output by 7 per cent is not possible because of:

a limited supply of an essential raw material, and
a lack of skilled machine operators.

These two constraints represent the problems which need solving. Check your view of the situation with others. Their perceptions may differ and their views throw valuable new light onto the picture.

Take care not to jump to conclusions when defining a problem:

Poor quality of service is commonly blamed on low wage levels which are said to attract low grade and poorly motivated staff.
Investigation may identify the real problems to be inadequate training and poor supervision.

Solution identification and evaluation of alternatives

You are looking to identify the *best* solution, not the *first* solution. This means taking time to consider the alternatives. In principle the more options you have, and the more carefully you assess their cost-benefits, the better the final solution will be.

Use the creative techniques from chapter 5 to help in generating alternatives. Remember that other people involved in different aspects of the operation will have different perspectives on the situation – and that these can be valuable. Your aim is to produce a refined list of viable alternatives which are not 'blinkered' in their scope.

This short list requires careful evaluation:

- Apply SWOT analysis to each option.
- Screen each alternative against criteria based on the 4 'R's.
    Resources – what would be required?
    Restraints – what restraints exist: legal, social, company policy etc.?
    Reaction – of influential groups: financial, public, media, customers, competitors, senior managers etc.
    Results – what are the likely outcomes?
        – what is the probability that this solution will work?

Providing quantification to considerations such as these will provide you with the basis of a cost/benefit analysis: *how* much will it cost, set against the value of *what* we will gain?

Do *not* be restricted to only financial benefits – use the concept of **opportunity cost** to consider other factors, such as valuable publicity and improved reputation.

Decision-making

Whichever system of evaluation and comparison used, you should aim to reduce your list of options to two or three. Assuming they are mutually exclusive, you will now have to make a decision between them. The science of Operations Research has provided a number of techniques which use sophisticated mathematical models to help develop solutions in the context of the organization. There are also techniques that can be used by the non-specialist manager which will help you make *effective* decisions objectively.

Weighting

Table 7.1: Weighting to compare options

Criterion	Rating (out of 100)	Weighting (%)			Value		
		A	B	C	A	B	C
Cheap	50	30	20	50	15	10	25
Fast	40	30	15	55	12	6	22
Least disruption	30	30	50	20	9	15	6
In line with company policy	60	35	45	20	21	27	12
Total					57	58	65

This is a good analytical technique which provides a framework that forces managers to make a systematic and balanced evaluation of each option across a spectrum of relevant factors.

- Re-state your objective and produce a list of relevant criteria against which solutions can be judged. For example, cost may be critical, or the time to implement may be more important. Consistency with company policy and the amount of disruption to the operation are also typical factors that have to be weighted. Whatever the relevant factors, you should give each a weighting and then rate each solution against each criteria. Multiplying the score for each criteria by its weight will allow you to make a comparison across all options under consideration (table 7.1). On this basis solution C is marginally better than A and B. Its success does depend, however, on the correct identification and weighting of the success criteria and the subjective forecast of each of the solutions' performance against that criteria.

  When several people are involved in a decision, and especially when individual items are seen at different times, this simple method of obtaining a quantitative result from subjective observations is invaluable. It is effective in selection interviews, evaluating the merits of new products – in fact, anywhere that one wishes to bring a more objective measure to the decision-making process.

Decision trees

A decision tree is a conceptual map which catalogues possible decisions and their

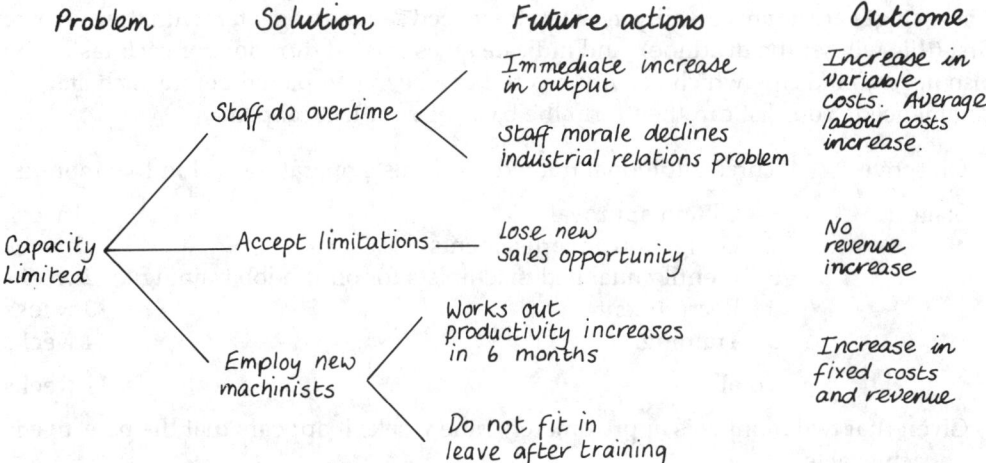

Problem	Solution	Future actions	Outcome

Figure 7.1 *Decision tree*

outcomes (figure 7.1). It is particularly useful if you are required to make a number of decisions, each affected by previous decisions.

The technique allows the knock-on impact of decisions to be considered. Used in conjunction with assessments of **probability** it is possible to make very sophisticated judgements that are supported by quantitative evaluation. As always, however, the quality of the numbers coming out depends entirely upon the reliability of the numbers assigned to each part of the decision tree – and to the mathematical accuracy of the calculations.

Decision implementation

The remaining chapters in Part One look in more detail at the management skills required for successful implementation, communication and control of plans. Here we are looking at the logistics of the process.

Filling the planning gap

The area between where you are now and your objective is known as the planning gap. This space needs to be filled with a series of planned actions which will implement your solution. Progress will be made by a series of short steps. Each step adds a link to a chain until eventually the chain reaches the target. Begin implementation of your decision by identifying the stages that have to be accomplished.

For example, if the solution to our earlier problem of increasing capacity was to hire three new machinists (see Figure 7.1) the steps might include:

- Getting approval
- Advertising the vacancies
- Interviewing the applicants
- Selecting on-the-job trainers
- Recruitment
- Training

These stages are not necessarily in order, they need sequencing. Start with the outcome first (this will set the deadline), and indicate an estimated duration for each task. You also need to indicate which activity has to have been completed before each stage is commenced. Your list can then form the basis of your tactical plan.

Objective:	Three additional trained machinists operating within two months.	
Stages:	1 Obtain approval	1 week
	2 Design job advertisements	1 week
	3 Identify qualified machinists for on-the-job training	2 weeks
	4 Recruitment	3 weeks
	5 Training	4 weeks
	Total	11 weeks

Given that two months is approximately nine weeks it appears that the objective is not achievable.

If the information is transferred to a Gantt, or bar chart, a visual picture of the activities makes the situation clearer (figure 7.2). A Gantt chart provides a different way of looking at the situation. It can now easily be seen that task 3 can happen concurrently with others and that this allows the task to be completed inside our time scale.

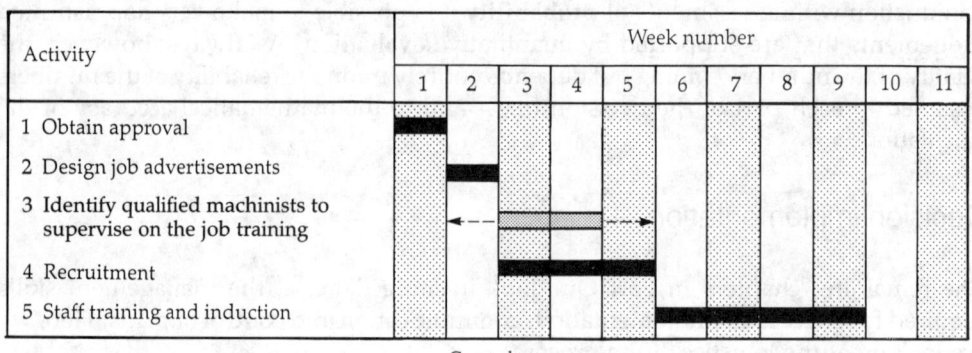

Gantt chart

Figure 7.2   *Gantt chart*

Another useful technique is *network analysis* or critical path analysis, which determines the critical elements in a sequence of stages so that the overall activity can be completed in the minimum amount of time. *Critical path analysis* (CPA) and *programme evaluation and review technique* (PERT) are the most widely used network analysis techniques. The difference between them is that CPA takes the assumed time scale of activities as reasonably accurate while PERT assumes that they are not and takes into account three possibilities, the shortest, longest and normal timings. Networks are usually lengthy and complicated and require a computer. They are particularly valuable when implementing long term plans and projects.

Simple techniques are the best for practising managers. Complex computer driven simulations are useful in their place, but most day-to-day decisions can be taken quite easily with the help of pencil, paper, pocket calculator and common sense.

When communicating decisions, especially in case studies and in presentations, it is very helpful to use diagrammatical representations of the processes. They are far easier to comprehend, and are very supportive of your oral explanations.

Decisions and objectives

Decisions are always closely associated with objectives. Without unambiguous objectives there is nothing for achievement to be measured against and the control function fails. Objectives must always be quantified, as we saw in chapter 6. They must be written against time. Rate these objectives:

1 To achieve an increase in sales.
2 To achieve a 10 per cent increase in sales.
3 To reduce staff turnover from 10 to 5 per cent by March.
4 To identify areas of high staff turnover by January.
5 To identify areas where staff turnover is higher than 15 per cent p.a. by end January.
6 To eliminate waste from the kitchen, immediately.

Comments

1 Any increase will do. Even 0.01 per cent over a year. What sales level is needed to generate the budgeted profits?
2 Better, but over what time frame? Ten per cent over same period last year? On a weekly, monthly, quarterly or annual basis? A rolling annual figure, or a calendar year? (If the latter the results cannot be known until the end of the year, far too late for corrective action.)
3 Better – but is the objective targeted upon an entity, a department or a section? Generally staff turnover is localized and an overall objective is counter-productive.
4 Much better – clear sense of purpose. Identify the problem areas, then decide what to do. And a time target given, but too loosely. When in January is the objective to be achieved?
5 The only good objective in the six.
6 Impossible to achieve. Laudable intent – but who defines waste? And it is simply not possible for a caterer to produce exactly the right quantities of everything even within a closed institution like a prison where there is a captive market (pun intended!). Set a waste objective along these lines: 'Waste to be reduced to not more than 2 per cent of purchases by 31 March, and then held at that level.'

It will be seen that a good objective has its control factor(s) built in. Thus the task of the **Management Information System** is to measure achievement against objective, and report back promptly. Areas where control is not possible are not 'no-go' areas, but they automatically become higher risk areas since there will be no way to know results in time for remedial action.

When dealing with matters of *quality* rather than quantity it becomes more difficult to set quantified objectives. Yet it is always possible:

- Production quality can be measured by skilled tasters, against a reject rate.
- Impression can be quantified along a numerical axis (see **semantic differential**).
- Staff behaviour can be measured by appraisal and assessment, although it must be noted that it is in the area of human relations that managers have the most difficulty in setting quantified objectives. The usually adopted method is to take a series of measurable yardsticks, such as timekeeping and absenteeism, and deduce an overall pattern of behaviour. With experience, and constant refinement, a workable model can be produced that helps in the difficult business of managing people.

Budgets and control

Once a decision has been made, appropriate resources must be allocated to its implementation. The analysis of what needs to be undertaken to implement the decision provides a detailed basis for forecasting the cost. Once the forecast of required resources has been approved, the budget becomes the control device.

Variances against budget should be reported, analysed and understood. It is often a dilemma as to whether to change budgets. It has to be a pragmatic decision taken in the light of the new information and the changed circumstances. A decision to change a budget should not be taken lightly, but flexibility must be evident when circumstances change.

An Exception Report, based upon variance analysis, will be found in chapter 8.

Guidelines for decision-making

- Expend energy, time and resources on decisions in direct proportion to the significance of the decision and the degree of perceived risk.
- Use formal frameworks and techniques to help ensure objectivity and clarity.
- All decisions should have built in control criteria allowing their progress to be monitored
- Monitor your personal decision-making skills in order to improve your performance.
- Decisions must be implemented. This requires developed interpersonal skills of communication and persuasion. This is discussed in the chapters that follow.

ACTIVITIES

1   Identify three small problems at work or home and, for each, go through the formal stages of decision-making to identify and plan appropriate actions.
2   Over the next month keep a record of the decisions you make and the methods you use to help you make them. Experiment using different techniques. Remember they may seem hard work at first.
3   Produce a Gantt chart for the implementation of your holiday plans.
4   Make a point of finding out what computer aids for decision-making are available to you. Find out which are of value, and how to use them.

Decision-taking is the prime skill of management.
It is rated higher than any other attribute
by senior European managers

8 *Implementation and control*

As we have seen, the function of management is to coordinate and use the resources of the organization to achieve predetermined objectives. The ability to 'make things happen' is the hallmark of a good manager. A manager needs to be more than a good strategist because success will be judged on results, not upon intentions. Success could, in the relatively near past, be achieved by administrators focused narrowly upon objectives – totally task-centred. The needs of management in the 1990s require an equal emphasis on the processes of how things happen. Task-centred management is no longer sufficient.

A plan is only a document that provides a focus for activity. Its successful implementation requires firm control and specific interpersonal skills that include leadership, delegation and motivation.

> Business is about leadership: it requires understanding, courage, single mindedness, drive and ability to persuade and lead others. To manage change one often needs to change managers . . . particularly managers who fail to involve their people and so secure their full commitment.
>
> Sir Michael Edwardes

These characteristics come more naturally to some than to others, but it is wrong to suppose that good managers and good leaders are always born, never made. The application of a few basic rules and techniques can improve the effectiveness of any manager.

Leadership and management

Management is concerned with task achievement and with control procedures. This is not to say that managers cannot be leaders – the best ones are.

Leaders tend to exemplify the qualities required or expected in their working groups, e.g. a medical leader would need to personify the clinical and caring qualities that underpin the profession. But the leader requires one other attribute – the ability to hold a team together as a working unity.

It is these two qualities – enabling the group to fulfil its mission and holding it together as a working unity – that identify the leader, that define the particular attitudes, knowledge and skills required to be the leader, and to be accepted as the leader.

> The only way in which the growing need for leadership in management can be met is to find the potential leader and then start his training and give him the chance to lead.
>
> Field Marshal Lord Slim

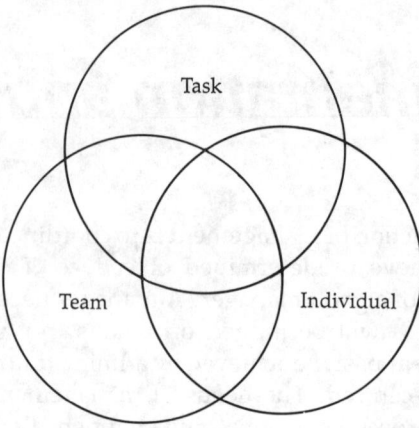

Figure 8.1

Action Centred Leadership has been developed over 30 years by Professor John Adair and is a widely accepted basis for modern day management/leadership training. Adair contends that there are three needs present in working groups or teams:

- the need to achieve the common task;
- the need for team maintenance;
- the needs the individuals bring with them to the working situation.

Adair's model represents each need by a circle, and the circles overlap (figure 8.1). Each contributes to the others – but if one of the needs is not handled effectively it will detract from both of the others (figure 8.2). A good leader will always have a considerable overlap between the three circles; a poor one may have circles that do not overlap at all!

Although this model is conceptual in that it is almost impossible to quantify, it is extremely valuable as it is easy to work with and individuals empathize with it without difficulty.

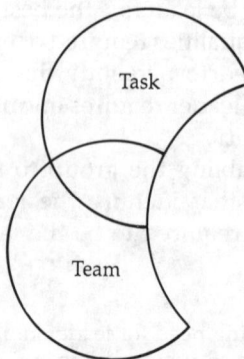

Figure 8.2

Delegation

> But of a good leader, who talks little,
> When his work is done, his aim fulfilled,
> They will say, 'We did this ourselves'.
>
> Lau-Tzu, sixth century BC

It is in delegation that the acid test of a manager–v–leader can be found. The manager retains a high degree of control and requires the subordinate to report back on matters of detail. The leader maintains sufficient control to help a particular individual, at a particular time, through any difficulties. The good leader does not take back control; he or she helps the subordinate and, between them, they solve the problem.

Managers usually start their working lives in an operational role doing a functional or supervisory job at 'shop floor' level. This tactical background, with responsibility for day-to-day detail, is frequently difficult to move away from. Often quite senior managers still like to 'get their hands dirty', much to the frustration of their subordinates, especially as they are often out of touch with modern day technical reality and no one dare tell them so! Another group who are almost inevitably guilty of a failure to delegate are managers who spend all their time fire fighting – reacting to unexpected developments. They have failed to spend sufficient time looking to the future.

Captains of industry have a lot in common with captains of ships – both have to be prepared to get out of the engine room and take their place on the bridge, charting the future course, monitoring progress through subordinates and taking the hard, not the routine decisions. The concept and importance of delegation is frequently hard for newly appointed managers to grasp. It is difficult to accept that they are no longer expected to do the job themselves, but to ensure that it is done with **effectiveness and efficiency**.

Delegation depends upon three factors:

- Assignment of responsibility – that is, specific to the task. It can be defined as *all of the duties that must be done in order to complete a given task.*

- Delegation of authority – the person who delegates *empowers the other person to act for the delegator*. It is not possible to delegate responsibility.

- Creation of accountability – subordinates incur obligations to carry out the designated work and properly use the delegated authority. Thus while the delegatee is accountable, the delegator is responsible.

Delegation is the tool of management which:

- Makes the best use of the organization's most valuable resource, its people. By matching the right skill level to the right task, everyone remains motivated and low grade tasks are not undertaken by overly qualified, highly paid workers.

- Ensures that there is a stream of people gaining experience by observation and practice.
- Prevents a duplication of effort. Everyone is clear about their role.
- Ensures there is time and energy being invested into planning for the future.

Are you a good delegator? Do you find there are not enough hours in the day to do your work? How well is the tool of delegation used in your organization?

ACTIVITIES

1 Assess your manager's skills of delegation:
   - do you have clear areas of responsibility and authority?
   - does he or she undertake activities that you or others in the department could do equally well?
   - are you often delayed while waiting for approval or authority from your manager?
   - are there clear guidelines and controls for reporting progress?
2 Now apply the same questions to yourself and to your skills of delegation.
3 Produce a list of all the activities you do, which could be performed by others:
   - equally well now;
   - equally well after some training.

Delegation guidelines

- Always delegate authority where you assign responsibility.
- Always ask for authority where you are assigned responsibility.
- Allocate time adequately to brief and debrief activities. Establish clear and agreed objectives – both personal and task-related. Set limits to the authority, establish criteria for control and an agreed basis for monitoring progress.
- Make sure the member of staff has the required training and support to undertake the required function.
- Accept that the task may not be performed exactly as you would have done it. Before asking for changes or amendments be certain they are necessary to achieving the objective and are not simply alterations to fit your personal style.
- Be prepared for mistakes – use them as a constructive basis for the individual's personal development.

Motivation

Leaders and managers are focused not just at getting a job done, but getting it done well. This requires a motivated workforce. Understanding the principles of motivation is important if the manager is going to ensure that his or her plans are implemented effectively and efficiently (see chapter 9).

Motivation can be described as *the internal driving force that impels the individual to activities which offer the opportunity for need fulfilment.* Once one need is satisfied it will be replaced by another: when your hunger is satisfied you need to rest, when you wake up you need activity, and then you are hungry again.

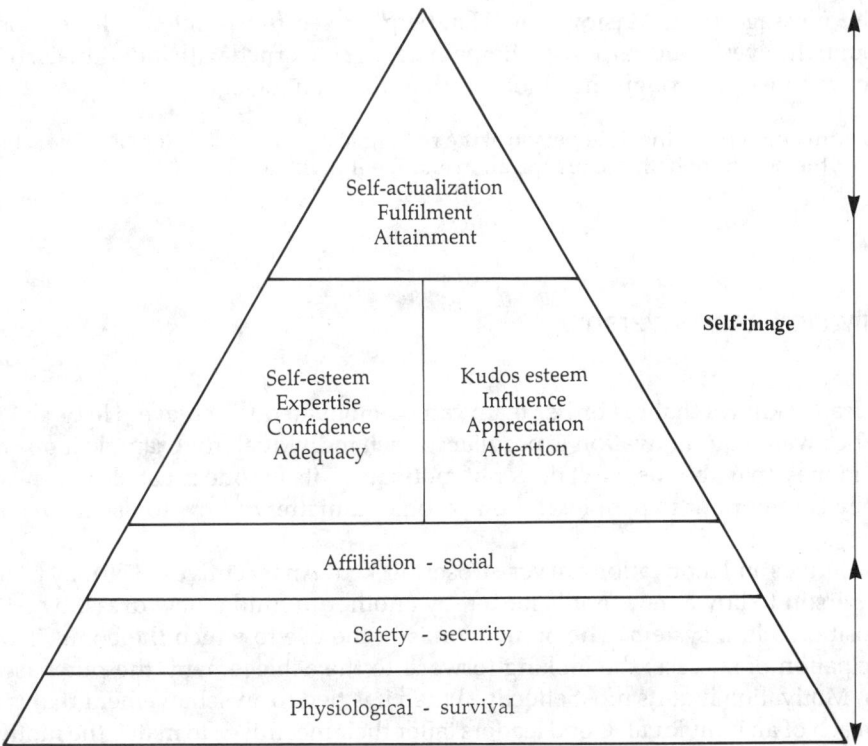

Figure 8.3 *Maslow's Hierarchy of Needs*

Maslow published his *Hierarchy of Human Needs* in 1943. It has become one of the most useful and widely quoted classifications that help us to understand the motivation of individuals. There are five areas of need, and they are often shown in the form of a triangle (figure 8.3).

Human needs ascend in priority. Only as each successive level is reached and fulfilled is it possible to move on to the next. Any diminution of achievement causes the individual to drop back through the levels until the motivational level of the moment is reached. It follows from Maslow that money is not a directly motivational force. What people choose to do with their money *is* motivational, but money itself is of value only to money collectors (who would be fulfilling their self-actualization needs!).

Herzberg's studies confirm what one can deduce from Maslow. They reveal that the factors which motivate people and satisfy them at work are not the opposite of those which dissatisfy them! Motivators and de-motivators are, in fact, separate items. Herzberg chose to use the term 'Hygiene Factors' for those elements that people regard as necessary to effective work. Changes in these have minimal, if any, effect on motivation. 'Motivators', however, pack a real punch.

Hygiene Factors are peripheral to the job itself. They include: pay, working conditions, company policy and quality of supervision. Hygiene factors, when positive, allow the Motivators to work.

Motivators are central to individuals. They include: self-improvement, responsibility, respect, status, achievement, challenge.

The message from Maslow and Herzberg is: see the problem, the opportunity, through the eyes of the employee. Empathize, be concerned with individuals. It is more effective to work through the emotions than through logic.

> Give the right job to the right person at the right time in order to develop his or her abilities – for the benefit of both the organization and the individual.
>
> John Adair

Motivation and leadership

The leader knows that his or her team can be motivated to achieve. He or she should also be aware that motivation is peculiar to each individual, for example if one accepts that money (pay, bonus, etc.) does not motivate of itself, one must also be aware that money is important to people! It then becomes a matter of how to use the *incentive* of money.

Incentives and motivation are very closely linked. An incentive of £50 may be used by one person to buy a new tennis racket, by another to fund a new dress, by a third as deposit on a hi-fi system. The motivation is in the use to which the bonus is put; the anticipation of success; the looking forward to the achievement; the purchase of the item. Motivation is at its most effective when it is tied to an achievement that is within the reach of an individual. Good leaders tailor their incentives to match the motivations of individuals.

ACTIVITIES

1 Carry out a small survey of friends or colleagues. Ask each of them in turn what makes a job good, and what bad.
   Compare the key factors that you identify with the work of Maslow and Herzberg.
2 Calculate how much time and energy you have spent in the past month on your hobby or leisure activities. Why? Many of them require as much energy and commitment as work. What is your reward? The professional musician, golfer or gardener does for a living what many regard as pure hobbies. How can this be?
3 Identify three incentives that tie into non-monetary motivations, e.g. a sales competition for a small physical prize but large kudos esteem.

Control

Managers and leaders need to be in control. They cannot delegate their responsibility for achieving organizational objectives although they do have to assign responsibility and delegate authority. It follows that they must have a form of control system that monitors achievement against objective *and* informs them of progress in time for remedial action where necessary.

Planning in a rapidly changing environment means that changes to proposed courses of action will need to be made if the overall objective is to be achieved. A system with clearly established processes, and criteria for control, is essential if managers are to be able to monitor progress.

Speed and accuracy are critical to the value of a review system. There is little point in having accurate information too late for action, nor in having inaccurate information in good time. Increased application of computerized information systems has improved the speed with which control information can now be available to managers, e.g. Electronic Point of Sale (EPOS) Systems in retailing provide up-to-the-minute stock inventories, but to be of value this data must be converted into information and flagged only when it requires management action.

A control system based upon exception reporting will help to focus management attention to significant variations in performance against expectation. Variations in performance are identified whether they are positive or negative. Excess performance can cause as many operational difficulties as under-achievement, for example exceeding a sales budget will cost profit and reputation if the production budget has not been upgraded. Only significant variations should be flagged to management, i.e. variations outside agreed levels.

Control system guidelines

- Controls must be set according to the nature of the job to be performed.
- Variances must be reported immediately in a style acceptable within the culture of the organization.
- Controls should show exceptions at points where management action can be effective.
- Controls should be flexible and economical in operation.
- Controls should be simple to understand and should indicate the necessary action, i.e. a manager achieving budget is due praise – the system should not seek out only those who fail.
- Control information must be 'user-friendly', i.e. presented in a way that is appropriate, helpful, clear and in time.

ACTIVITY

This activity demonstrates the process of exception reporting. It is, of course, normally carried through on a computer, but for simple sets of data it is still just as efficient to hand plot it using graph paper. Note that for a computer to generate information it is first necessary for the programmer to be briefed carefully by the manager who needs the information.

AN EXERCISE IN EXCEPTION REPORTING

THE DAVID DUNWELL PARTNERSHIP

Figure 8.4 represents sales and cost data for the David Dunwell Partnership during period 4. It is of little use to management since it provides no indication of which branches are doing best, and which need management support. To extract management information from this data prepare a revenue/costs graph, and apply exception criteria by drawing dotted lines on the graph (figure 8.5).

Apply exception criteria (by drawing dotted lines on your graph, figure 8.6):

– allow 3 per cent plus or minus variation from revenue;
– allow 3 per cent plus or minus variation from cost below revenue budget;
– allow 4 per cent plus or minus variation from cost above revenue budget.

These variance criteria should be changed over time. (With experience an organization will work to tighter and tighter limits.)

You will find that some branches fall within the criteria, and some outside. It is the exceptions – the ones outside – that are your prime concern. (In Figure 8.6 we have shown only those branches that fall outside the exception criteria.) It is a straightforward operation to produce a management document that provides the general manager with a list that gives the same information as in the original, but which ranks it in order of the priorities that he or she has established (figure 8.7).

THE DAVID DUNWELL PARTNERSHIP
SALES & COST ANALYSIS – Period 4

Store	Target £'000	Revenue Achieved £'000	%	Target £'000	Controllable costs Achieved £'000	%
Arundel	120	117.6	98	24	21.6	90
Bagshot	150	162	108	30	33.6	112
Croydon	120	122.4	102	24	24.5	102
Dartford	200	184	92	40	43.2	108
East Grinstead	150	148.5	99	30	30.3	101
Farnham	160	158.4	99	32	31.7	99
Guildford	300	279	93	54	50.8	94
Hassocks	220	224.4	102	39.6	34.8	88
Kingston	240	235.2	98	43.2	41.5	96
Larkfield	310	325.5	105	55.8	53	95
Manston	260	291.2	112	46.8	45.4	97
Newhaven	180	189	105	36	32.4	90
Petersfield	240	216	90	43.2	44.9	104
Ramsgate	170	171.7	101	34	33.3	98
Sevenoaks	210	222.6	106	37.8	36.3	96
Tonbridge	220	215.6	98	39.6	42	106
Uckfield	190	193.8	102	38	36.5	96
West Wickham	180	162	90	36	35.3	98

Figure 8.4 *Initial presentation of sales and cost data for David Dunwell Partnership*

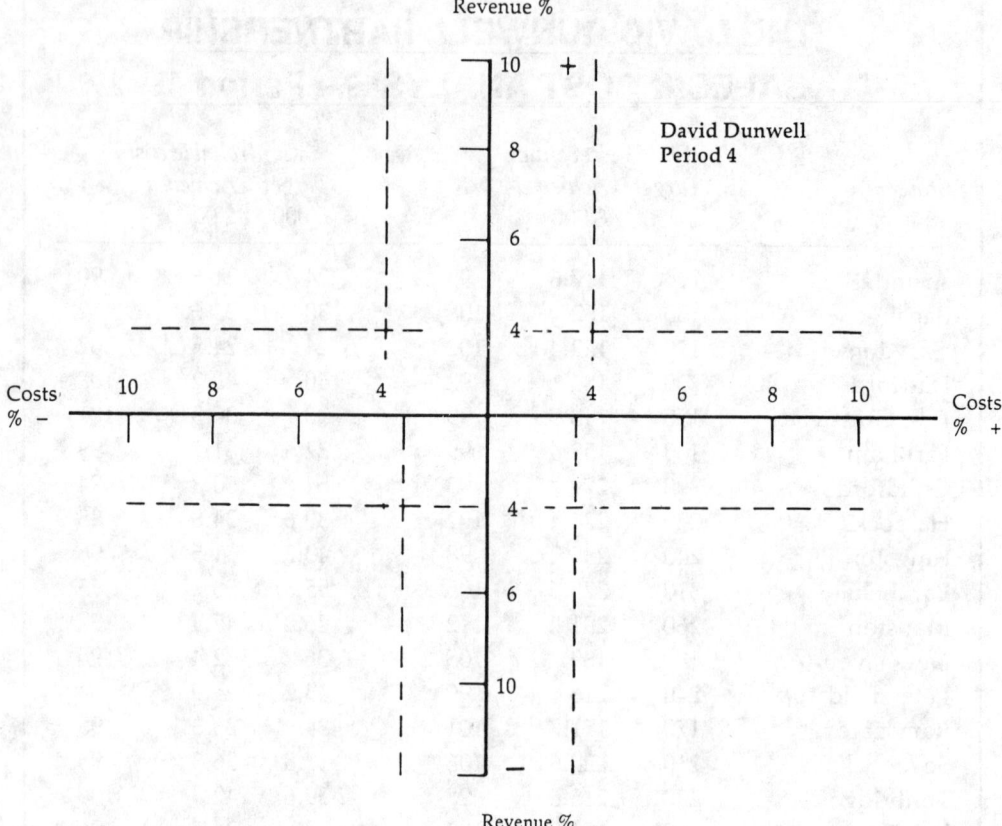

Figure 8.5   *Revenue/costs graph*

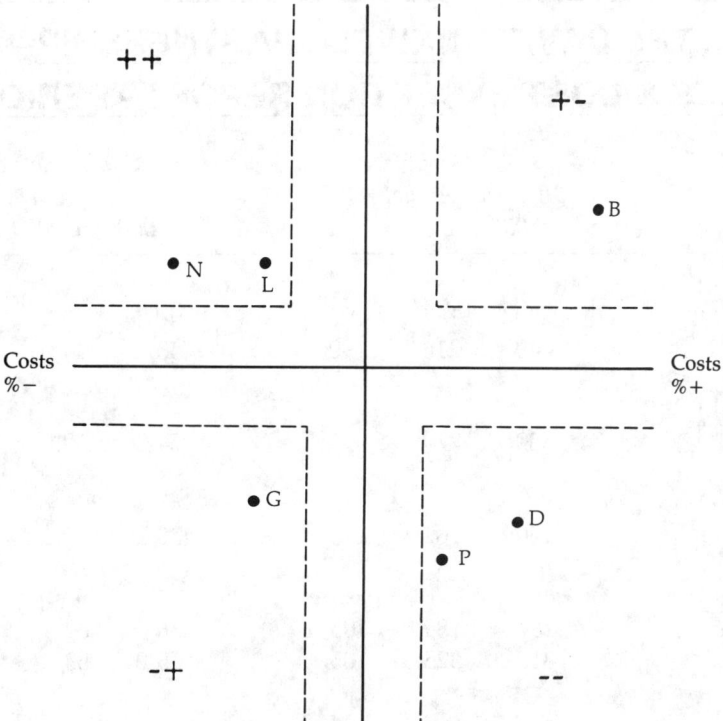

Figure 8.6 *Exception report graphically showing the branches outside control criteria*

THE DAVID DUNWELL PARTNERSHIP
SALES & COST EXCEPTION REPORT - PERIOD 4

PRIORITIES	Revenue				Controllable costs		
	Target £'000	Actual £'000	%		Target £'000	Actual £'000	%
R (−) C (−)							
Dartford	200	184	92		40	43.2	108
Petersfield	240	216	90		43.2	44.9	104
R (−) C (+)							
Guildford	300	279	93		54	50.8	94
R (+) C (−)							
Bagshot	150	162	108		30	33.6	112
R (+) C (+)							
Newhaven	180	189	105		36	32.4	90
Larkfield	310	325.5	105		55.8	53	95
Others							
Manston	260	291.2	112		46.8	45.4	97
West Wickham	180	162	90		36	35.3	98
Hassocks	220	224.4	102		39.6	34.8	88
Arundel	120	117.6	98		24	21.6	90
Kingston	240	235.2	98		43.2	41.5	96
Tonbridge	220	215.6	98		39.6	42	106

Figure 8.7   *Detailed exception report on David Dunwell Partnership*

Management controls must be planned
as objectives are set

9 *Internal marketing*

The success of planning is not the production of plans, but their successful implementation. Over recent years there has been an increasing realization that anyone can plan ... to the level of an academic paper exercise. Management is about getting plans operational.

Preparation of plans is undoubtedly a function of management, but in organizations where the planning *process* has been emphasized, rather than the *benefits* of planning, the results have become sterile planning cycles. Coupled with the bureaucracy that is generated by an academic planning cycle the result is to stifle creativity and flexibility, and to undermine morale. Much time is spent in debate over the niceties of the plan, with little regard to the practicalities of implementation. Thus elaborate menus can be planned without consideration for, or appreciation of, the necessary skills and attitude required in the kitchen staff if they are to be produced effectively.

To implement plans effectively they need to be 'sold' to those who will be involved in carrying them out. This management task requires many other skills: leadership, motivation, delegation, communication and control. But for those organizations able to focus on the benefits of planning, as a framework for dynamic change and growth, success in the rapidly changing marketplaces of the 1990s is much more certain.

Management is about leadership and leaders sell concepts and objectives just as the salesperson sells products. Both are equally essential to the continued health of the business.

Both management and marketing are about raising people's perceptions – of generating a commitment to go one better. Internal marketing is a way of 'selling' plans to your staff and your colleagues so that as the plans become operational there is commitment to their achievement. Internal marketing applies to all managers, it is crucial that every manager secures acceptance and support.

Internal marketing is a tool of motivation and support. It builds morale, and provides the rationale for the plans. Otherwise there is the serious danger that plans will be written by 'them' and not accepted by 'us'. 'Them & Us' operations are doomed to misery: high staff turnover, autocratic demands and staff resistance to change are typical results of the failure to market internally.

Internal marketing takes the concepts and techniques of marketing and applies them inside an organization. This is normally not a big budget operation – but the principles of selling a package hold true. The plan or objective is the package, the employees are the customers. Staff will be more committed to a plan's objectives if they believe in it; if they have 'bought it'. Committed staff who believe in the organization's plans have a focus, a common purpose. Conflict and misunderstanding are reduced, effort and resources are directed to the achievement of the plan.

One of the barriers to this more open style of management lies in our culture, especially our style of leadership, which is borrowed, as we have seen, often with little modification, from the armed services. Ideals of obeying without question and working to a 'need-to-know' principle are less appropriate in a rapidly changing business environment, where the contribution of everyone is valuable.

Many companies still fail to make plans available to employees and do little to market their strategies – seeing such actions as unproductive. In fairness they also can be concerned with security, but by the time planning has advanced to the level that it can be made public internally there is generally little of which alert competitors are not already aware. One, of course, guards sensitive managerial information extremely carefully.

People are by far the most important resource in any organization and so activities which improve motivation and increase effective use of the human resource should not be underestimated. Only people have the ability to deliver the competitive edge. Security is a matter of trust, and people can be trusted if well motivated, involved and committed. Today's manager has to be a leader of people and the tool of internal marketing is available to help maximize the value of the people resource.

The internal customer

Marketing's view of the customer as a complex unit of individuals and influencers affecting a decision, is equally valid in the process of internal marketing. Each of the target audiences must be identified and researched. The principle is exactly the same as when making a sale of a product or service to a customer. The tools and methodologies are also basically the same.

Decision-making units (DMUs) must be identified. They will vary in nature and complexity depending on organizational size and structure. Each Manager will have a unique perspective of the organization, and will identify DMUs in the light of his or her own need. It follows that the DMUs for manager A may well differ from those perceived by Manager B. One should be careful to handle internal marketing from one's own perspective, and not be seduced into accepting the definitions of others.

Associated with every DMU will be a **decision-making process** (DMP). It is essential to understand and allow for the needs of the DMP as well as the DMU.

In the public sector, schools, hospitals and local authorities all have elected members acting as decision-makers at senior level. Some of these will be politically supported, many will have particular interests and needs of their own. Most will have little (if any!) actual knowledge of how line managers operate. Managers in organizations with elected members having decisive powers need to present plans in a way that satisfies the needs of these groups. Lobbying often plays an important part in securing approval for plans and authority to proceed.

The role of the shareholders can be equally powerful; ensuring their support for management plans and strategy is essential if managers are to retain their positions on the board. Direct communication with shareholders, well-organized shareholders' meetings and effective public relations strategy are key elements in the internal marketing to this segment of the market. The financial press is a frequently used channel of communication, and the role of the Annual Report has changed considerably over recent years as managers have realized the need to 'sell' their organizations, and their plans.

The availability of finance is frequently a stumbling block to plans as resources are always limited. Competition for them will come from a number of sources, all of whom will have compelling reasons why their needs are paramount. Knowing clearly the benefits of your strategy for the organization and spelling these out to the budget holders will increase your chances of winning the needed resources.

The finance department is an audience of high priority when marketing your plans. Financiers see the world far more pragmatically than most – especially marketing, who can get carried away into 'blue sky' thinking. Tailoring plans to meet the tough needs of cash flow and profitability is good discipline, and essential if the support of the financial department is to be won.

The experienced manager soon learns that the best people to help convince any department are the members of that department itself. If help is asked for as the plans are developed it is possible to incorporate the thinking and needs of each involved department. 'Would it be acceptable if . . .?' is an excellent question. Once plans are finalized they are much easier to steer through given that each involved department has had a hand in their preparation.

Pre-thinking is essential. There is time to be taken in the winning of help from each department, but time spent early in the planning process is justified by the results when it comes to presenting the entire plan. It is now a shared plan, all have had a part in its creation. Much more difficult for anyone to be critical; and nobody will be difficult simply through hurt feelings!

The requirements of each department are different. Their ideal package will not suit other departments. It is for the instigator of the plan to ensure that it is blended to offer as much incentive to each involved department as possible; and to sell acceptance of the less acceptable elements. The functions tend to respond kindly to:

Finance	– improved returns on capital employed, improved efficiency, confidence that creditors will pay, budgetary control leading to acceptable risk.
Production	– volume throughput in existing plant, time to commission new plant, confidence in estimates, good quality control.
Personnel	– consistency of employment and of employment policy, warning of changes that will affect employees, adherence to employee legislation.
Marketing	– new packages that meet identified needs, variety and choice, wide margin to allow good promotion and flexibility in pricing, continuance of existing packages, total reliability in delivery and use, and with good after sales service.

Within the workforce various groups with common needs and interests may be represented by functions, subsidiary companies or trade unions. Each sector will have influencers and opinion leaders who need to be identified and targeted. Methods of communication will vary from meetings and staff newspapers to letters and notice boards.

Once the internal DMUs and DMPs have been identified, and the various customer groups segmented and researched to clarify their needs, it is possible to develop a marketing plan targeted to satisfy the needs of each group. The variables which can be modified to influence the degree of support for a plan are known as the 4 Ps – the **marketing mix**.

Product

The plan itself is the product. Its objectives, strategy and tactics will be viewed differently by the various audiences. Objectives will need to be seen as achievable and realistic by those expected to deliver them.

Most of the audiences reading the plan will have a need for security and belonging. Does the plan threaten my job, my prospects or my dividends? Does it include my function, my division?

Managers need to remember that when producing plans the over-riding question in the reader's mind will be, 'What does this mean to me?'

Price

It would be naive to assume that in the case of internal marketing there is no price to pay. The price tag may not be immediately visible, but there will be a price. The cost to the company of adopting my plan is the benefit lost by not being able to implement your plan – the **opportunity cost**.

To the shareholders and owners the cost may be lower profits this year for the benefit of higher next. For the workforce, increased productivity now, and job losses, may be the cost of future security or higher wages.

The manager, like any salesperson, needs to think carefully about how to handle the issue of price. Trying to ignore it will not be successful. Presenting it clearly in terms of cost benefit will be more effective.

Place

This variable refers to the availability of the benefits being offered. Timing of the planning process and communication of the plan may affect its implementation. Introduction during the annual pay round may place an unnecessarily high emphasis on productivity details.

Equally, the time scale involved will influence acceptability. Jam tomorrow may be saleable, but jam in five years' time will be much less attractive. Western business cultures seem to share a characteristic preference for shorter term strategy and quick returns rather than a longer term approach with the objective of maximizing returns. Identifying ways to make the benefits of a long term plan more attractive will be a management challenge for the years to come.

Promotion

Some of the various methods of communicating plans to internal audiences have already been mentioned. The approach to promoting plans is the same as promoting products. Be clear about the objectives:

* to create awareness;
* to change attitudes;
* to generate action.

Select the most suitable communication tools and make sure you transmit a series of consistent messages. A strategy of cost saving will be damaged by the production of a glossy four-colour report. Calling for economies in photocopying is useless if it is done on an A4 photocopied sheet addressed to each individual in a company. People react to what they see, not what they are told. Actions are noticed, they have to be consistent with the basic message. Take care in your selection of language and symbols to communicate your message. Negative aggressive language is likely to result in a surly response. Your message will set the tone. It has to be received, understood and acted upon.

After sales service

Reporting back after the plan has been implemented, reviewing progress and providing feedback are essential to continued success and participation by all in future plans. Planning is a continuous process, all involved have to be *involved throughout*.

Internal marketing guidelines

- Take internal marketing seriously.
- Identify the elements and needs of your DMUs and DMPs.
- Develop a communication strategy for each of your audiences.
- Use the most appropriate communication tool for each audience.
- Sell to the various audiences in terms of their needs.
- Do not forget the after sales service; you will need to approach each audience again and again as new plans develop. Each must become a 'repeat customer'.

ACTIVITIES

1 Review how plans are marketed within your department. Try to find out if the process is different in other departments.

   Frequently the sales function will have highly developed internal marketing techniques because the awareness of the need for motivation has been long accepted, and natural selling skills will come automatically into play. They can, however, unwittingly overplay their hand. If they are the only team selling internally a resistance can develop into a resentment very quickly.

2 Produce a schematic showing the DMUs and DMPs for your section, department or company. Beside each audience indicate your perception of its needs and the alternative channels of communication you could use for access.

3 Try using the principles of internal marketing at home. Choose an objective – to convince the family to holiday at your favourite location, or the children to tidy up their rooms. Devise a marketing plan to convince all of those involved. Try it out and remember the controls: Why did it (or didn't it) work? What will I do differently next time? Why?

Plans made
but not accepted wholeheartedly
can never achieve their full potential

10 *Reports and presentations*

Analysing a situation, identifying alternative courses of action, deciding and developing the best strategy are skills critical to the successful manager. But a manager's thoughts and recommendations have to be communicated to others: to seniors for support, approval and authority; to juniors for understanding and action. Your skill with the tools of communication, report writing and presentation in particular, will directly influence how you and your work is judged. Unless you make other people notice your management skills the only person aware of them will be you. This part of your duties is a little like putting icing on the cake; cake looks and tastes better if it is well iced, and it is more likely to be selected in the first place.

Packaging your thoughts and recommendations clearly and effectively is the key to both your reputation as a manager and a successful examination pass. People equate:

- Muddled recommendations with muddled thinking.
- Untidy presentation with an overall approach that is slipshod.
- Careless presentation with a lack of concern.
- Personal grooming with effectiveness.

In these matters there is no time pressure excuse. A management presentation has to have a flair, a style. If short on time by all means short cut; reduce the number of transparencies, but never their quality.

You will be well advised to take time and trouble to perfect your handling of the tools of report writing and presentation – both are fundamental to your success as a manager. Like the other tools, real competency will only come with practice, but an understanding of the basic principles is essential as a foundation upon which to build.

Reports

The function of a report is to carry information. The presentation style, the format, varies. The Annual Company Report has to meet the requirements laid down by company law, a management report has established terms of reference to meet.

Organizations tend to have preferred styles for their reports. It is good sense to discover, very quickly, how reports are formatted when you join a new organization. Adopting a common style is effective in communicating information. One is not writing a novel, nor an essay. There should be no twists to the plot. Everything should flow smoothly, and be written in grammatical Business English using simple words. There are no bonuses to be earned for using a long or unusual word unless there is distinct need. Clichés should be avoided.

Managers and examiners like to receive what they have called for. Make sure you know exactly what style is required.

What is a management report?

A management report is a written, action planning document. It should:

- Clearly report on a situation.
- Make positive recommendations for action.

It is normal for reports to be written in the third person and they must be logical and clear. This requires a degree of planning before starting to write. Although the elements of a report need to be the same, how they are combined and the order in which background and recommendations are sequenced changes the emphasis and balance.

Before starting any report be sure of your focus. Write down:

- Who is this report for?
- What action do I want it to result in?
- What are my objectives in writing it?

These are, in effect, the terms of reference – the rationale of the report. One should never write a report without knowing specifically what one expects it to achieve.

If you are a case study student you are writing for the senior examiner, who will be acting in the role of a senior manager. You want your work to result in a pass mark at least and therefore you must look at examiners' reports to discover what kind of written report they need from you. You will find their comments on the failure of candidates to write reports very helpful.

As a management student your objectives underpinning the report are to provide a vehicle to demonstrate to the examiner your skills of analysis and decision-making, in the context of the given case study and questions. Remember that you have to answer the questions asked. Just as a manager reporting to a managing director must give the MD specific answers, so must a case study candidate. There is no provision for intellectual indulgence.

A clarity of focus will help you make judgements about what should be included in your report, how much detail to put in and in what order to use your material. It will also indicate what must be left out.

You may find that your report is destined for a number of different audiences. One possible way to deal with this is to produce different versions – each customized to the needs of its readers. For example, you could write a full report to your line manager, but a summary report for other department heads.

Report writing guidelines

There are certain basic rules for report writing that you need to follow. Within them you have the opportunity to modify the structure of your report to suit practice in your organization, your objectives and the needs of your audience.

- The report must always be headed with the name of your organization, department or section.
- At the beginning state: who it is for, who it is from, and the date.

- Always start with a heading, a title.
- Use numbered paragraphs and sub-paragraphs, each headed as necessary. There is likely to be a customary system of numbering used in your company. For examination purposes the simple decimal system is excellent. Number each main point and then sub-number subsequent points within the main point, for example:

  1 *Background*
  This report was commissioned by the Board of Directors to provide information of value in considering new acquisitions:
  1.1 The company wishes to adopt an aggressive stance to the market for its premier product, Widgets Mark XXII;
  1.2 The market is approaching saturation. Expansion is likely to be most easily possible by acquisition;
  1.3 Financial support for acquisitions up to a value of £50m is available.
  2 *The market*
  etc., etc.

- Present the contents in logical order, i.e. logical to the reader not yourself. Complete everything that relates to one point before moving on to another. It is then possible to cross reference within your report, e.g. 'see Appendix D', 'this is developed in 4.5 below' or 'as was stated in 3.2 above . . .'. The beauty of using the decimal system in an exam is that you are able to insert additional points if you think of them later, as footnotes but referenced from the report. In real life they would, of course, be inserted into proper order on a word processor.
- Take care to structure your material logically. There is no opportunity for the reader to ask for clarification of a point. Your material has to stand alone. You may find that your points fall into a natural sequence: chronological, spatial, order of importance or complexity. Use diagrams and illustrations where they help to clarify points or communicate information more effectively. It is easy when you have been working on a problem for a long time to forget to include the basic background, explanation of terms or parameters of the project. Take the state of mind, experience, intelligence and interest of your audience(s) into account.
- Structure your report to take your reader(s) through the stages:
  Awareness – familiarize the reader with the basics, relevant facts and background. Clarify the nature of the problem.
  Attitude – outline your analysis of the position and the pros and cons of the available options. Back this by facts and evidence as necessary. Detailed supporting information should be included in appendices and clearly referred to in the main text.
  Action – lead the audience logically to the action you recommend. Always include clear recommendations for action.
- Recommendations must always be included. They have to be firm, clear, unambiguous and decisive. To achieve these characteristics you will find recommendations usually encompass quantified objectives:

  It is recommended that two new production supervisors are appointed and trained before September.
  Recommended sales force targets are 2,000 cases per month for July, August and September.

Commonly you will find a summary of 'conclusions and recommendations' at the front of a report. This is in recognition of the fact that a busy manager may not get further than page one. (Nor need to if you are trustworthy and thorough.) Your job is to make it easy for your manager to take decisions. He or she should find clear recommendations for action – one of which could be to delay or re-think – and clear signposts to the body of evidence that supports each recommendation, for example:

2.3   It is recommended that the Widget pressing machine in Unit 7 be replaced no later than December 31st. (See 4.1)

2.4   It is recommended that *no* action be taken concerning the Widget packing machine in Unit 9. (See 4.3)

An example of a short management report

THE PLASTIC BAG COMPANY PLC

TO: Operations Director
FROM: Day Shift Production Manager
DATE: 12.3.9X

SUBJECT: Appointment of Production Supervisors

1.   Background
     Over the last 12 months:
     1.1   output has increased by 22%;
     1.2   machine capacity has increased by 30%;
     1.3   2 new production processes are now available;
     1.4   9 more operatives are employed on the day shift.

2.   Marketing has indicated that sales growth is forecast to rise by a further 6% during the next year.

3.   At current staffing levels we will be unable to maintain the required level of quality control checks.
     3.1   Currently there are 4 full time production supervisors rostered for the day shift.
     3.2   One of these, Shanna Peters, is scheduled to take maternity leave from August 15th.

4.   Available options
     4.1   Reducing the level of control checks to 1:2,000 was considered.
           Appendix A provides information of current quality status.
           Appendix B summarizes the marketing manager's report of January 18th on Client Quality Needs.
     4.2   Appointing additional production supervisors has been considered. Analysis of the required staffing levels needed to meet the projected production level at the required quality control standard is in Appendix C.

5. Recommendations:
    5.1 Quality control standards should be maintained at the agreed level.
    5.2 A total of 6 full time production assistants should be available for the day shift roster by September 199X.
        5.2.1 4 should be recruited from the labour market, as usual,
        5.2.2 2 should be recruited direct from the local College at end of term. A special training programme should be devised with the College, using work placement – which is in line with the company's good neighbour policy.
    5.3 New production supervisors should be appointed from the current production staff, to reduce training time and cost.
    5.4 In addition a temporary appointment should be made to provide maternity leave cover, see 3.2 above.

6. Urgency
    It is emphasized that to allow adequate training of the new supervisors, selection needs to have been completed by June lst.

Signed

Appendices Attached [not included in this illustration].

ACTIVITIES

1 Find four management reports at work, produced by different people or departments. Consider each critically and produce a list of:
   –   three good points of each,
   –   three ideas for their improvement.
   Now carefully examine the last report that you produced – did it do justice to the quality of your work?
2 Write a management report to the chairperson of your local resident's association. You would like to organize a Crime Watch operation for the area and need to convince him or her of its value.
3 Next time you have to write a report at work, or for a college assignment, make a point of reviewing your work against the guidelines for report writing. Take time to modify and improve.

Report writing is another skill that develops over time. The mental processing of information into logical, brief, cohesive chunks is not easy – but the benefits in terms of mental discipline, ability to think through problems, and to be organized are valuable skills in your life both in and outside business.

Presentations

Writing a management report and presenting the same material orally requires markedly different communication tools. For managers in the 1990s the ability to present is essential – whether it be to a single person, a small intimate group, or a large formal session. Presentation performance is based upon preparation and structure – exactly the same mental skills and disciplines as are needed when writing reports.

Presentation skills are directly interpersonal. To be successful you need to be practised, rehearsed and confident. Confidence can only come from practice, but an awareness of some of the rules of presentation will help you to make improvements immediately in your effectiveness.

You will be required to make many presentations throughout your career. They are popular because they force the essence of a situation to be distilled, and presented succinctly. A management report may run to 10,000 words, you may have to reduce it to key factors in order to cover it in 20 minutes. It seems that it cannot be done – yet many management presenters achieve it regularly.

As always it is crucial to begin planning for each and every presentation with a written focus:

- Who is this presentation for?
- What action do I want it to result in?
- What are my objectives in making it?

It may very well be that your aim is to make the work sufficiently attractive that those present go through your recommendations in detail. This may be a major achievement! You may be competing with other managers for the attention of senior management, and for approval of your budget. You have to know exactly what constitutes success . . . before you start to plan in detail.

A presentation is a much more immediate style of communication. It allows you to respond to feedback, to clarify and modify the message *and/or* the style to meet the perceived needs and mood of the audience. You can therefore provide yourself with alternatives – areas to follow through in depth if interest is evinced; and areas to jump across to if the audience is not sufficiently involved. (Using these alternative routes takes confidence and skill, but both will come with time.)

The audience will receive messages not just from the words, but from you directly. Your body language will add emphasis and power to your message. Poor presentation technique will detract from the message and weaken your case. If you let your nerves show, do not look directly at the audience nor appear apologetic, your message will seem unconvincing and will be less likely to win support.

It will be encouraging if you confirm for yourself that all presenters are nervous before they start. It is true, but you need to talk with people that you admire, and ask them. *You* have to be convinced that it is normal to be nervous; that without a degree of 'nerves' you will not be sharp; and that the flutters in the stomach go away once you have got started – the adrenalin is necessary to a good performance.

As you gain experience you will learn exactly how your 'nerves' work. Exactly when you ought to be feeling nervous. For some it is only in the last few minutes, for most it is an hour or more ahead. (If it is more than an hour ahead you should do a lot more preparation and rehearsal!) From these two factors come the basis of confidence.

Presentation guidelines

- Research your audience: find out to whom you will be presenting; their level of knowledge and expertise; why they will be in the audience; who are the key people that you have to concentrate upon?
- Prepare thoroughly.
    Know your subject and the material to be presented.
    Structure your delivery of the material.
    Pre-write the first sentences – and thoroughly rehearse them. That guarantees you a good start.
    Prepare and rehearse your closing point(s). Then you can cut to a positive close if you find you are running short on time.
- Refine the content. The most common mistake is to put too much into a presentation. Keep refining, keep throwing out material ruthlessly until you have a punchy, structured and short presentation.
- Simplify. Never try to achieve too much.
- Structure logically. Your audience must be able to follow you – they will be new to material you have worked on for weeks or months and you must not expect them to be immediately familiar with it. It is fatal to lose an audience simply through an unexpected change of direction that you understand. Try to imagine you are directing a foreign visitor who speaks little English through the town or suburb in which you have played as a child. No short cuts!
- Visualize. Tell the story in pictures and graphs when you can. Visuals must not be complex, and the audience must have time to absorb them. Above all *stop talking* when you show a new visual. Watch the audience and pick up your presentation only when most are back with you. This takes courage – but people cannot read and listen at the same time.
- Remember that questions can throw presenters.
    Think through the most likely in advance so that you are as well prepared as possible.
    Say at the beginning whether you will take questions at any time, or whether you prefer them at the end.
    When you do not know the answer always say so – but follow up with 'but I will find out and let you know'. Then carry out your promise.
- Prepare yourself. Decide which clothes will be most appropriate, ensure they are sent to the cleaners and come back in time. Check your hair and all aspects of personal presentation. You must look the part or you will lose credibility before you open your mouth.
- Rehearse. Make time to go through your notes and visuals. Check them carefully for errors. Number 35mm slides so you know which order and which way up they go into the projector. Always double check they are in correctly. Even if they are sealed into the magazine with masking tape always double check, especially if you are supported by a technician.
    Time your presentation several times. Work in front of a mirror and try to hit the pace you want. (You will be too fast, so be prepared to cut down your material even further.)
    Key point prompts are all you will need, supported by your report that will act as a security blanket. 6 × 4 index cards are good. They are small enough to hold in one hand, and large enough to hold key points. Best to have one point per card. Number

the cards in case you drop them, and/or punch the top corner and loosely tie them together.

Remember Sod's Law – *If it can go wrong, it will*. Your job is to cover as many of the possible disasters that could befall you.

Run through your presentation to a colleague or friend who has the task of suggesting improvements. Best to use someone who is not involved with the project and, preferably, has no direct interest in your success. Welcome the comments, and learn from them.

Make sure you find time to check out the presentation room early. Is it laid out the way you want it? Can you use the equipment provided?

Presentation structure

Although this can be very much a matter of personal choice which will depend upon the personalities and subject concerned, a proven structure which works very effectively in most circumstances is as follows.

1 Introduction. A clear statement of who you are and where you are from. What you are going to present and *why*. Outline the structure:

- Good morning, I am . . . from . . .
- Thank you for inviting me to present the facts about our XYZ project.
- I understand that you are considering a similar project, and I will be happy to show you where we went right, and where we went wrong!
- I would like to take questions at the end, please, because I will be taking you through the project from concept to turnkey, and I believe a lot of early questions will be answered automatically.

2 Body. In the body of the presentation you are dealing with the facts. You have them well structured, you match the speed of the audience, you do not talk over a visual aid.

3 Conclusion 1. The end of your formal presentation. End on key points that summarize. Then take questions.

4 Questions. Handle them one at a time. *Never* say 'I covered that earlier' because if you did the questioner did not understand and that is your fault.

5 Conclusion 2. Re-summarize the position, probably end with *brief* thanks, the key is that *you* close your presentation so that it is packaged as a unit in the minds of the audience.

Presentation hints and tips

- Attention span is very short. As much as 10 minutes is good in an adult (figure 10.1). Therefore change the style and pace of your presentation as you progress. At the beginning there will be very high attention from the audience, so get key facts across early. Towards the middle there will be a decline in attention, so change style to re-kindle the response. This is the time to use a short video. As your time is running out there will be a natural, and unconscious awareness, and a lifting of the attention threshold. Another opportunity to hammer key facts across.
- Beware of using humour! A joke that falls flat, or a situation that is not appreciated as funny will kill a presentation, and your confidence. With experience you will be able to build in some humour, but not when you are a relative beginner.

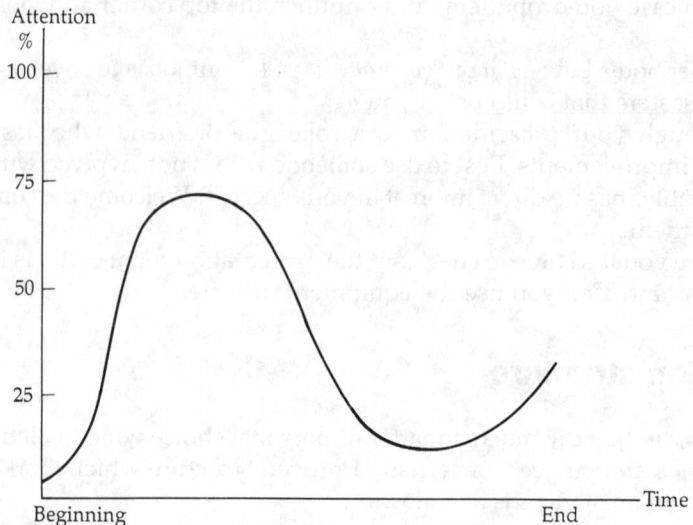

Figure 10.1   *Attention given by typical audience unless preventative action taken*

- Avoid information that is too detailed. Put tables or figures into graphs and bar charts. Round large numbers. 'Sales will be £10 million in 1994' is far better than 'Sales revenue is forecast to be £9,875,500 in 1994'.
- Present one fact at a time. Build from fact to fact. Secure understanding of each as you go along.
- Give details and supporting materials in a report or handout.
- Always attempt to check the presentation room, and the equipment. Whether it be the day before or half-an-hour before, check it. Working with professional technicians is no guarantee that all will work (they may have only got onto site three hours before the conference, and you may be the first to use a piece of equipment that tested OK).
- Be prepared to revert to flip chart and pen if the electrics fail. If you have pre-thought this it is most unlikely to occur, but in a long career it will happen several times.

Media

Understand that the techniques for effective presentation via TV/video and radio/tape are very different from those needed for face-to-face work. Not everybody can cope with a range of media and, certainly, each is better in one form or another.

Do not be tempted to make a video or audio tape without training and *never* go on to a TV or radio interview without thorough preparation from a professional.

Meetings

Meetings are a very important part of a manager's internal communications task but fall outside the scope of this book. It would not be possible to do justice to the subject within the space available; there is, however, a wealth of readily available material for consultation and there is no shortage of internal training courses.

ACTIVITIES

1 Make a point of critically watching or listening to recordings of public speakers. Note how they use carefully rehearsed phrases that you will hear repeated in different situations: for example, on any one day compare early morning radio current affairs programmes and midday, early evening and night-time news bulletins and current affairs programmes on BBC1 and 2, ITV and Channel 4. The phrases will also appear in newspaper interviews, in weekend newspaper colour supplement features and in the House of Commons. Speakers repeat phrases like this because it works. It takes time to refine a compelling phrase – but the 'stickability' makes the effort worthwhile.

2 Identify an opportunity within the next six weeks when you can make a presentation. Call a staff meeting or offer to do a careers talk at a local school. Work hard, but do not be over ambitious. Ten to 15 minutes is best.

3 Take every opportunity to improve your presentation techniques – are training courses available at work or at your local college?

4 Critically review amateur videos, and compare them to those professionally made. The difference is exactly the same in principle as between an amateur presenter and a professional. Your aim is to achieve professional standard in your field.

5 Compare the body language of professionals and amateurs appearing on TV chat shows ... watch for a time with the sound off, and run a video tape of the interview at high speed.

Your actions speak far louder
than your words!

Part Two

Aide-mémoire of Selected Terms

11 *Glossary of selected terms*

From 'audit' to 'working capital', here you will find summaries and reviews of key techniques, activities and tools from across the business spectrum.

This is not intended to be an exhaustive glossary of management and marketing terminology; simply an *aide-mémoire* which will be of value as a quick reference guide.

The material is presented in alphabetical order, with cross-references indicated in bold type as appropriate.

Audit

A financial audit is a rigorous examination by an independent and well-qualified accountant. The term 'audit' has been adopted in a far looser way by management to indicate a *situational analysis*. Thus it is possible to 'audit' any aspect of management activity.

See also **management/marketing audit.**

Average

See **quantitative analysis.**

Awareness, Attitude, Action

Advertising, it is said, can sell anything – once! After that the product stands or falls by its ability to deliver to the promises made in its presentation. Consumers often need help to become aware of their need for a specific good or service, at a specific time. The awareness of need must then be turned into a positive purchase decision. That decision must be acted upon. Thus there are three major stages through which every purchaser passes: awareness, attitude and action.

> Research indicates that promotional activity concerned with protecting the British public from the spread of AIDS has successfully generated a high level of awareness. Sales of condoms showed a marked increase. Yet the number of condoms *used* did not change. Nor did the number of sexual partners show any decline.

Advertising is most effective at creating Awareness. It is very ineffective in generating Action. Thus the Promotional Mix consists of specific tools that are used to create and maintain awareness, to develop and sustain a positive attitude and to motivate action in terms of both purchase and use.

Brand manager

A brand manager, sometimes called a product manager, is a junior marketing manager with responsibility for one or more brands, or products. Typically in his or her mid to late 20s, he or she will have authority far beyond his or her level of management. This is because the authority is *derived* from the marketing manager or marketing director.

A brand manager will not last long in post if he or she loses the confidence of senior marketing management. In larger firms there will often be one or more group brand managers, each responsible for a range of similar brands, through whom the brand managers report. Authority will still be derived from the marketing manager or director. See **structure**.

The young manager is close to the corridors of power, and makes recommendations for both strategic and tactical action. There will be very few in the marketing team, and the exposure is high. It is therefore a post in which a considerable amount of learning is achieved and from which careers can be built.

Acting as the advocate of their brands, they will have contact with every function in a firm. Actions will typically be taken on the basis of a telephone request, thus the delays inherent in a bureaucratic system of memos and formal requests will be short-circuited. (The formal request will, naturally, have to proceed through channels for the protection of all concerned.)

As prime contact for the brands, these managers will carry responsibility for the achievement of budget – which will include working with outside agencies for research, advertising and PR.

Typically, successful brand managers will take responsibility for more significant brands as time passes. Often they will spend time as a sales person before gaining a senior post as a sales or group brand manager.

Note: Various titles are used by different concerns, e.g. Marketing Executive (Coffee), but the principle does not change.

Budgetary control

See **budgeting.**

Budgeting

Budgeting is the process of managing the balance of expenditure against income. Under *budgetary control* a series of **objectives** – statements that provide clear targets for achievement within each operating section of a business *and* allow a **control** mechanism to measure achievement against plan.

Budgetary control is the process by which performance is regularly monitored. The time span depends upon the type of concern. In the financial markets positions are monitored by the second, e.g. foreign exchange. Government programmes are often measured over a period of years. Companies tend to look at one-year time periods, with monthly reviews.

It is important to have a continual awareness of how a business is performing. The annual statutory documents are accounting records *not* management control documents. Under budgetary control potential problems (or benefits) are identified as they arise.

Operating units can be a *cost centre* or *profit centre*. A cost centre operates against a budget forecast of cost. A profit centre is expected to generate a forecast amount of profit.

Dependent upon the concern's internal invoicing policy, every centre can be profit-oriented. Each section can charge for the added-value that it gives to the product or service. Profit generation is shared throughout the concern with, under effective systems, no split between those perceived as profit earners (i.e. marketing and sales) and those who spend money (i.e. production, administration and central services).

One of the problems that have to be faced under profit-centred management is the requirement of each manager to make a profit, and thus to want to buy from the source of best value. Internal strife can be generated by a manager finding an external source of supply that offers better value. In theory this should spur the internal department to improve its service, but it may be unable to do so for reasons outside its control.

Budgets are not *targets*. Generally it is considered good to beat target but under budgetary control it is necessary to meet budget. It is equally bad to exceed budget as it is to fall short. Production is geared to a manufacturing budget that is tied to a sales budget. If both are not running in synchronization there will be a surplus or shortfall of production. Under budgetary control variations from any one budget should allow others to be amended in time to minimize damage and maximize efficiency.

See also **promotional budgeting**.

Cable television

See **satellite and cable television.**

Cash flow

See **financial analysis.**

Charts and diagrams

Pictorial representation of information often make points more obvious. Bar charts and pie diagrams are the most commonly used *pictures* . . . they are not statistically reliable representations of information. They are best used in support of an argument, to illustrate key points. Decisions should be made on numerical information, its diagrammatic representation should be taken as a simplified version that may very well mislead.

A **graph**, whether simple or logarithmic, should always have its origin at zero. Both axes should be clearly labelled, it should be titled, and the source and date of the data identified.

A **matrix** is a most useful tool. It allows data to be combined into one table to yield information that is not apparent from the individual tables.

Contingency planning

The purpose of contingency planning is to provide management with a set of action plans ahead of need. Planning takes time, and 'fire-fighting management' spends its time rushing from problem to problem. With a system of contingency planning the managers attempt to visualize every eventuality that could befall, and decide what to do in the event. Good planning ensures that the basic materials for each of the contingency plans are ready ahead of need.

Most contingency plans are never needed, but without them management is vulnerable.

Control

A term used to indicate that decisions, once taken, have to be implemented and monitored. A *control process* is a monitoring and reporting system that measures achievement against intention and flags *variance* to management.

See also **budgetary control** and **objectives.**

Cost centres

See **budgeting.**

Costs

Costing is a technical subject on which clear policy decisions must be taken. The key costing terms are:

- Direct costs   – those that can be charged directly to a cost or profit centre.
- Indirect costs   – costs that cannot directly be attributed to a cost or profit centre and which are apportioned between centres, as appropriate.
- Overhead   – the total of indirect costs.
- Prime cost   – direct materials, direct labour and direct expenses.
- Factory cost   – prime cost plus factory overhead.
- Cost of sales   – factory cost plus overheads of: administration; research and development; selling and distribution.
- Sales price   – cost of sales plus profit.
- Fixed costs   – costs that do not change with the level of activity.

- Variable costs   – costs that do change with the level of activity.
- Marginal costs   – the costs involved in producing extra units *given that existing revenue covers fixed costs.*
- Contribution   – the difference between sales revenue and the variable cost of those sales. A positive contribution helps to pay for fixed costs.
- Break-even   – the point when sales revenue is just sufficient to cover total costs.

See also **opportunity cost.**

Customer or consumer?

The terms 'customer' and 'consumer' are often used indiscriminately, and thus confusion is caused. It is necessary to be clear that a customer is a person who buys. A consumer is a person who uses up a product or service.

Obviously one person can be both customer and consumer – but on many occasions a customer is buying on behalf of one or more consumers.

Marketing has to understand the behaviour of those who can, those who could, and those who do buy a particular product or service. It is necessary to think very clearly through the problem, to identify exactly who are the prospective and actual customers; who are the prospective and actual consumers.

A child may not like vegetables, but a mother will buy them, and insist on their consumption because 'they are good for you'. Child = consumer, mother = customer.

The term 'final consumer' is sometimes used to designate the person(s) who will use up the value of the goods or service. This is not necessary – nor is it necessary to invent an 'intermediate customer'. Quite simply a customer can also be a consumer, a consumer can also be a customer.

Corporate purchases, and some domestic high value purchases, involve groups who jointly make the purchase decisions. Thus it is necessary to investigate the *decision-making unit* (DMU) and the *decision-making process* (DMP). Once that is done it becomes obvious that a DMU is present within every decision whether or not to purchase. There are six elements to the DMU, best visualized as a SPADE stuck into a heap of Fertilizer (see figure 11.1).

S = Starter;   P = Purchaser;   A = Adviser;
D = Decider;   E = End-user;   F = Financer.

No purchase will be made without consideration of all six elements.

The DMP refers to the systemized procedure followed, formally or informally, in order that a decision regarding purchase can be made. The DMP can be extremely complex and time-consuming – as in a decision to commission a civil engineering project; or simple and fast – as in an individual choice between a bar of milk or nut chocolate from a vending machine.

Sales research is much concerned with identifying both the DMU and the DMP, and should be the basis upon which strategic and tactical selling decisions are made.

The Japanese have been particularly assiduous in gaining a thorough understanding of consumer and customer needs, and in using the results of their sales research.

Figure 11.1   *SPADE mnemonic*

Data and information

It is easy to confuse these terms. Data is both singular and plural. A single number and a complete research study are 'data'. Data is the presentation of facts.

Information is hidden in data. Usually one has to manipulate data to locate and clarify the information that is needed. *Secondary data* (see **marketing research**) must always be manipulated.

Data should always be approached in a doubtful frame of mind. It must be tested for **validity** and **reliability**. Data must never be assumed to have value; it must always prove itself.

Basic rules

1 Data should be read from a position of disbelief.
2 Data may have been prepared for a specific purpose. Confirm that the information it contains is actually relevant to present needs – not just 'useful', or 'interesting'.
3 Data should be manipulated and combined to extract relevant information; or to prove that it does not exist.
4 Confirm:
   4.1 That the source and date of the data are given.
   4.2 That it is presented fairly.
   4.3 That the data that has commonality – e.g. ice cream purchases for the North West of England are not necessarily comparable with ice cream sales in Lancashire and Cheshire (which comprise *part* of the North West).

See also **information**.

Decision-making process (DMP)

See **customer or consumer?**

Decision-making unit (DMU)

See **customer or consumer?**

Decisions

Managers exist to make decisions. That is their fundamental role, underpinning leadership and the management of resources.

Decision theory requires that:

1 Problem(s) are defined.
2 Alternative solutions are identified.
3 Alternative solutions are evaluated.
4 Decision(s) is/are taken on the basis of the information available.
5 The decisions are acted upon.
6 Results of action are monitored, and remedial action(s) taken as necessary.

Effective decisions can only be taken if managers have access to appropriate **information** in sufficient time.

Directors

The title 'Director' is correctly used to describe one of the senior officers of a limited company. 'Production Director' and 'Director of Production' are not of the same seniority despite the similarity of their titles. This is important when one is visiting, or about to entertain, since it may be necessary to field an executive of appropriate seniority to welcome a visiting director.

It is less important when accepting authority to do business from any person in a concern. If the person gives every impression that he or she is acting in good faith on behalf of their organization and if they are not obviously too junior to have the requisite authority, it is likely that a contract will be enforceable. It can, however, become both embarrassing and time-consuming to go to court, therefore it is better *when possible*, to check the actual authority of any person, director or not, with whom one is about to do business.

Non-Executive Directors are invited to sit on a Board of Directors for the special benefits that the chairman and members of the board feel they bring with them. They have no day-to-day responsibility for the business and its operations but, as with all directors, they have a statutory responsibility to ensure that the concern is operating legally and that it does not continue to trade if insolvent. (See **statutory accounts**.)

It is very important when selling to establish most clearly the areas and degree of authority enjoyed by all that one needs to become involved with, either directly or indirectly. In particular it is necessary to discover exactly who makes the final decision, and who are the strongest influencers.

See also **customer or consumer?**

Discounted cash flow

Different cash flows, extending over a period of time, can be compared as single numbers by discounting the amount in each cash flow using the organization's internal cost of capital. The number which results is called the cash flow's net present value (NPV). In simple terms the cash flow with the highest NPV *may* be the most attractive. If an organization can take on a finite number of new projects it may rank them by NPV and then select as many as it wants to undertake.

Distribution

Delivery trucks, multi-stationery, scheduling, efficient warehouse usage, cost of storing stock . . . these elements are important within the logistics of delivering a product, but they are not the totality of distribution.

Distribution encompasses every aspect of the channel(s) that take a product or service from point of origin to final consumption. Thus distribution is equally important to a service supplier and to a product manufacturer. The service, and the product, have to be where the consumer needs them – fit and ready for use – at the time of consumer need. It is the task of **physical distribution management** to ensure that the logistical task works effectively. It is for management to set distribution policy.

Strategic decisions about distribution are always made by those who hold power in the distribution channel(s). When there are many small retailers the grocery distribution channels are controlled by the manufacturers and (possibly) the wholesalers. As fewer but more powerful retailers dominate the market, the power in the channel shifts to them.

Profits come from repeat business and so distribution is not complete until the product or service is consumed. Those holding power over distribution therefore hold the whip hand in negotiations with every other interested party.

Key concepts are:

- Without availability customers cannot buy the product or service. Demand generated, but unsatisfied, will yield both no profits *and* customer dissatisfaction (that may spread across a whole product range).
- Products available when and where customers want them provide added value and can directly affect demand.
- **Packaging** has a role to play within distribution, as well as within promotion, in addition to its basic role of protection.
- Changing distribution patterns open up new market segments.
- The length of the distribution channel(s) will directly affect the control of the marketing of the product and the amount of capital committed to distribution.
- Distribution costs represent a significant part of the total cost. Improved distributive effectiveness can significantly influence profit.
- A channel of distribution will naturally contract to a point of **minimum total transactions**. As technology advances, so the choice of channels is in constant change.
- Distribution decisions affect costs and demand and should not be made in isolation.
- Distribution needs to be in harmony with the rest of the marketing mix and with overall product positioning.

Effectiveness and efficiency

Management objectives should cover both *effectiveness* and/or *efficiency* in addition to being quantified against time. Effectiveness is doing the right things: efficiency is doing things right.

'Doing the wrong things right' – Efficient without being effective.
'Getting the result, but at what cost?' – Effective without being efficient.
'Doing the right things right.' – Both efficient and effective.

This objective covers all the requirements:

Defective equipment shall be restored to full working condition within 6 hours of receipt of complaint.

The quality of the repair is specified as is the efficiency of response required. Provided there is a **control** system to ensure that complaints are accurately logged on receipt, and that the workmanship is supervised it will be possible to measure success against objective. Compare the laxity allowed to repair teams if the objective is written thus:

To repair defective equipment promptly.

Note: Efficiency is often loosely described as 'greater productivity, better administration'. But, to an engineer, efficiency means the measurable relationship between the work done by a machine and the energy supplied to it. It is extremely difficult to measure efficiency in non-quantifiable areas of a business. The tools of weighted averaging and semantic differential are most helpful.
See **quantitative analysis**

Exception reporting

See **financial analysis**.

Feasibility study

A feasibility study is a thorough examination of one or more alternative courses of action. Using **What if?** techniques and supported by detailed planning techniques one or more **scenarios** are worked through with the intention of determining the most viable course of action in the light of identified internal and external constraints.

Inevitably feasibility planners suffer from the problem that they are working into an unknown future. Whatever safeguards are built into the planning process it is most unlikely that a totally accurate plan will evolve. The benefits of a feasibility study, therefore, are not a perfect plan. Instead they are the benefits associated with reconnaissance – a foreknowledge of the type of problems and opportunities that are likely to be faced; and rehearsal – tackling a series of problems and opportunities through What if? scenarios.

Financial analysis

Financial analysis is the process by which data in the statutory accounts is transformed into *meaningful management information*. This is particularly so when measuring a concern's performance over time, and also when comparing performance with that of competitors. This information is vital to management at strategic level.

Good financial analysis will provide management with information in time for decisive action to be taken. Accounts as history have value – but not to a manager in a post of responsibility.

Individual departments build up financial pictures of their performance at the tactical level. Costs of production and of marketing will be analysed as individual budgets. Other departments, such as finance, legal, personnel etc., will all monitor their own costs against budgets. All the individual budgets are consolidated into a company's **statutory accounts**.

Cash flow

One of the key concerns of management is *liquidity*. A business can trade for a considerable period while making a loss – quite legally if it has an asset base to cover the debts it is incurring. It cannot continue once it has insufficient liquidity (cash or assets quickly turned to cash).

The shortage of *working capital* (i.e. cash and quick assets) is the spectre that haunts all management. The management of liquidity is therefore a key management task. A *cash flow statement* is an indispensable tool since it breaks every aspect of a concern's operations down into a cash-in/cash-out time matrix. An internal cash flow statement is a highly confidential document. More than any other it reveals the true success and viability of a business.

Variance analysis

Once a budget has been established, as a forecast, it is relatively simple to set up a system that monitors performance against budget. Performance that falls outside predetermined *variance criteria* is flagged for management attention. Thus an experienced manager can be allowed a larger variance than one new in post. Operations critical to the concern can be monitored more tightly than those of less immediate importance.

To prevent management being swamped with data a system of *exception reporting* will ensure that only areas that fall outside the variance criteria are flagged. This information should be presented in order of importance. It is desirable to establish a flagging system that brings forward excellent performance as well as adverse variations. Otherwise management will be continuously dealing with problems, and may be seen to be super-critical and intolerant.

Financial ratios

It is important to identify trends from year-on-year changes; also to compare results for different years and to measure the comparative performances of different operating divisions. In the main, financial ratios eliminate inflationary effects and are equally accurate in whichever currency the accounts are prepared.

Financial ratios have the advantage that they, generally, eliminate the difference in size of businesses and so they allow comparison of different companies.

There are a large number of generally used financial ratios, but those most commonly used fall into three categories: stock market ratios, performance ratios and financial status ratios.

Stock market ratios
These are not generally a concern of operating management, but are most valuable when considering acquisitions. Top management need to be aware of how the company is performing and, of course, the relationships with the shareholders and financiers are affected by stock market performance. There is a plethora of literature to turn to in case of need.

Performance ratios
These measure how well a business is being run. Commonly used ratios are calculated thus:

Profit margin   = profit/sales.
Return on equity   = profit/equity.
Return on net assets = profit/net assets.
Stock turnover   = sales/stock.
Debtor turnover   = sales/debtors.
Creditor turnover   = sales/creditors.

Financial status ratios
These consider the ability of a company to meet its liabilities. They are subdivided into *solvency ratios* (longer term) and *liquidity ratios* (shorter term). The main ratios for general management purposes are:

Debt ratio   = Long term debt/debt + equity
(solvency)   (target result less than 50 per cent).
Current ratio   = Current assets/current liabilities
(liquidity)   (target result greater than 2.0).
Acid test   = Liquid assets (debtors + cash)/current liabilities
(liquidity)   (target result greater than 1.0).

Fire fighting

Managers are said to be 'fire fighters' when they rush from problem to problem with no overall plan. The expression originates from an analogy with brush fires, where a series of spontaneous combustions occur and urgent actions are needed to prevent a small fire turning into an inferno.

See also **contingency planning**.

Forecasting

The only thing certain about a forecast is that it will be wrong! Made with the best information, the most advanced software programs and with the best of intentions the strong probability is that any forecast will be inaccurate.

A forecast is a statement of expectation, made into an uncertain future. Most forecasts cannot be correct. Yet they are essential for an entity to survive. The system of *budgetary control* (see **budgeting**) monitors achievement against expectation and should flag variances *in time for corrective action to be taken*.

The key aspect of forecasting is to be aware of its unreliability and provide for that in planning. Forecasts must be subject to ongoing review and there must be no hesitation nor embarrassment if/when changes are needed.

Forecasts should be over appropriate time scales. Bank dealing rooms can produce forecasts for a day's activities while aircraft manufacturers produce forecasts which extend for many years.

Franchising

A *franchisor* licenses one or more *franchisees* to make or use something in exchange for some form of payment. This can be direct – in the form of a fee and/or royalty, or indirect – an obligation to buy a product or service in which the franchisor has an interest.

Franchising has become extremely popular in recent times because it allows an operation to expand very quickly without undue risk, and without the need for a substantial amount of working capital (see **financial analysis**). Franchising will succeed, given market demand, where there is careful *mutual* selection of the parties to a franchise contract, an effective manual of operations that is enforced, and both parties are engaged in long term association for mutual benefit.

A franchise offers a proven business formula which helps to ensure that a franchise start-up is considerably safer than an independent entry to the marketplace.

The franchisee provides the advantages of working capital, motivated local management, market knowledge and contacts. Franchisees have been particularly attracted to, and successful in, service sector operations. Many well-known High Street names that appear to be a national chain are, in fact, franchises: Prontaprint, Kall-Kwik, Fast-frames, Holiday Inns and McDonalds. Coca-Cola operate through franchisees, as do Hertz, Avis and Budget Rent A Car.

Gee wiz statistics

Gee wiz statistics abound in the financial pages of our newspapers. It is essential that you are able to recognize and discount them.

The technique of mis-information, which is the point of gee wiz statistics, is to present data in a compelling way such that you are inclined to accept it at face value. An

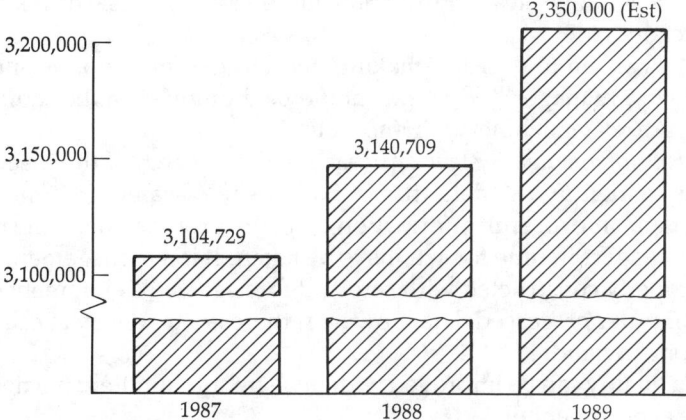

Figure 11.2 *Gee wiz bar chart*

example will suffice to demonstrate a typical approach (figure 11.2). You will see that there is a very healthy growth in the figures – but look at the vertical scale. It does not start at zero. If you plot the same data on a graph which is to scale you will find that the line is virtually flat! When you go back to the original data you will see that the actual increases year on year are 1.16 per cent and 3.48 per cent, far behind the rate of inflation.

The technique for handling any statistics is simple. Start from a position of disbelief. Require the statistics to prove themselves. Always check their reliability; ensure that pictorial representations do not over-simplify.

Graphs

See **charts and diagrams.**

Image

See **positioning.**

Incentive

See **motivation.**

Information

Information provides signposts to help managers take decisions. It must never be confused with *data*, which is information presented in a general, and sometimes confusing way. Without clear information there is a high **risk** of taking the wrong strategic direction.

Information is an aid to decision-making, therefore information is one of the major tools available to a manager. It can and should be thought of in the same way as other resources: workforce, machinery, finance, etc.

A *Management Information System* is pro-active in its search of the macro- and micro-environments to identify the data that is likely to be of value. Its function then is to convert raw data into useful information, and to provide that information to the appropriate managers in time for actions to be taken. It is a management service that is vital since, properly constructed with care and foresight, it is extremely cost-effective. As with all computer processed data, however, there is a tendency to call for more than one needs – or can handle.

Information quality can be improved with investment, but there is a need to evaluate cost and time against benefit.

Information management can give a strong competitive advantage. It should be taken seriously and looked upon as a valuable corporate resource that requires planning and managing to ensure it is used effectively. A manager should be able to access information that is current, relevant to the decision, reliable and accurate.

Information should be *needed* not simply *nice* to know.

See also **data and information.**

KISS principle

Keep It Short and Simple, a guiding principle that is too often ignored by managers when they write reports and make presentations.

Also known as Keep it Simple, Stoopid!

Leadership

> 'Leadership is getting extraordinary performance
> out of ordinary people.'
>
> Sir John Harvey-Jones

Leadership and management should not be confused. They are distinctly different concepts. 'Lead' has its root in 'laed', a word common to all old North European languages. It means a road, path, course of a ship at sea, journey. A leader accompanies people on a journey, guiding them to their destination. He or she holds them together while leading them in the right direction.

'Manager' only entered the English language in the sixteenth century. The root is 'manus', a hand. The father of our words manager and management was the Italian verb for handling, or 'managing', a war horse.

The military introduced the term to Britain, with specific reference to the handling of armies in the field, to handling swords and to handling ships. These were all areas where a strict hierarchy and a rigid code of discipline were needed. In the eighteenth and nineteenth centuries the terms 'manager' and 'under-manager' began to appear in industry and commerce. The current understanding of management is shaped by the mis-conceptions that have grown into perceived truth through constant repetition over some two hundred years.

Managers, in the nineteenth century, were administrators of enterprises that were owned (and led) by others. They were responsible for the efficient operation of their concerns. They were focused upon objectives to be achieved rather than upon *processes*. The processes by which the objectives were identified, and the processes by which working groups were formed and maintained were not a concern of management. See **chapter 8**.

Legal matters

Legal matters are very dangerous country, country that should not be explored without a known and trusted qualified guide. A manager is best advised to achieve three things:

- Sufficient knowledge of the law to be aware before he or she is in need of help.
- Self-confidence to turn for help before it is needed.
- Contact with a lawyer who can be trusted to give sound advice and to achieve the right results; one who is aware of the need to call in specialist help, if and when it is going to be needed.

All managers must be aware of the law in three specific areas:

- Law of contract   – to the point where they do not commit themselves or their concerns without conscious decision.
- Consumer protection   – to ensure that every proposal is checked thoroughly and that legal requirements are complied with.
- Employee legislation   – all aspects are vitally important to the management of a contented and successful team.

Incidentally, no manager should contemplate going into court, however good his or her case, without thorough preparation – including rehearsal.

Liquidity

See **financial analysis**

Management accounts

Management accounts are produced in addition to financial accounts. Whereas the financial accounts are required to be produced by law, and have to follow a prescribed format, management accounts have no such limitations.

Management accounts take whatever form an organization requires. Their sole purpose is to provide relevant information, in a form and at a time when it will facilitate decision-taking. They are highly confidential, operational documents, containing prize information such as **cash flow** and **budgetary control** details.

Management accounts should flow within the **Management Information System**, and be accessed only on a 'need to know' basis.

Management Information System

A **control** system that exists to provide management with relevant information, in an easily digestible form, at a time when possession of the information allows management to take action.
See also **information**

Management/marketing audit

A management and a marketing audit is carried out in much the same way as a financial audit, but because of marketing's need to work with subjective judgements a marketing audit can provide only a reasoned view on all the external and internal factors which interact with marketing and the organization.

A marketing audit is a means of identifying problems and opportunities. A commonly used tool is the SWOT analysis.

Audits should be carried through as a matter of routine discipline at intervals to suit the organization – but it is usual to conduct a full audit at least annually, as an aid to the production of the next year's budget. Partial audits are taken when they are needed, and can relate to specific areas of a manager's duties. In fact, the SWOT tool is so useful and easy to use that it becomes second nature to approach any management situation via an informal SWOT analysis.
See **chapters 2 and 3.**

Manager

See **leadership.**

Marketing communications

A global term which covers all communications of a marketing nature (without and within the organization). Tools of **promotion** are used to achieve marketing communication objectives.

Marketing Information System

A **control** system that is a sub-set of a Management Information System to provide specific information that is of assistance in the management of marketing. Given that the system is set up correctly it will ensure that data from the marketing environment flows through the Information System and emerges in the form of information in time for action to be taken.

Note that **marketing research** is one of the tools that contribute to both the Marketing and Management Information Systems.

See also **information**.

Marketing mix

Identified and named by Jerome McCarthy, an American advertising executive in the 1960s, the marketing mix comprises four 'P's. They are: Product, Place, Price and Promotion, and together they are the controllable factors which influence demand. These, together with planning and marketing research, make up the entire 'Marketing Toolbox'. No marketing plan is complete without each of the six elements being thoroughly covered.

The 4 Ps are inextricably linked, and are unsurpassed as a basis for developmental thought. They provide an excellent framework around which to present a marketing plan. Each of the 4 Ps is a technical term that should be used correctly.

Product includes service, and refers to those aspects of a concern's offering that are consumed by the end-user. Thus the protective aspects of packaging are included, but not the promotional element.

Price covers every aspect of the charge made for a concern's products or services. Thus discounts and long term incentive deals fall within the P of price – but not time-bound, short term incentives which are charged to the sales promotional budget.

Place refers to the delivery of the product or service in all its detail. The logistics of delivery are covered under **physical distribution management** (see also **distribution**). Strategic decisions regarding availability, and quantity, fall under this P.

Promotion is a technical term that should be used correctly. It encompasses advertising, public relations, sales promotion and personal selling (see **promotion**).

Marketing research

'Marketing research' is the global term that embraces many forms of research. *Market research* is research into the market only. Advertising research, promotional research, sales research ... any type of research to do with marketing is encompassed by the global term. Its purpose is to fill an *information gap* that has been identified by management.

The acronym CATS identifies the four research constraints: Cost, Accuracy, Time, Security.

Accuracy: Bias should be guarded against but occurs naturally through the use of biased sample bases. *Error* refers to statistical error and exists in all research. Sampling error can be given a mathematical value, a 'level of confidence' and will fall as the sample size increases. Mistakes must be monitored and corrected through systems of checks and controls managed by experienced researchers. It is for the manager who commissions the research to determine how accurate the results need be. The researcher will work to brief. Inaccurate information is far worse than no information at all. It is essential to select carefully, brief thoroughly, and monitor carefully.

Time: If there is insufficient time to conduct an accurate survey before the decision must be taken it is necessary to question the viability of a research exercise.

Security: Research can reduce the opportunity to be first on the market. Much will depend upon what is known of the competitors and their likely speed of response.

Secondary data is data that is gathered for a different purpose. It can be relatively inexpensive, because it is data which already exists. The cost is simply that of extracting the required information. Secondary data should always be used before the need for primary data is considered. *Primary data* is new information. Its collection can be expensive, but may be necessary. Primary data, once collected, immediately becomes secondary data for use in other situations.

The marketing research process

There will usually be another party involved in the process of filling the information gap. This may be a member of an internal research department, or an external agency. A close working relationship is essential. The nature of the problem has to be clearly thought out and the information gap defined. The accuracy of the information, and the timeframe, must be clearly identified so that the researcher can produce a realistic proposal.

The quality of information provided by researchers depends on the manager's attitude and approach from the briefing onwards, and upon the quality of the research brief.

The stages of a marketing research investigation are:

1 Information gap – identified and evaluated.
2 Research brief prepared.
3 Research organization selected and briefed.
4 Research proposal accepted.
5 Collection, analysis and evaluation of data.
6 Preparation and presentation of research report.
7 Management decision(s) taken.

Checklist for a research brief:

1 Clear definition of the marketing problem being examined.
2 Background to the problem and any information currently available.
3 Objectives of the research – as a basis for discussion and agreement with the researcher.
4 Constraints: cost, accuracy, time, security.

Motivational research (often called *depth research*) provides qualitative data and helps to answer the question 'Why?'. Attitudes are so subtle and complex that specialist and highly skilled researchers are necessary. This sort of research is usually conducted on a small scale and the most common techniques are group discussions and in-depth interviews, but there are many other tools of qualitative research. Select researchers very carefully since there is often a degree of controlled subjectivity in motivational research.

Market segmentation

It is necessary to examine a potential market to identify particular parts of it that share a common need, have a similar psychological make-up and can be reached with *both* promotion and product. When this is done one has segmented the market.

Segmentation can be consumer- or product-centred. Normally one would use consumers as the centre but sometimes one is forced to segment by product.

- Market segmentation
  – division of the market into specific groups of consumers (targets) who share common needs.
- Market targeting
  – evaluation and selection of one or more of the targets to enter.
- Product positioning
  – establishing the 'package' clearly in the minds of the consumer (see **product or service?** and **positioning**).

Segmentation bases

- Geographic – the market is divided into geographic units: a nation, a country, a city, a town. More likely, now, to be a TV area. Certainly an area for which secondary data sources exist.
- Demographic – *people*-based segmentation. The market is divided on criteria such as age, sex, family size, income, etc.
- Psychographic – *mental* based segmentation, based on social class, life style, personality characteristics, behaviour.
- Behavioural – segmentation by attitude, knowledge, response. People within clear geographic and demographic segments can and do display totally different life styles.

There is no right nor wrong way to segment a market, but whichever method(s) one chooses it is essential that three more criteria are used:

- Measure – Can the segment be measured? It is possible to know, to believe, that a market exists, but can information be obtained so that a manufacturing forecast can be prepared?
- Access – Can the customer get to the product?
  – Can the promotional messages reach the customers and the consumers?
- Size – Is the segment substantial enough to be profitable? If not, is there any other reason to justify working with it – the need to maintain continuity of service across a range, perhaps.

EMPLOYERS/
SPONSORS

	Large	Medium	Small	Individuals
Existing clients	1	2	3	4
Probable clients	5	6	7	8
Possible clients	9	10	11	12
Cold contacts	13	14	15	16

Segments 3 and 7 will be targeted immediately. Segments 10 and 14 will be
targeted in three months if the initial campaign meets budget.

Figure 11.3 *Segmentation matrix*

A *segmentation analysis* can be presented visually (figure 11.3). This allows clear
recommendations as to which target(s) to hit first as shown – the exact composition of
each segment must be specified and there should be a statement indicating the purpose
of the visual.

Geo-demographic segmentation

By cross-referencing post codes with census data from the government it is now
possible to classify areas of about 150 houses using some 40 geographic and demographic variables – a system known as geo-demographic segmentation. Without computer power this would be an impossible task.

ACORN – A Classification of Residential Neighbourhoods – were the originators of
this system, although several competitors have joined them in the marketplace. Choosing between them is a question of matching one's need to their exact provision.

The success of the technique depends upon the high probability that like people live
together, and that like people behave in similar fashion. A grouping, once identified,
labelled and its behaviour studied, is likely to be replicated elsewhere in the country.

It is known, for example, that the purchasers of Morris Marina cars were found
mainly in ACORN groups B, J, A and E. Ford Granada owners came from groups J, I
and B. The least likely to buy Marinas were in group H whereas Granadas were rare
in group G.

Socio-economic groupings have been used for many years, but are very clumsy when
compared to geo-demographics. SE groups are based upon the occupation of the head
of the household (accepted to be the man whatever his partner's occupation). They
divide the population into six groups: A, B, C1, C2, D, E.

A and B are usually taken together and account for about 16 per cent of the population, C1 has about 23 per cent, C2 some 31 per cent. D has around 19 per cent and
group E about 11 per cent.

Working with a single classifier that can account for 31 per cent of the population (and
that inaccurately) is far from ideal, especially when ACORN offers accurate and reliable

splits of no more than 4 per cent of the population. Modern technology is providing the alert marketer with a more powerful tool to supplement those that have been in the toolbox for years, although SE groups will continue to be used in a broad, overall way.

Matrix

A matrix allows information from several sources to be brought together on to one chart and is highly effective as an analytical tool. (For examples, see **product life cycle** and **positioning.** Note that a **cash flow statement** is a financial matrix.)

Mean

See **quantitative analysis.**

Median

See **quantitative analysis.**

Minimum total transactions

A channel of distribution is made up of several links. Goods move through 'middlemen' from supplier to user. Middlemen are only justified if their presence and service minimizes the total costs of effecting the distribution of the goods. In the examples given in figure 11.4 the total transaction costs are £320 and £200. Thus the middleman will survive. Traditional grocery wholesalers went out of business in the UK as the large retailers gained sufficient outlets to justify taking over their own distribution.

Mix

A term now in common use that originated with **marketing mix** but has spread to include any combination of factors required to achieve a given objective.

Mode

See **quantitative analysis.**

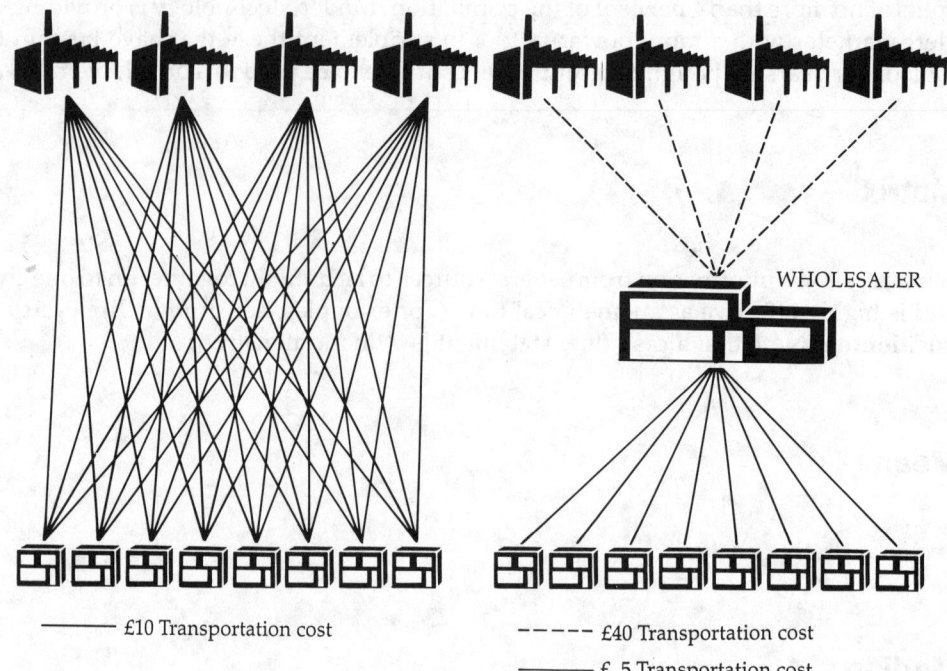

Figure 11.4   *Principle of minimum total transactions*

Motivation

Maslow published his *Hierarchy of Human Needs* in 1943. *Herzberg's* studies confirm what one can deduce from Maslow. They reveal that the factors that motivate people and satisfy them at work are not the opposite of those which dissatisfy them! Motivators and demotivators are, in fact, separate items.

Incentive and motivation should not be confused by the working manager. Incentives are offered: a bonus, time off, a special favour. Motivation is internally generated: how to spend the bonus (how important is it to *me, now*?), how to use the time off (or do I really want to be here getting that other rush job finished?). Linking incentives to motivations is a key management skill.

> Correction does much, but encouragement does more.
> Encouragement after censure is as the sun after a shower.
>
> Goethe

Motivation and the customer

The principles of motivation and incentive hold true for customers and consumers. Incentives can easily be offered as inducements to purchase but they will be ignored unless they lock in to a motivational force that lies within the target group of customers and consumers.

See **chapter 8**.

Motivational research

See **marketing research**.

Need or want?

Needs are something one must have. Wants are things one would like. A purchase is possible when a want becomes a need. Wants are easily generated. Converting them into needs is usually affected by discretionary income. For many the interest or the ability has been lost by the time a want can be afforded!

Wants and needs are very personal and it is easy to allow one's own perception to colour the approach to a prospective customer. For example, car salespeople tend to be very bad in this regard. Simple sales research would tell them that the young woman is in the showroom to buy a car for her handicapped father, but too often they neglect to ask the few questions that would elicit this key information and start straight in to sell what they think she should want.

Net present value

See **discounted cash flow**.

Objectives

Objectives are clear statements of intention. They should always be set against time – and quantified as specifically as possible.

- Bad objectives:

  To increase sales of XYZ brand.
  To increase sales of XYZ brand by 5 per cent.

- Good objectives:

  To increase sales of XYZ brand by 5 per cent over the same period last year.
  To generate £350,000 sales of XYZ brand in the Anglia TV region in the three months January/March, 1991.

See **effectiveness and efficiency**.

Opportunity cost

Opportunity cost is the cost of one course of action expressed in terms of the *alternative foregone*. It is difficult to quantify as it includes non-financial costs and benefits, but it is a very valuable concept to aid decision-making.

An example: if you have opportunities to enter two markets, but the resources to support only one, in opportunity costing one would quantify each alternative in terms of its own potential *less* that which could be achieved by the alternative. Additional considerations such as future orders, expected speed of payment and publicity benefits would also be added to the equation. The one with the greatest net value should be the choice.

In real life management the *concept* tends to be used rather more than the quantitative model.

Package

See **product or service?**

Packaging

The packaging of a physical product, or of certain aspects of a service (e.g. hangers and bags used by dry cleaners), has to achieve much more than simply provide physical protection to the contents. It should provide *sufficient* protection – note the qualifier 'sufficient'; much money can be wasted through over-protection. It must meet legal requirements (e.g. baby-safe bottles for medicines).

Packaging can also be used creatively as a media vehicle that carries a promotional message. Packs now commonly carry sales promotion offers, they routinely carry the overall image for the brand through to point of sale and of use, and they provide added value to the purchaser. The creative use of packaging is of value even in industrial markets.

Perception

A product exists in the perception of the consumer. It has a perceived difference when the consumer believes it to be better or worse, perhaps against all the evidence. Thus simple aspirin may not clear a headache, but a branded version of aspirin may work.

A firm held in high regard is 'allowed' the occasional mistake: 'Fancy that, not a bit like them!' The same error, perpetrated by a firm in low esteem would result in: 'Typical of them, you can't trust their products, I've always said so!'

Selective perception allows the target unconsciously to blank out uncomfortable, unnecessary or unwelcome messages. Hence the 'Don't Drink & Drive' campaigns tend to miss their targets, motor car advertising is missed unless one is in the process of choosing a new car and some smokers are not deterred even by incontrovertible evidence involving their own health.

Physical distribution management

No physical distribution system can simultaneously maximize customer service and minimize distribution cost. Maximum service implies large inventories, in close

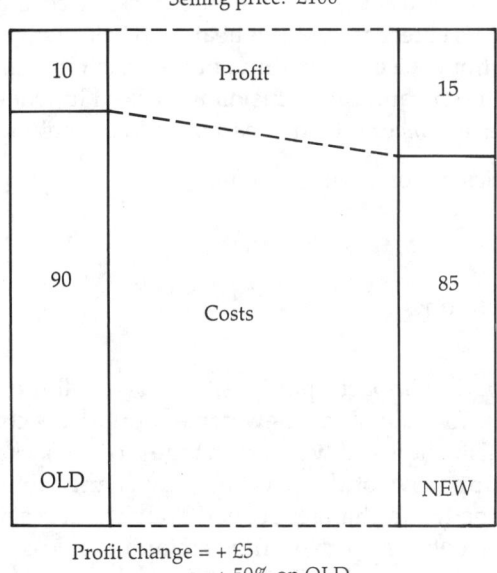

Selling price: £100

Figure 11.5   *Profit leverage through cost reduction*

proximity to the customers, with flexible transportation availability. Minimum cost implies slow/cheap transportation, low stocks and few depots. It is therefore vital to set clear objectives covering the level of customer service. This is a key area of competitive activity and it behoves one to be clear and specific in establishing policy.

It is essential to research the relative importance of these various customer services *to the target customers*, and to discover what competitors are offering – and achieving. Then it is necessary to decide upon a competitively viable mix of customer services. Only then is it possible to design a physical distribution system. Even a small saving in distributive costs can have a major impact upon profits.

In figure 11.5 a profit change of + £5 = + 50 per cent on old profit. To achieve the same profit increase through sales it would be necessary to increase turnover by 50 per cent! The 'gearing effect' of the cost reduction from £90 to £85, just £5 on £90, produced a 50 per cent profit improvement.

Positioning

Often the term 'product positioning' is used. This is technically incorrect since positioning has to do with the minds of the members of a target audience. Every person who is aware of a product or service, brand or personality has to some degree 'placed' it/them into a mental category. 'She's a typical Volkswagen driver' reveals levels of unconscious positioning. It says everything about how the person and the motor car are perceived.

A package with a unique position has a clearly defined personality, with which consumers within its target market have some form of relationship. They are most clearly aware of its existence, and have a formed attitude towards it. Those outside the target market may be totally unaware of the package. For example, Mars is positioned not as a chocolate bar, but as a social, nourishing snack. According to the adverts (the pictures not the words) its eaters are young, healthy, virile, active, fit and happy. Mars is found on the confectionery counters, in vending machines, in cafes, and it is also bought to be served at home and for inclusion in packed lunches.

Positioning generates an *image* which is based upon a combination of factors:

- Product characteristics or consumer benefits;
- Price/quality/value.
- Use.
- User.
- Product class/competition.
- Cultural symbolism.

The channels of distribution impact upon position, as do all the support services.

An offering is 're-positioned' when a new perception of it is created in the minds of the target audience. This will probably mean changes to the packaging, perhaps to the recipe, but these are supportive of the psychological change that is sought.

Positions can be mapped, and changes actively sought – or resisted. The lawnmower battle of the early 1980s between 'hover' mowers and Qualcast's traditional cylinder mowers provides an excellent example of successful re-positioning by Qualcast – in two stages over two years (figure 11.6).

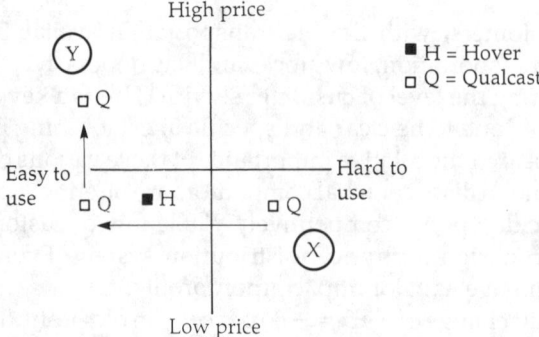

Figure 11.6   *Repositioning: by taking it in two stages, Qualcast management successfully repositioned the product over two years from position X to Y*

Positioning statements

The exact position that the package is to take in the minds of the target market is expressed in a positioning statement. The statement must be accurate and detailed. It will focus all marketing effort and so the creative management time devoted to it will be repaid in long term benefit.

It is difficult to challenge a competitor who holds a position; usually it is better to define, establish and protect a position that is unique in the market.

Price

If a business is to survive price must always equal or exceed marginal cost. The lowest justifiable quotation is normally marginal cost, although too much business 'on the margin' will force a business to close. Full costs have to be covered, and a quantity sold at the margin contributes nothing to fixed costs. Therefore the other sales have to be at a price that recovers their own share of *contribution* (see **costs**), plus that not earned by the marginally costed sale(s).

Price should not be confused with **value**. Customers buy on value, not upon price – although the two terms are often confused.

Price is the actual sum paid by the customer. Recommended retail prices are often discounted. Manufacturers make allowances from list price under a variety of guises. It is important to discover exactly what net price a competitor is charging. It is not sufficient to work from published price lists.

Price wars result when very similar products (e.g. petrol) are put into price competition. The result appears to be good for the customer in the short term, but is disastrous for the manufacturers since all competitors can and probably will match price reductions. The end result is that retail prices are lowered, with no additional volume to reduce costs of production.

Taken to the extreme a price war can force one or more suppliers out of the market whereupon it is quite likely that prices will return to their previous level, if not higher.

A decision on price has considerable implications for every aspect of a concern's operations (figure 11.7). Simple price-setting formulas based just on cost or demand are inadequate, although they are easy to understand and apply. They are inadequate because they try to treat pricing as a science, which it cannot be since it depends so much upon the subjective values of the customers and of the **positioning** established by Marketing.

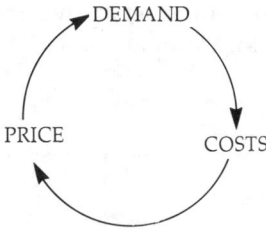

Figure 11.7 *The price/costs roundabout*

Primary data

See **marketing research**.

Probability

See **quantitative analysis**.

Product life cycle

The product life cycle concept is a useful descriptive shorthand for managers. It is drawn as an S curve, with its point of origin well before launch (figure 11.8). Profitability

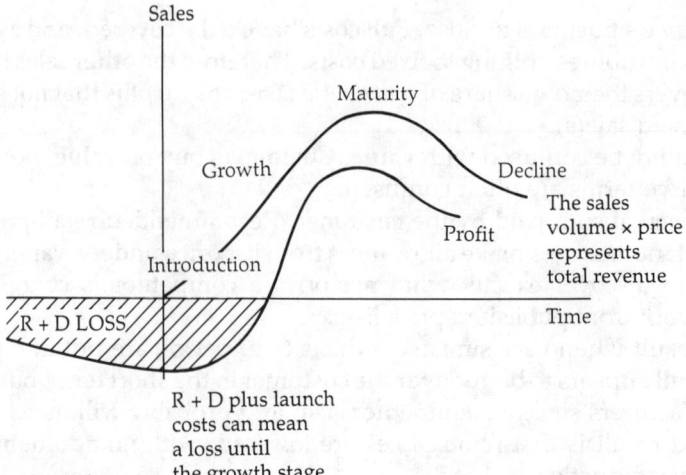

Figure 11.8   *Product life cycle*

does not follow the same curve as sales. It is necessary to invest at the introductory and growth stages – too often firms take profits out when they should be putting investment in. In most markets the aim should be to achieve market share, and then to hold it. From high share comes long term volume sales, and from sales come profits. Towards the end of the life cycle profits will be lower because there will typically be many competitors, the product will be dated, the production facilities well worn and the maintenance budget high.

With the advent of computers it has been possible to present the concept in a form that allows for quantification (figure 11.9) By quantifying each axis, using a logarithmic scale, it is possible to plot the current product life cycle position of each product, model, brand, range, within the portfolio. Comparison can be made with competitors, and

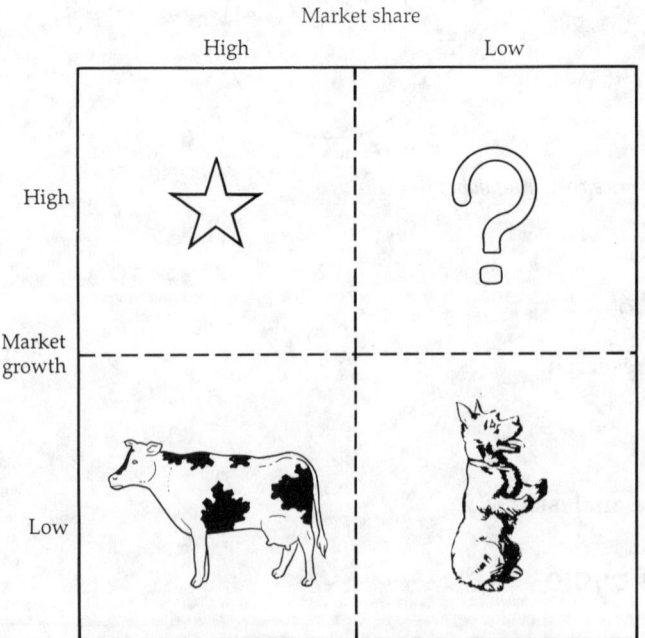

Figure 11.9   *Boston matrix: basic*

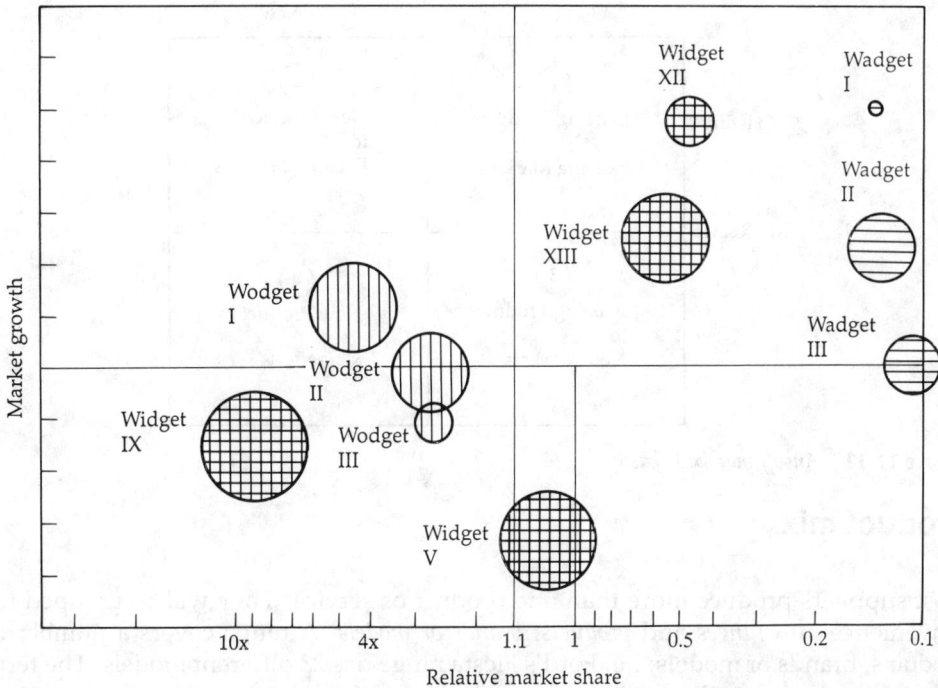

Figure 11.10 *Boston matrix: business portfolio*

What if? scenarios can be played through (figure 11.10) The Boston Matrix is designed for markets that are in growth. Alternative matrices have been produced for other market situations, but none has the immediacy and power of the original.

Extending the product life cycle can be achieved by a strategy of modification. The Sony Walkman has been modified and extended almost beyond recognition from its origin. Add-on products – speakers, special earphones, etc. – have broadened its appeal and it continues to set the standard for others to attain. (This conforms with the quality **positioning** that Sony have secured and which they protect.)

Product manager

See **brand manager**.

Product/market opportunities

The *Ansoff matrix* is an excellent planning tool. It is apparently simplistic, but it demands very careful consideration if it is to be used effectively (figure 11.11). The matrix has great value in planning, especially as a tool upon which to work out **What if?** scenarios. It is also an excellent way of communicating strategy to any audience (figure 11.12).

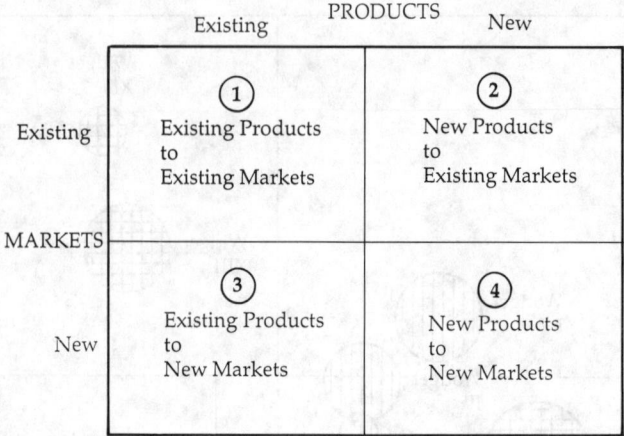

Figure 11.11   *Ansoff matrix 1: basic*

Product mix

Most suppliers produce more than one product or service. They will be grouped for convenience into *ranges* and *products, brands or models*. A range covers a number of products, brands or models, i.e. Ford's Fiesta range has 23 different models. The term 'product mix' refers to the combination of products offered by the company. A product mix is described, somewhat subjectively, using three adjectives: depth, width and consistency.

Depth refers to the number of products, brands or models offered within any range. An eight-model range would be described as deep.

Width refers to the number of lines or ranges which are offered. An electrical wholesaler carries a very wide range.

Consistency refers to the amount of apparent synergy between the products produced. A kitchenware manufacturer would have consistency to a very high degree if all products were electronic.

There is nothing intrinsically good or bad about a product mix which is deep or shallow, consistent or inconsistent. These adjectives simply *describe* the mix, they contain no value judgements.

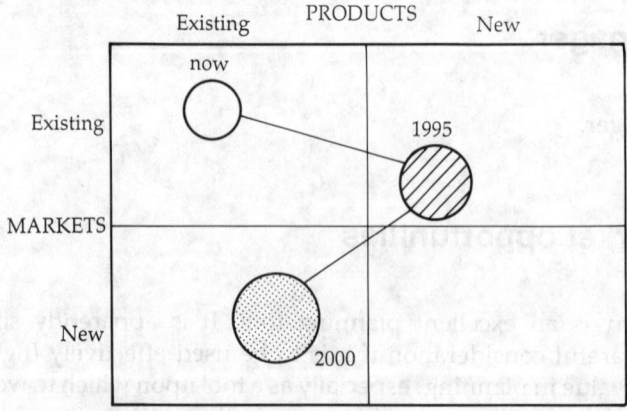

Figure 11.12   *Ansoff matrix 2: in use*

Product or service?

Quite clearly a *product* has a tangible presence, whereas a *service* does not. There are grey areas – such as catering – where one offers both a tangible product and a supporting service. This has confused business people for decades, without need. The difference is purely academic. Of practical concern is how to package and supply whatever one is selling. Whether it is a product or service should not come into the discussion.

Package means more than 'packaging'. Putting a 'package' together to make sales and profits is part of the creative side of a marketing manager's work. A package must contain, and feature, all the elements of the offering that are appealing to the customer and to the consumer. It is the package that one sells, the package that customers buy. Purchases are made to satisfy identified needs. The needs are not for the product, they are for what the product does. For example, a washing machine is bought because it promises to provide clean clothes quickly and with maximum convenience and minimum effort. Nobody buys a washing machine for itself!

Product planning

Organizations achieve their objectives by selling their products or services. It may not be immediately apparent that a sale is taking place, but good presentation will help even a patient in hospital to be psychologically better prepared to accept and benefit from treatment. Presentation in the interests of the consumer is a keystone to good salesmanship.

Products or services are *packages* that make up the raw material with which the concern has to work (see **product or service?**). They can be moulded, modified and represented to the market in a variety of guises, but at the end of the day the concern achieves its objectives by selling its packages.

Current production capacity is always finite – only in time can it be expanded, contracted, modified. Organizations have to operate within a current range or **mix** of packages. Planning is therefore a critical and fundamental task of management.

Key questions are: what to produce, when, how many?

- What to produce will be determined by the concern's experience, resources and assessment of the market, both historic and current. The current product mix has been determined by the quality of past decision-making.
- Timing can be both tactical and strategic. At a tactical level this can refer to a decision about launching a range in March or in April. Strategic decisions concern the commissioning of a new range, or the discontinuation of an existing one.

    Often the launching of a new product will mean the end of an existing model. Management skills are crucial to the timing so that earnings from the old range are maximized.
- How many to produce is a critical decision – one that is almost impossible to get right since demand is unpredictable despite the best efforts of **marketing research** and the sophistication of **forecasting** techniques. There is always need to provide for the dual contingencies of over- and under-demand. Both should be planned for well before the launch.

Budgetary control should ensure that achievement is monitored against objective – but it is very easy for the information not to reach the right manager, in time; or for it to be misunderstood.

The skill in product planning lies in getting the demand/supply balance correct for each product/market opportunity.

Profit

Profit, in a marketing-orientated company, comes through satisfying the consumer. With obvious exceptions the requirement is for long term profit growth. This means a need, sometimes, to sacrifice short-term profit opportunities to the greater good of a long term strategy. To have a chance at sustained long term profit growth it is necessary to re-invest a proportion of income so that a replacement range of products is constantly going through **Research and Development** and coming forward to the marketplace.

Marketing is no less valid in non-profit making organizations. For them the attainment of their organizational objectives provides the 'profit' motivation. A Health Education Authority may have long term 'profit' objectives expressed in terms of increasing average life expectancy, and short term ones in terms of reducing the incidence of lung cancer or AIDS.

Profit centre

See **budgeting**.

Promotion

Academic definitions are of little practical use. It is far better to understand what the terms mean in actual use, what benefit is gained from each element.

Promotion tools are used to achieve *marketing communication* objectives, which include all the internal and external communications emanating from marketing to assist in the achievement of specified objectives.

Promotional mix

Four major tools make up the promotional mix:

Advertising — communication through paid-for media space.
Public relations — communication through unpaid-for media space.
Sales promotion — activities to generate action at the point of sale.
Personal selling — person-to-person contact.

Advertising is the art of condensing the key message to a form that will reach and be noticed by the identified target audience. It is paid for, and is identified as biased in favour of the package it promotes. The audience expect advertising to 'puff' its claims, and allow for such over-statements. It is extremely effective in creating and maintaining awareness, and in reminding existing users of the benefits of the product or service they are using.

Public relations (PR) generate *publicity*. The terms are distinct, but are commonly misapplied. PR is *not* free . . . although it uses media space. There has to be a budget for PR because press releases and photo opportunities have to be created and these are tasks for highly skilled personnel. Many entities employ a PR consultancy since the costs of operating an internal PR department can be high.

PR creates and maintains awareness, but it can also have a strong effect on attitude.

Sales promotion operates at the point of sale. Its aim is to generate purchases – now! A temporary inducement is added to the proposition – 5 per cent extra; 25p off; zero interest on credit sales; collect six labels and get such-and-such free etc. Sales promotion can be applied to all products and services. The principle remains the same, the method of applying it differs. Activity is sales promotion if the offer is time-limited, if it offers extra benefit for specific action and is targeted upon people. Sales promotion as we know it today only came into the UK around 1960 and yet more money is now spent on it than upon advertising.

Personal selling: In every buying/selling situation both personality *and* role have to be dealt with. The same person, with the same personality, has to be treated differently dependent on the role he or she is currently fulfilling. The potential purchaser will not realize this, nor even care, but it makes a crucial difference to the seller.

The trend to self-service outlets apparently negated the need for personal selling in the retail marketplace. Yet the booming demand for customer care training indicates that person-to-person contact skills are still very much needed. As one moves up into higher **risk** purchases there comes a stronger need for salesmanship. A purchaser is looking for advice, for guidance, for specialist demonstration. A good salesperson is sought out by a potential buyer. In industrial selling the role of the salesperson is paramount. A sales campaign will be laid out after *sales research* (see **customer or consumer?**) has determined the DMU and the DMP. It will be crucial in large value purchasing to ensure that each member of the DMU is targeted with a contact of matching personality, suitable seniority and with appropriate specialist skills. All contacts need to be monitored, and results fed back into the team so that progress against objective can be measured.

See also **packaging**.

Promotional budgeting

Objective(s) are a prerequisite of budgeting but promotional objectives can tend to generalizations if management is not firm. The setting of promotional objectives is not difficult if basic segmentation practices have been followed and there is understanding of the role of each of the promotional tools.

Identification of a segment will necessitate a knowledge of its size. This allows a determination through research or estimation of the number in it who have achieved each successive stage in the process of purchase: Unaware; Aware; About to buy; Buying and liking; Have bought and didn't like.

Note: There is always attrition, and the need to attract new potential users into the Awareness stage; e.g. parents of young children are only interested in 'baby products' for a finite time, yet there is a constant stream of about-to-be parents coming forward who are Unaware of the range of products and services available.

Promotional objectives can then be written in achievement/time terms: for example, By 30 June to:

generate awareness in 35 per cent of the target segment;
develop a positive attitude in 25 per cent;
convert 12.5 per cent to regular users.

Converting to and from percentages and real numbers is essential. Hard numbers are required in order to calculate the finance; percentages are easier to work with in general planning.

Promotional budgetary control relies upon continuous research, that is, upon research before, during and after each campaign. A *tracking study* maintains a constant watch on a target segment and feeds a constant flow of information to management. Budgets can be set in a variety of ways – the best being *Objective and Task*. By far the most difficult to introduce, but by far the most valuable, it depends upon clear communication objectives being set and specific plans being made to meet those objectives.

Effective controls are paramount to ensure that the promotional budget's effectiveness is known. A firm may decide it will increase awareness of Brand X from 35 to 40 per cent at latest by 1st July next. It follows that it has to know the level of awareness now, and be able to monitor change. It has to have an effective research operation. It can then decide which promotional tools to use, and how much needs to be spent to achieve the objective.

Promotional mix

See **promotion**.

Quality

Quality is a relative concept that rests on the implied understanding of 'Quality for the purpose' – a highly subjective judgement made by each customer/consumer. Building quality into a product will add cost, but the added value if valued by the target market will ensure that the cost is more than justified in profitability. It is counter-productive to offer a quality product to a segment that sees no need for it.
See also **positioning**.

Quantitative analysis

Managers need an awareness of the value of quantitative analysis, but do not necessarily require detailed skills of statistical manipulation. With personal computers readily available, and a support team of specialists, the modern manager needs to know *how* but not *do*.

He or she must know *what* and *why*.

What information is sought, and why it is needed are the key contributions required from managers before any sifting of data to extract information can cost-effectively begin.

Key terms

Average

Average is a measure of central tendency. It is a measure of location, a value around which other values are distributed. Management commonly use three kinds of average: mean, mode and median. A *mean* is an arithmetic average and is calculated as the sum of a group or series of items divided by their number. A *weighted mean* is calculated by multiplying each item by a suitable 'weight' and dividing the total of the products by the sum of the weights (see **chapter 7**). A *mode* is what most people understand by 'average'. It implies the item that is most commonly found, the most frequent item in a series, the position of greatest density. The *median* is a position average, the value of the mid-case in an array. The median has the same number of items above it in the array as below. It is therefore not a mathematical average but is of use when no mathematical measure is applicable (i.e. the ability of employees).

Two arrays of numbers may easily have the same average. In one group the individual items may have values near to the value of the average, in the other the values may be widely dispersed. It is necessary to be able to measure the extent to which the values of individual items vary around the average. Various techniques are available; the most commonly used in management being *standard deviation* (see below).

Probability

More managers are confused by probability theory than any other statistical technique. Yet it is not necessary to be confused since probability models are now freely available via the computer.

Events are graded for their probability from 0 indicating impossible, to 1 indicating certainty. Assessment of the likelihood of an event taking place is carried out by assigning a probability between 0 and 1.

Confusion arises when one starts to consider the various types of probability, and the general manager needs to decide whether to study probability theory thoroughly or to rely upon the technical experts for assistance if and when needed.

Regression and correlation

These are specialist statistical techniques that the manager needs to know about, but *not to learn*. They are used to calculate the equations for the 'line of regression' and the 'correlation coefficient' for sets of data. Such techniques are not really necessary for the working manager who is able to use graphs and charts to produce close enough approximations.

Regression is concerned with the establishment of a trend. It is used as a forecasting tool, and with computer back-up it is very easy to use, especially in **What if?** planning. If necessary a reasonable approximation can be obtained from a simple graph, with the trend line added by hand.

Correlation measures whether there is a commonality between sets of data. Is one affected by the other? For example is the sale of umbrellas affected by rainfall and/or

sunshine? It could be that more are sold when it rains and less when the sun shines –
but are some used as parasols? Is there potential to sell in the summer also? Correlation
techniques help to match weather conditions to umbrella sales as a guide to management decision-making. Again, correlation can be worked out sufficiently accurately for
general purposes on a hand-drawn graph.

Skew

A pattern of distribution is said to be negatively or positively skewed when it tails off to
the negative or positive side of the mean. A normal curve of distribution – a bell curve –
has an equal number of events above as below the mean (figure 11.13).

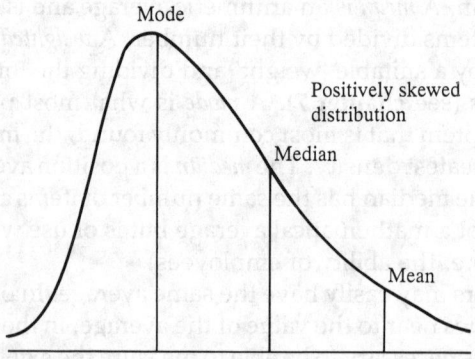

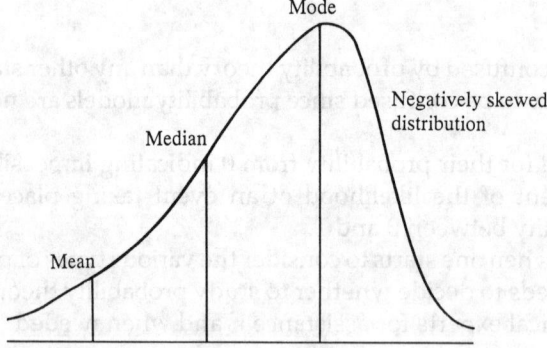

Figure 11.13   *Skew diagrams*

Valuable tools

The tools of analysis that many managers find of most direct value – because of their
straightforwardness and ease in use – are:

Weighted average (mean)

This technique assigns a weight to data, in order to indicate importance. It can greatly
facilitate the extraction of useful information (see **chapter 7**).

Trends

Trends, which are a highly significant part of management decision-making, can easily be obtained once a methodology has been established. As a continuing series of results come forward, from the same statistical base method, they may be compared and usually an underlying trend will be detected. It is important to retain the same base for surveys since only then can a degree of reliance be placed upon the information. Confidence develops over time. It is essential that statistical information prove itself before it is trusted. (See **data and information**.)

Standard deviation

This is a technique of weighted averaging which indicates how far the end result, the weighted mean, is truly representative. The larger the standard deviation the more of the sample who scored away from the mean; the lower the standard deviation the more that were in close agreement. Standard deviation is easily calculated on a pocket calculator and very quickly indicates the reliability of a mean as a basis for decision.

Semantic differential

This scaling procedure measures the connotative meaning of concepts. (Connotative: referring to the qualities, attributes and characteristics of an object designated by a word.) It takes into account both the more obvious meaning, which can readily be given, and also the more subtle and difficult to describe connotative meaning.

Respondents are asked to rate designated concepts along a continuum that can be either bipolar (active/passive) or descriptive (likes to entertain/likes a quiet life). Five-, six- or seven-point continuums are used and weights are assigned to each point. It is therefore possible to assign a numerical value to qualitative information. These numbers should not be taken to indicate absolute value as the original scale points cannot be assumed to be equally spaced. A continuous research study does allow the results of each individual component to be compared.

Semantic differential is a very useful tool as it is simple and very adaptable. It is used in marketing research to obtain qualitative information and is also of great value to personnel management when there is need to measure prevailing attitudes within an organization.

Be careful with numbers

It is extremely easy to confuse numbers, and to confuse numbers and percentages.

1,234 mn is the same as 1.234 bn – but *not* the same as 1.234 mn.

1.234 mn	=	1,234,000
1,234 mn	=	1,234,000,000
1.234 bn	=	1,234,000,000

The two changes are from 'mn' to 'bn' and from a comma to a full stop. Also be very careful when working in a foreign system – the French, for example, reverse the use of the full stop and the comma!

Percentages also require care. For example, 8 per cent of 1,000 is 1,250, but it is very easy to think it is 800, especially when working under pressure, and more especially when faced with a skilled negotiator.

It is the apparently small matters, such as the misplacing of a decimal point, or the reversal of a percentage, that are of most immediate concern. Such errors must be guarded against.

Ratios

See **financial ratios**.

Regression and correlation

See **quantitative analysis**: key terms.

Reliability

Data is said to be reliable when it can be shown that the research, if replicated, would produce a similar result. A 'split test' is one method of determining reliability: if data is split at random into two sets and each analysed the expectation is that both sets will produce similar results. If they do, the research is reliable.

Research and development (R&D)

To everything there is a life cycle; there is a beginning, a middle and an end. The middle might very well be extended, the end postponed, but nothing will last for ever.

It is essential to commit resources from successful trading into developing new products. Some operations thrive out of their ability to mimic the success of others. Even so, they need to allocate resources to the technicians who make this fast mimicry possible.

Not every new offering can be a success. The ratio of new ideas that make it through to market success is said to be as low as 1:100. It is very important, therefore, not only to generate many new ideas, but also to develop an effective screening process.

Risk

Not to be confused with 'gamble'. In normal usage the two terms are employed incorrectly as synonyms. Risk is defined as 'Hazard of loss, where the probability of loss is known'. Gamble as 'Act in the hope of'.

A manager is paid to take risks. Taking decisions on the basis of the evidence available is a required duty. Complete information is never likely to be available and so the manager's job is to evaluate the risk of alternative actions, and choose between them.

Sales force

One of the key factors in the success of a concern is its sales force, its person-to-person contact with its customers and its consumers. Just as the average salesperson has no concept of life on a production floor, so the majority of people in any concern have little, if any, concept of the job of selling.

It is important that management treat the salespeople as integral and important members of the team, and scotch any rumours that the sales people have it easy. An 'us and them' attitude can develop astonishingly quickly, to the detriment of all.

Non-profit making organizations should be equally concerned with their selling. It is important both that the service is managed effectively *and* that people know it is. The need and importance of person-to-person (sales) contact must not be ignored, nor undervalued.

Sales force strategy is concerned with achievement, not determination of sales volume. Clear promotional objectives (see **promotional budgeting**) allow:

- Sales force size to be calculated.
- A sales expense budget to be set.
- Establishment of sales territories.
- Determination of control mechanisms.
- Allocation of resource effort.
- Development of call strategy.
- Evaluation of results.
- Establishment of a training plan.

Sales force size can be calculated in a variety of ways, the most effective being by workload.

- Determine the number of effective calls to be expected from each salesperson (allow for 'notional' calls to take into account travelling, etc.).
- Determine how many calls will have to be made (grading customers on a scale so that key accounts receive more calls than those of lesser importance).
- Divide salesperson's calls per day into total calls.
- Result – the minimum number of salespeople needed.

Sales expense budgets must include all the costs necessary to achieve the sales objectives set out in the marketing plan. All sales support staff must be included, together with overhead apportionment. Allowances for entertaining, etc., will be included, but they more properly should be shown within the overall **promotional budget** along with the costs of sales attendance at exhibitions etc. (Unless these are specifically the responsibility of sales management.)

The budget should show the headings where sales have a degree of control. No functional manager should be held responsible for decisions outside his control.

Sales research

See **customer or consumer?**

Satellite and cable television

Satellite TV takes no account of boundaries of nation, colour, religion or language. Thus the opportunities (and the problems) for promotional planners are extensive. Global branding is becoming a necessity since promotional budget is wasted if neighbouring countries sell the same product under different brands. Further, with borders opening, and a mobile population it is important that a brand be recognized by its users wherever they may be.

A major repositioning exercise started throughout Europe in the late 1980s, and will continue until all pan-national brands have become 'European'. This is likely to be only a part of the story – global branding is almost certain to follow.

Zipping through a recorded programme – especially the adverts – has long been known in the United States, as has *Zapping* from channel to channel in search of the most suitable to watch. Both Zipping and Zapping have to be taken seriously since it is vital to ensure that adverts grab the viewers, and hold them at least long enough to communicate the main message. The audience is no longer passive!

Cable television, where individual homes are joined by cable to a central provider, offers the opportunity to use direct marketing in a very cost effective manner. It is now possible to target specific adverts to individual households. This is not yet a serious offering in the UK, mainly due to the relatively low penetration of cable television, but as more households are connected the marketing implications should not be underestimated.

Scenario

'Scenario' is a well-worn term in management that has been taken, along with much of modern management jargon, from the military. Scenario means 'An imagined sequence of future events' and therefore perfectly describes the duties of a management planner. Conceptualizing a series of possible scenarios, and working through the actions and reactions implicit in each, is a worthwhile activity. It allows both reconnaissance – a foreknowledge of the type of problems and opportunities that are likely to be faced; and rehearsal – tackling a series of problems and opportunities through **What if?** scenarios (see **feasibility study**).

Secondary data

See **marketing research**.

Segmentation

See **market segmentation**.

Semantic differential

See **quantitative analysis**.

Standard deviation

See **quantitative analysis**

Statutory accounts

By statute every company must produce accounts for its shareholders. Required are: a balance sheet, a profit and loss account and a source and application of funds statement (a cash flow statement). These documents enable shareholders to assess the performance of their investment. They do not, however, assist management in the day-to-day running of a business.

The *balance sheet* provides a statement of the assets and liabilities of a company at a moment in time. It resembles a snapshot rather than a movie film. Statutory regulations cover the style, presentation and content of a balance sheet. Each EC country has adopted an identical presentation and a form of words that describe each element. Note, however, that the base concepts from which the figures derive vary from country to country. Great care must be taken in interpretation.

The *profit and loss account* is an account of the trading activity that has taken place within a period. It amalgamates data to present costs against revenue over a stated period.

The *sources and application of funds statement* provides vital data concerning liquidity. A business is technically insolvent if it cannot settle its debts as they fall due. It is unlawful to continue trading if a management knows it is in this position. The balance sheet and profit and loss account are not designed to give much information about the cash position and so it is now mandatory for professional accountants to prepare a sources and application of funds statement for all firms whose turnover is in excess of £25,000 per annum.

Strategic business unit

A strategic business unit (SBU) is a division of a concern which is sufficiently large and well founded to be able to operate as an entity in its own right. Conglomerates, being much too unwieldy to manage as a single entity, operate through SBUs, although they may use their own descriptive term. Note that an SBU does not have to be a formalized entity under company law; SBUs work perfectly well within a public company, but usually as designated divisions of that company. There is no prescribed size; SBUs are governed simply by their ability to operate independently.

Structure

Every concern has some form of structure. There may be a formal hierarchy – there will always be an informal understanding of relationships, and of power. When both formal and informal structures exist it can become very confusing, and there is considerable potential for damaging internal politics.

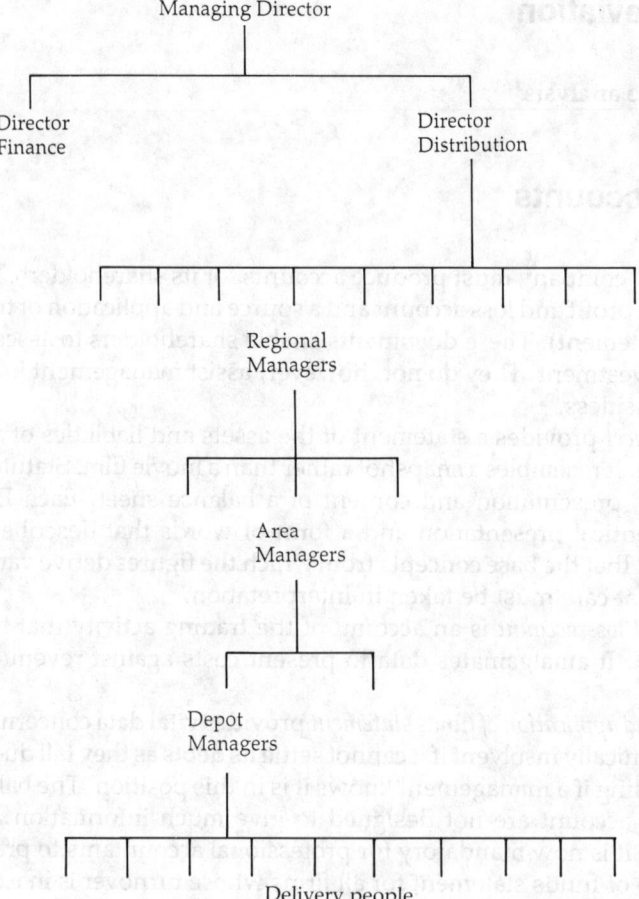

Figure 11.14   *Hierarchical management structure*

Hierarchy

Typically a structure is shown in the form of a pyramid, with the Chief Executive at the top. This indicates *line* authority and responsibility. It is based upon the model developed by the Roman army, and is very effective in a discipline-based entity where every person knows his or her place, and boundaries of authority are clearly delineated. It is inflexible and unworkable in modern operational conditions.

Within a structured hierarchy (figure 11.14) a series of informal networks will establish themselves simply because it is necessary to communicate quicker than the structure allows if jobs are to be done effectively. It follows that people working outside their given role are insecure, and management that insists upon strict adherence to the hierarchy and the procedures it lays down will find that the more creative and active personnel are not inclined to stay.

A hierarchy is necessary, in the background, to ensure that everybody has but one manager, and that administrative details of pay etc. are carried through smoothly.

Line and Staff

An entity has two major functions: to achieve the task and to administer and control. *Line* managers hold direct responsibility for the achievement of strategic or tactical objectives to do directly with the achievement of an entity's plans. *Staff* managers operate in support. The delineation of the posts also comes from the military where staff officers in headquarters behind the lines are responsible for strategic planning and logistical support.

Task achievement is the number one priority. An organization should be built around the need to achieve. But behind that is the need to administer and to control; to ensure that the rations get forward, as it were. The two must not be confused. A hierarchical structure is excellent for its purpose – administration.

Matrix

Tasks are achieved by teams of people working together. Often an individual works in a range of teams over a period of time, and will be a member of several teams simultaneously (see figure 11.15). This is a normal human response to task achievement. It is likely to happen informally, and so it is wise to formalize the process. Individual leaders are designated along the axes of the matrix. Any person so designated can bring together a team that has a clear focus. Thus one manager may lead a team and, at the same time, be a follower in another that is composed of the same individuals.

Matrix organization recognizes and rewards specialist knowledge and skills but clarity of purpose is essential to ensure that control is not abrogated.
See **leadership**.

GPs	Gen. nursing	Sisters Ante-natal	Physio	Family Planning	Counsellor	Health Visitor
Dr Carter						
Dr Bryan						
Dr Alexander						
Dr Shane						

Figure 11.15   *'Westfield Surgery' management matrix*

SWOT

Strengths, Weaknesses, Opportunities and Threats. A valuable tool of analysis.
See **chapter 3**.

Targets

Targets should not be confused with *budgets*. Generally a target is something to aim for. Often it will be set deliberately high. A budget is to be achieved. It is equally bad to under as to over achieve budget (see **budgeting**). Incentives are often linked to achievement, with a bonus for exceeding target. In conditions of excess supply this technique can be valuable, but it is likely to engender a volume sales ethos which may not be the best attitude to foster given that long term profit achievement is the usual aim.

Tracking study

See **promotional budgeting.**

Validity

See **marketing research.**

Value

The concept of 'value' expresses the intangible package of benefits that the **decision-making unit** believe attaches to the product or service under consideration. Value is always subjective in nature, and is completely misunderstood by the average purchaser. 'Price' is commonly used in unconscious substitution for 'value', and many serious mistakes have been made by managements who have not grasped the need to understand what the customer wants, as distinct from what he or she is saying. 'I buy at the lowest price' usually translates into 'I buy at the lowest overall price when I have taken all my needs over a period of time into account'.

Value includes such factors as:

- benefits offered;
- useful lifetime of the product;
- after sales service;
- reputation of the supplier;
- status attached to the brand;
- price asked, gross and net;
- guarantee/warranty period.

Variance criteria

See **financial analysis.**

What if?

Asking 'What if?' is an excellent management exercise. What if a competitor came into the market? What if we reduced price by 5 per cent? Using computer simulations it is now possible to work through many 'What if?' scenarios as an aid to decision-taking. The data base should, of course, be constantly reviewed and improved in the light of experience.

Even without a computer simulation 'What if?' scenarios are a most useful tool that management is well advised to adopt.

Working capital

See **financial analysis.**

Part Three

Management Tools in Use

The scenario and *sequence* for success set out in Part Three give a step-by-step guide for tackling a practical business problem or opportunity and provide both a clear framework and a systematic approach to follow.

Any practising manager is continually living within a series of case studies. In the broadest sense a case study is any situation that can become the subject of analysis and decision. As managers spend their working lives analysing and deciding it follows that they are continually living out case studies. A case study is simply a chunk of real life that has been extracted from its context and written up into a scenario. The technique is widely used, and is effective, simply because good case studies have a ring of truth – they come from reality, and it shows.

The scenario, the case, which you will find in chapter 12 is typical. It places you in context, within a contemporary situation, and provides all the data needed to carry out the specified tasks. What you do with the data, how you approach the scenario, what solutions you come up with, all are matters that will vary with your level of experience. Working with a good scenario provides the practising manager, and the student, with opportunities to experiment and to learn. Read through the scenario in chapter 12; in chapter 13 we show you a sequential way of handling a management problem. This sequence will be helpful with everyday management problems, and, of course, for case studies of all types.

Chapter 19 is specifically for management students, who should read it immediately after chapter 13, and before starting work on the case in chapter 14. Chapter 19 outlines the requirements of examiners, and shows how to pass a case study examination. Chapter 20 contains an examination paper based upon Hollins Holidays, and chapter 21 holds our suggested answers. Practising managers will find the examination paper and suggested answers of value since they replicate the kind of immediate short term progress report that a senior manager is likely to call for whilst a main feasibility study is being worked up.

To work with the Hollins Holidays scenario in chapter 12 it is necessary for you to imagine that you are employed by a large conglomerate which is interested in diversification. There are two things to note:

1 You have to accept the scenario as presented. Pick up the sense of the market from the case. Do *not* try to relate it to your contemporary situation.
2 All necessary data is contained within the case – and within your brain.

Work with us through 'Hollins Holidays'. It is a challenging case, with much scope for creativity.

12 Hollins Holidays: a management opportunity

You are to assume the role of Chris Knight, Head of New Products Development at ICCC. Your senior management position is described in the case, and you will be required to make clear recommendations based upon the data provided. Your manager will tell you precisely what you are to achieve.

Remember, all necessary data has been provided. There is no need for further research outside the case. Historical data is presented as it relates to the current year, i.e. two years ago is shown as Year −2; 11 years ago as Year −11, and so on.

The scenario

It was an unpleasant Monday morning in January when Chris Knight faced,	1
and triumphed against, the apparent conspiracy to prevent workers reaching	2
their jobs. Not for the first time the thought was vocalized all over London . . .	3
'Why, oh why are the British so unprepared for winter weather?'	4
Damp and bedraggled Chris reached the offices of ICCC (the International	5
Cigarette and Cigar Corporation). The lifts were not working, since the week-	6
end storms had disrupted the power supply – it was, of course, 14 floors up to	7
Chris's office!	8
On reaching the corner desk, earned by five years' seniority, Chris found a	9
message: 'see Kim Medway – immediately'.	10
What could the Marketing Director want, and why such a stress on urgency?	11
Surely it couldn't be that Chris was in trouble? Not likely, since Chris's team	12
had wrapped up their latest project in the middle of December, and Kim had	13
been very complimentary.	14
Pausing only to tidy up, Chris grasped the blue folder that was, in ICCC, a	15
mark of status, and walked quickly down the corridor. Jay, Kim Medway's	16
secretary, was obviously not yet in and so, unbriefed, Chris tapped on the door	17
to the inner office, and entered. It was 9.35 a.m. on a routine day.	18
'Good morning, Chris . . . glad you made it through the weather . . . well	19
done, again, on that job you put to bed last month. The Managing Director was	20
most pleased. So much so that he wants your team to handle a most confiden-	21
tial project that ICCC are determined to mount.	22
'What do you know about the UK holiday market?'	23
'Only what I've read in the press,' Chris replied. 'I believe that a fair number	24
of package holiday firms have gone to the wall . . . and there is interest in	25
developing new concepts . . . Vacation Villages and US style theme parks.'	26
'Not enough,' said Kim Medway sharply, 'dig a bit deeper.'	27
Chris considered the matter . . . here was an obvious opportunity to make the	28

step up that was so necessary to career development, after all the M.D. had   29
specified Chris for the new project. It was time to organize thoughts, and to get   30
away to a good start.   31

'There has been a major shift in holiday patterns, I'd say. Gone are the   32
days when the majority of the British spent two weeks each summer in guest   33
houses at the seaside. The jet aircraft opened up the potential for package   34
holidays; and brought the travel time and inconvenience down so that ordinary   35
families can holiday in the Mediterranean as easily, and as cheaply, as in the   36
traditional holiday resorts. In fact many established British holiday centres,   37
Scarborough, Skegness and the like have been very hard hit. Even Blackpool   38
has had to bring its illuminations programme forward to late August, from late   39
September/October. There has been an upsurge in self-catering and caravan   40
holidays.   41

'Holiday camps, I think, have suffered. The Costa del Sol must have been a   42
nightmare for Billy Butlin and Fred Pontin . . . although I believe they have   43
opened up over there. Certainly I know that Trust House Forte is now a huge   44
international hotel and holiday chain.'   45

Kim Medway interrupted. 'What's been happening recently, Chris?'   46
Recently? Chris thought . . .   47

'I suppose the most important recent developments have been the falling   48
numbers of Brits taking their holidays abroad (but I'd like to check if my   49
impression is correct); then there is the increase in prices in Spanish hotels   50
which, coupled with the falling pound, must be very bad news for the holiday   51
trade – at least for the package holiday trade.   52

'There is also, of course, the development in taste of the average holiday   53
maker. A fortnight in a caravan outside Bognor is not so exciting now as my   54
parents tell me it was when they were children. Food too, and wine. The Brit on   55
holiday has become used to a much wider menu, and cheap booze, without   56
British opening hours.'   57

Chris paused, and Kim asked, 'Any thoughts about overseas visitors to the   58
UK?' 'Well,' Chris answered, 'they must be going up, and be projected to   59
continue to rise. I can't see the pound recovering in the short term and, unless   60
there is sustained terrorist activity, that must make the UK attractive to Ameri-   61
cans and Japanese in particular.'   62

A thought struck Chris – routine monitoring of the trade press was paying off   63
. . . something about a Dutch Company . . . OH YES . . .   64

'There is a Dutch operation now open in the UK.' Chris said. 'I can't recall the   65
details, but I believe they operate specialist sporting villages and have opened   66
one in Sherwood Forest . . . and . . . haven't Butlins been very successful with a   67
Water World (or something) down in the West Country?   68

'If I can check out the details, and my memory isn't failing me, it could be that   69
there is a new trend in vacations, just beginning. Let me investigate, and I'll   70
come back to you.'   71

Kim smiled. Chris was obviously the person for the job. And it could only   72
reflect credit onto the whole of marketing. The MD was right, of that Kim was   73
sure. All that was needed now (all) was to get the project rolling.   74

'Chris,' Kim began, 'I must remind you that everything from here on   75
is totally confidential. We must keep the wraps on everything, and very   76
tightly too.' Chris nodded. This was standard, but it did no harm to have it   77
stated.   78

Kim continued 'We, that is the Board of ICCC, are convinced that there is a 79
major gap in the UK holiday market. A gap that we intend to exploit. A Board 80
level decision has been made to activate a company that we have owned for 81
many years, but which ceased trading over 20 years ago. We shall change its 82
name in due course – for the moment we shall refer to it as "Hollins Holidays". 83

'The decision that must be made is whether or not to enter the UK market 84
with a series of holiday centres that will be custom-built to meet the perceived 85
needs of a segment of the public. We have decided that we must be specific, 86
that is good marketing theory that actually works in practice(!), and that we 87
have to commit ourselves from the beginning. We cannot afford to test market. 88
So we have to be very sure that we are making the best decisions possible. Do I 89
make myself clear?' 90

Gosh, yes, thought Chris. What an opportunity to shine. With the M.D. 91
taking a personal interest in the project – the Chris Knight project – this was one 92
opportunity not to be taken at less than full commitment. 93

'Kim, I'll be very happy indeed to look into this, and come up with firm 94
proposals. I take it that is what you require?' 95

'It is indeed, Chris. From now on you are 100 per cent on this project. If we 96
decide to proceed the first holidaymakers must be on site in 27 months. At the 97
start of the UK summer – although in view of the weather today I'd perhaps 98
better say 30 months!' Chris laughed, it wasn't very funny, but it was the best 99
Kim could do; and it is wise to laugh at the jokes of one's boss. 100

'One last thing, Chris,' said Kim Medway, walking across the office and 101
opening the door to see if Jay had arrived . . . NO! Frowning Kim turned back to 102
Chris. 'The Board has also discussed the idea of having holiday centres with 103
different identities. They could, for example, feature historical themes or focus 104
upon sports. We thought that if we went for history we could set up one as 105
Norman, another as Tudor, another as Victorian, and so on. That way we 106
would attract customers year after year. Alternatively we could go for Bat and 107
ball, Sea and Surf, etc. You have the choice as to whether or not to include a 108
section on these ideas in your proposal. I know that you would omit it you 109
found it to be impractical. No doubt the Board would not be put out if you felt 110
that its ideas had no future.' 'Oh Yes!' thought Chris. 111

Kim Medway continued 'We need from you specific proposals on the struc- 112
ture of the holiday centres, the size of the operation, target market segment(s) – 113
you know . . . a full, preliminary proposal, well thought through and costed. 114

'A secondary data search has been completed and the documentation is here 115
for you to take away. Let's now go and get a well-deserved cup of coffee as Jay 116
still hasn't made it in through the traffic.' 117

Note:
Case studies do not arrive with numbered lines – it is good practice to add the
numbers yourself since this facilitates quick referral.

APPENDICES: DOCUMENTATION

Appendix A

ICCC

INTERNAL MEMORANDUM

TO: Kim Medway
FROM: Group Economic Research Department
DATE: 2 December

In accordance with our discussions, we have prepared the enclosed tables of information to assist you and your team in the preparation of your proposals for Hollins Holidays:

i) Economic Indicators
ii) Foreign Exchange Rates
iii) Comparison of international costs.

The sources of information include *The Financial Times*, *British Business* and *The Economist*.

A/1: Economic Indicators

Year	Gross domestic product (Based on year −7)	Consumer's expenditure (£bn at year −7 prices)	Balance of payments (£m at current prices)	Output of production industries (Based on year −7)
−6	99	137	6159	97
−5	100	138	3978	98
−4	104	144	3133	102
−3	107	147	1612	103
−2	111	152	3602	108
−1	113	160	(365)	113

A/1: cont.

Year	Retail sales (Based on year −7)	Retail price index (Based on year −7)	Tax and price index (Based on year −7)	UK unemployed (m)
−6	100	116	116	2.3
−5	102	126	127	2.6
−4	107	131	132	2.9
−3	111	138	137	3.0
−2	115	146	144	3.1
−1	121	152	147	3.2

A/2: Foreign Exchange Rates

Country	Currency	Year −3	Year −2	Year −1
Australia	Dollar	1.4035	2.1140	2.1650
Austria	Schilling	25.6400	24.9500	20.3150
Belgium	Franc	73.30*	72.4500*	60.10*
Canada	Dollar	1.5315	2.0138	1.9760
Cyprus	Pound	0.7425	0.7910	0.7320
Denmark	Kroner	13.0800	12.9125	10.9050
France	Franc	11.1700	10.8825	9.4725
Germany	Mark	3.6500	3.5450	2.8900
Greece	Drachma	149.2000	213.9000	203.0600
Irish Rep.	Punt	1.1720	1.1610	1.0585
Italy	Lira	2242.0000	2417.5000	2000.5000
Malta	Pound	0.5650	0.6115	0.5320
Netherlands	Guilder	4.1200	3.9950	3.2650
New Zealand	Dollar	2.4315	2.8735	2.7753
Norway	Krone	10.5325	10.9175	10.8500
Portugal	Escudo	196.4500	228.2400	214.2300
Spain	Peseta	201.3800	221.9800	194.1800
Switzerland	Franc	3.0150	2.9235	2.4350
USA	Dollar	1.1590	1.4390	1.4325

All exchange rates are per one pound sterling
* Commercial rate of exchange

A/3: Comparison of International Costs (Year −1 prices)

Country	Currency	Hotel room	Meal	Bottle of wine
Australia	Dollar	45	25	3
Austria	Schilling	710	366	50
France	Franc	426	125	6
Greece	Drachma	2400	1000	150
Italy	Lira	40000	16000	3000
Norway	Krone	500	275	65
Spain	Peseta	1700	600	300
Switzerland	Franc	145	45	30
UK	Pound	40	10	6
USA	Dollar	40	12	9

Appendix B

ICCC

INTERNAL MEMORANDUM

TO: Kim Medway
FROM: Group Economic Research Department
DATE: 5 December

Further to your telephone request, would you please find detailed below the breakdown between Visibles and Invisibles in the figures which we recently supplied for the UK balance of payments.

Please contact this department if you require any additional information.

B/1: Balance of payments (£m current prices)

Year	Visible	Invisible	Balance
−6	3360	2799	6159
−5	2332	1606	3978
−4	(836)	3969	3133
−3	(4384)	5996	1612
−2	(2111)	5713	3602
−1	(2256)	1891	(365)

Appendix C

ICCC

INTERNAL MEMORANDUM

TO: Kim Medway
FROM: Lan Dagent
DATE: 7 December

Following our discussions I now confirm my best estimates of the costs in the areas of your concern:

CAPITAL EXPENDITURE

Land	South East England	£50,000 per acre
	South West England	40,000 ,,
	The Midlands	30,000 ,,
	North East England	15,000 ,,
	North West England	20,000 ,,
	Wales	15,000 ,,
	Scotland	15,000 ,,
	Northern Ireland	10,000 ,,

Note: 1 square mile equals 640 acres.

Building costs: £340 per square yard, per floor.
Note: Costing includes provision of services, but does not include furnishings.

Landscaping: £1,500 per acre.

REVENUE EXPENDITURE

Decorations: £30 per sq yd of building every 2 years.
Maintenance: £3 per sq yd of building each year.
Power: £4 per guest, per week.
Food: £30 per guest, per week.

Rates (Business & Water) (per sq yd of building per year).

England	South East & South West	£10
	The Midlands	£9
	North East & North West	£8
Wales & Scotland		£7
Northern Ireland		£6

Appendix D

ICCC

INTERNAL MEMORANDUM

TO: Kim Medway
FROM: Research Librarian
DATE: 10 December

THE BRITISH TOURISM SURVEY

As requested, herewith relevant extracts from the most recent British Tourism Survey –
Yearly.

This research (BTS-Y) is carried out by personal interviews with a nationally
representative random sample of adults (+16) resident in Great Britain. Interviewing
takes place in November to cover the holiday year ending 31 October.

BTS-Y is concerned only with holiday travel. 'Holiday' generally refers to a holiday of 4
nights or more.

NOP Market Research Limited carried out both fieldwork and data analysis.

D/1: Volume and Value of Tourism

Year	Tourism to Britain/UK			Tourism to England		
	British	*Foreign*	*Total*	*British*	*Foreign*	*Total*
Trips (million)						
−11	132	8	140	107	8	115
−10	114	8	123	92	8	100
−9	117	10	127	96	9	105
−8	121	11	132	101	10	111
−7	121	12	133	98	11	109
−6	119	13	132	95	12	107
−5	118	13	131	97	12	109
−4	130	12	142	106	11	117
−3	126	12	138	104	10	114
−2	123	12	135	101	11	112
−1	131	13	144	110	11	121
Nights (million)						
−11	500	116	706	460	102	562
−10	535	119	654	415	105	520
−9	550	129	679	430	113	543
−8	545	134	679	435	117	552
−7	545	149	694	420	131	551
−6	530	149	679	405	129	534
−5	525	155	680	415	136	551
−4	550	146	696	435	129	564
−3	520	135	655	415	120	535
−2	505	136	641	400	120	520
−1	545	146	691	435	127	562
Spending (£m)						
−11	1 145	725	1 870	1 150	675	1 825
−10	1 800	900	2 700	1 375	825	2 200
−9	2 150	1 200	3 350	1 700	1 100	2 800
−8	2 400	1 750	4 150	1 925	1 575	3 500
−7	2 625	2 325	4 950	2 000	2 125	4 125
−6	3 100	2 475	5 575	2 400	2 250	4 650
−5	3 800	2 775	6 575	3 025	2 525	5 550
−4	4 550	2 925	7 475	3 525	2 675	6 200
−3	4 600	2 950	7 550	3 675	2 700	6 375
−2	4 500	3 125	7 625	3 600	2 850	6 450
−1	5 350	3 625	8 975	4 300	3 300	7 600

THE BRITISH ON HOLIDAY

D/2.1: Proportion of British Adults Taking 4+ Night Holidays

Year	−10 (%)	−9 (%)	−8 (%)	−7 (%)	−6 (%)	−5 (%)	−4 (%)	−3 (%)	−2 (%)	−1 (%)
Any holiday in:										
Great Britain	52	49	49	49	47	45	42	41	43	40
Ireland	1	1	2	1	1	1	1	1	1	1
Abroad	13	12	15	17	19	21	22	23	24	23
One holiday	44	42	42	43	43	40	40	38	40	37
Two	14	12	14	14	14	15	14	14	13	14
Three +	4	5	6	5	5	6	6	6	7	6
One holiday	61	59	61	63	62	61	59	58	61	58
No holiday taken	39	41	39	37	38	39	41	42	39	42

D/2.2: Profile of British Holiday-/Non-holiday-takers (Year −1)

Age	Adults (pop. %)	No hol. (%)	Hol. GB (%)	Hol. abroad (%)
16–24	18	19	15	18
25–34	18	16	18	20
35–44	15	13	16	18
45–54	15	14	14	19
55–64	15	13	16	16
65+	20	25	21	9
Social class				
AB	17	9	19	36
C1	22	18	25	27
C2	31	32	32	23
DE	30	42	24	15
North	6	8	4	4
Yorks and Humberside	9	8	10	11
North West	12	11	13	11
East Midlands	7	6	9	5
West Midlands	9	10	10	8
East Anglia	3	4	3	3
London	13	13	12	16
South East	18	16	18	23
South West	8	8	7	8
Wales	5	6	5	4
Scotland	9	10	9	8

D/3.1: *Estimated Number of 4+ Night Holidays Taken by the British*

Year	Britain (m)	Abroad (m)	Total (m)
−10	37.50	7.25	44.75
−9	36.00	7.75	43.75
−8	39.00	9.00	48.00
−7	38.50	10.25	48.75
−6	36.50	12.00	48.50
−5	36.50	13.25	49.75
−4	32.50	14.25	46.75
−3	33.50	14.50	48.00
−2	34.00	15.50	49.50
−1	33.00	15.75	48.75

D/3.2: Estimated Total Holiday Expenditure (4+ night holidays)

Year	Britain (£m)	Abroad (£m)	Total (£m)
−10	1 460	1 210	2 670
−9	1 570	1 360	2 930
−8	1 700	1 860	3 560
−7	2 380	2 570	4 950
−6	2 420	3 510	5 930
−5	2 710	4 320	7 030
−4	2 500	4 730	7 230
−3	2 640	5 000	7 640
−2	2 970	5 560	8 530
−1	3 080	6 140	9 220

D/4.1: Region Stayed in for One Night or More on 4+ Night Holidays in GB (Year −1)

Country	Region	%
England	South West	20
	Southern	10
	Yorks and Humberside	9
	East Anglia	7
	North West	7
	South East	6
	East Midlands	5
	Heart of England	4
	Cumbria	3
	Greater London	2
	Northumbria	1
	Thames and Chilterns	1
	Isle of Man	1
		76
Wales	North Wales	5
	South Wales	4
	Mid Wales	2
		11
Channel Isles		2
Scotland	North Scotland	5
	South Scotland	3
	Mid Scotland	3
		11

D/4.2: Countries Stayed in for one Night or More on Holidays (4+ nights) Abroad (Year −1)

Region	Country	%
Europe	Spain	31
	France	13
	Italy	8
	Greece	8
	West Germany	4
	Austria	4
	Portugal	4
	Yugoslavia	3
	Republic of Ireland	2
	Malta	2
	Switzerland	2
	Cyprus	2
	Netherlands	2
		85
North America	USA	3
	Canada	2
		5
Rest of world		10

D/5.1: Month in Which Holiday Started (Year −1)

Holiday began in	Holiday in GB	Holiday abroad (%)
May	8	11
June	15	12
July	21	13
August	25	16
September	13	14
Other months	19	34

D/5.2: Type of Accommodation Used on Holiday (Year −1)

	Holiday in GB	Holiday abroad (%)
Licensed hotel/motel	19	55
Guest house	6	4
Friends'/relatives' house	23	18
Caravan	21	2
Rented house/flat	13	16
Holiday camp	5	1
Camping	5	3
Paying guest private house	3	1
Youth hostel	1	1
Boat	2	2
Own villa/flat	1	4
Other	3	2

D/5.3: Mode of Transport and Type of Holiday Arrangement (Year −1)

Holiday in GB (%)		Holiday abroad(%)	
Transport		Transport	
Car	70	Plane	70
Coach	14	Boat	28
Train	10	Hovercraft	2
Other	6		
Type		Type	
Package	12	Package	62
Independent	88	Independent	38

Appendix E

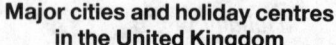

**Major cities and holiday centres
in the United Kingdom**

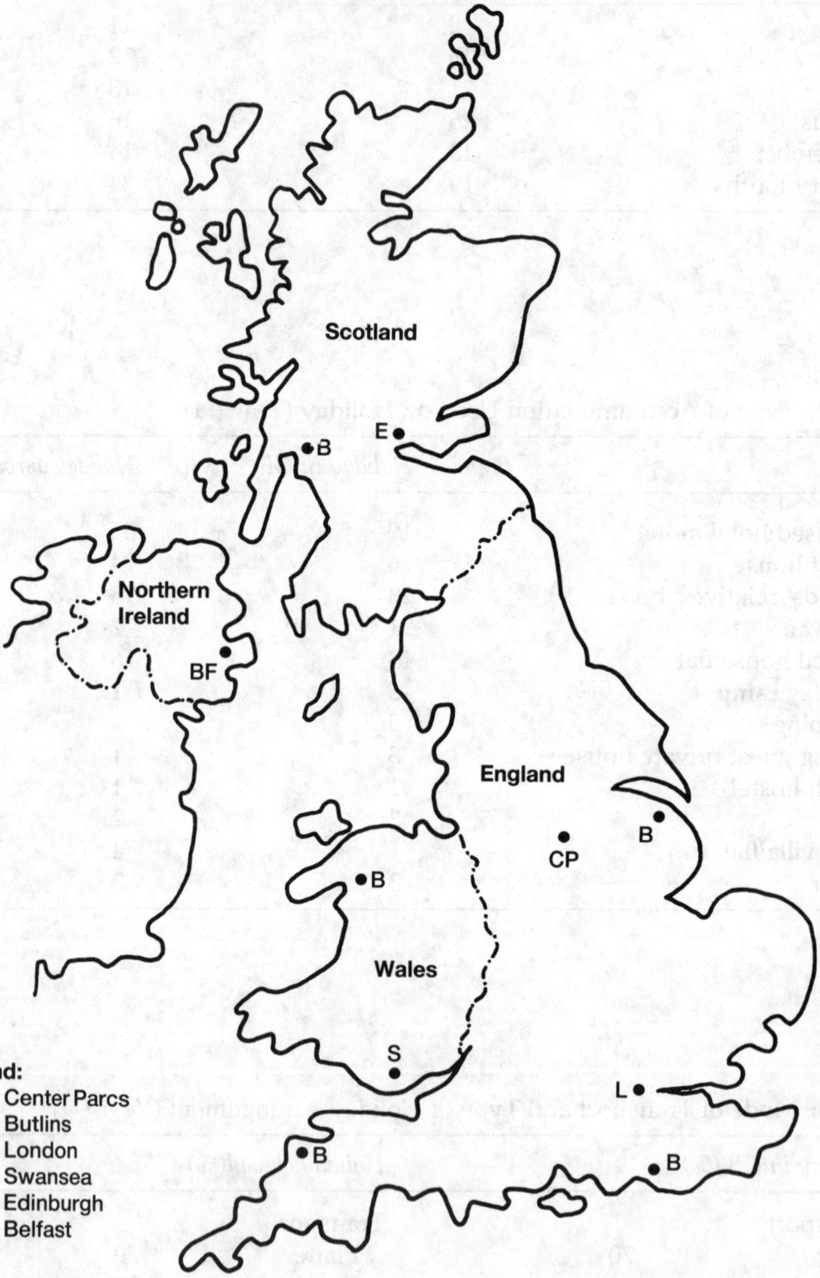

Scotland

E

B

**Northern
Ireland**

BF

England

CP

B

B

Wales

S

L

B

B

Legend:
- **CP** Center Parcs
- **B** Butlins
- **L** London
- **S** Swansea
- **E** Edinburgh
- **BF** Belfast

Appendix F

ICCC

INTERNAL MEMORANDUM

TO: Kim Medway
FROM: Research Librarian
DATE: 20 December

HOLIDAY CAMPS

1. Holiday camps were born as a result of the 1935 Holiday Pay Act that gave employees paid holidays.

2. There was huge growth after the Second World War, but there was poor investment and by the 1980s they were not equipped to handle the decline in the UK holiday market, especially with the music hall image that they had acquired. Even so some 2.5 million people visit holiday camps each year.

3. Currently there is a major re-positioning taking place. It is acknowledged that they have been too far down market and each of the three major operators is moving more up-market.

4. BUTLINS – the biggest operator, and the first – have five 'Holiday Worlds' and five hotels. They offer a total package including half-board chalets, self-catering suites and de-luxe caravans.
   Each of their Worlds is fully self-contained. Holidaymakers can obtain everything they need without leaving the site.
   All entertainment is gratis . . . funfairs, cinema, cabaret, sports, late night disco. One World offers a 'multi-million sub-tropical water complex'.
   The largest Butlins World accommodates 11,000 holidaymakers, the smallest, 5,000.
   Butlins have been owned by the Rank Organization since 1972.
   Investment has been in the region of 10m per centre. Profits apppear to be some 8.3 per cent of turnover.
   Butlins are quoted as saying that 'accommodation is the holiday ingredient that holidaymakers are most likely to talk about'.

5. PONTINS were taken over by Bass in 1980. Immediately £30m was earmarked for investment.
   With 25 camps, accommodating from 250 to 4,000, they see the main problem as keeping up with the expectations of the consumer. 'A private bathroom is now the minimum . . . full-board customers expect, and get, tea making facilities.'

6. LADBROKES have 17 centres from Yorkshire to Cornwall.
   The smallest has 88 chalets and caravans, the largest holds 5,000.
   Ladbrokes claim to have led the market with fun pools, and the introduction of BMX cycle tracks.
   Investment is running at some £2m a year.

7.   WARNERS is the smallest of the big four. It is owned by Grand Metropolitan. Investment is believed to be in the region of £7m.

Warners have always believed that small is beautiful, and so have 10 centres, mainly on the south coast, all with sea frontages. Typical size: 500–600 people.

Warner's flagship is Sinah Warren on Hayling Island near Portsmouth. It has upgraded this top-of-the-market holiday centre and added a futuristic sports complex that includes a gym of exclusive health club standards, a sauna and a jacuzzi. It claims to offer 'the facilities you would expect from a top class hotel'.

Warners are more up-market than their competitors. They are positioned to attract 'proportionately more Cs than Ds'.

8.   Image
The 'Hi-di-Hi' image of the holiday camp feeds upon the folk memories of mass catering, of loud speakers waking the whole camp each morning, of organised sports. It is something every operator is trying very hard to expunge.

Travel agents are a major target for image conversion, with the expectation that they will transmit the modern reality to their clients.

Brochures are very attractive, and every effort is made to stress the 'total experience' to demonstrate how each firm has redesigned its centres with client expectation in mind.

9.   Bookings are made roughly 35/65 per cent direct/travel agent.
Agency commission is 10 per cent. The average holiday price in mid-summer is £150 per adult, children go at half price. In May and October the price falls to £125 per week.

10. Second holidays are opening up as a significant market. Ladbrokes are quoted as saying 'People spend two weeks in Majorca with Thomson and then a week in Devon with Ladbroke'.

Short breaks, often centred on special events, are also becoming a feature of importance.

11. Sporthuis Centrum Recreatie of Holland have built a 600 bungalow village in Sherwood Forest, near Nottingham. They operate under the name Center Parcs, and I am preparing a separate memorandum for you as they seem to be of considerable significance in this market.

Appendix G

ICCC

INTERNAL MEMORANDUM

TO: Kim Medway
FROM: Research Librarian
DATE: 24 December

CENTER PARCS

1. Sporthuis Centrum Recreatie, of Holland, operate a new concept holiday village in Sherwood Forest, just outside Nottingham. Occupancy is believed to be running at over 95 per cent.

2. They also operate nine holiday villages in Belgium and Holland, attracting 1,500,000 visitors a year. Occupancy, it is reported, is 95 per cent throughout the year.

3. The following are extracts from their brochure:
    What we are offering is so entirely new that we ask you to read it with a fresh and open mind. Put aside all pre-conceived ideas about holidays in Britain.
    Out of season breaks in Holland and Belgium are now a way of life. The weather is no more relevant than the time of year – there are no unpredictable factors.
    The Sherwood Forest Holiday Village provides, quite simply, a holiday with almost every imaginable facility built in, at an economic price.
    None of the conventional words and phrases really sums it up. There's something of the country club; something of the sports complex; something of the health farm; something of the holiday villa. An immense range of activities for all ages, 365 days a year.
    We are talking about lifestyle – that is why the all-weather aspect of the new village cannot be over-emphasized.
    At the centre, will be the Subtropical Swimming Paradise; a giant, almost futuristic dome that simulates Caribbean conditions all year round... Move outside and you can have energetic sport or utter tranquillity.
    High quality private villas cluster among the trees in 450 acres of woodland, and most villas overlook water as well.
    The English Tourist Board have described its arrival in England as 'The most important innovation in British Tourism since the war'.

4. In addition to the 'Swimming Paradise' which contains 22 different features from wild water rapids to a solarium, there are:

Outdoor sports	–18 to choose from;
Indoor sports	–13 to choose from;
Health & beauty	– 4 services;
Shops & services	–15 on offer.

    Conference facilities are also available.

5. The villas are each fully equipped to high standard, with central heating, wall to wall carpeting, colour TV with teletext and two video channels, an open fire and a patio.

6. Reservations are made either direct or through a travel agent.

7. Price is by villa, not by person. Three booking periods are offered:
    Week (Friday to Friday), Weekend (Friday to Monday) , Midweek (Monday to Friday).

    Prices are:

	January			July		
	Week £	W/end £	M/Week £	Week £	W/end	M/Week
1 Bedroom Villa	*104*	*72*	*57*	*249*	*No*	*No*
2 Bedroom Villa	*160*	*112*	*80*	*319*	*No*	*No*
3 Bedroom Villa	*176*	*128*	*90*	*349*	*No*	*No*
4 Bedroom Villa	*185*	*133*	*100*	*379*	*No*	*No*

Dogs are charged for at £6.00 per week.

Villas accommodate 2, 4, 6 and 8 people, respectively.

Price will include:

> *use of the villa, and all its services*
> *cot, playpen, highchair*
> *free use of the Subtropical Swimming Paradise*
> *bed linen*
> *use of the playground.*

Appendix H

ICCC

INTERNAL MEMORANDUM

TO: Kim Medway
FROM: Research Librarian
DATE: 2 January

TARGET GROUP INDEX

The attached are extracts from the latest Target Group Index as compiled by the British Marketing Research Bureau.

	POPULATION '000	ALL HOLIDAYMAKERS A '000	B % down	C % across	D index	ALL HOLIDAYS IN U.K. A '000	B % down	C % across	D index	HOLIDAYS ABROAD A '000	B % down	C % across	D index	PACKAGE TOUR ABROAD A '000	B % down	C % across	D index	HOLIDAY CAMP A '000	B % down	C % across	D index
ALL ADULTS	44599	27611	100.0	61.9	100	18345	100.0	41.1	100	11883	100.0	26.6	100	7266	100.0	16.3	100	2594	100.0	5.8	100
MEN	21418	13234	47.9	61.8	100	8809	48.0	41.1	100	5769	48.6	26.6	101	3480	47.9	16.2	99	1217	46.9	5.7	96
WOMEN	23181	14377	52.1	62.0	100	9537	52.0	41.1	100	6114	51.4	26.4	99	3786	52.1	16.3	100	1377	53.1	5.9	102
15-24	8868	5153	18.7	58.1	94	3180	17.0	35.9	87	2506	21.1	28.3	105	1430	19.7	16.1	99	699	26.9	7.9	135
25-34	7679	4653	16.9	60.6	98	3121	17.0	40.9	99	1982	16.5	25.8	99	1212	16.7	15.8	97	537	20.7	7.0	120
35-44	7440	4910	17.8	66.0	107	2486	19.0	46.9	114	1962	16.5	26.4	99	1172	16.1	15.8	97	597	23.0	8.0	138
45-54	6058	3901	14.1	64.5	104	2597	14.2	42.9	104	1962	16.4	32.4	122	1242	17.1	20.5	126	279	10.8	4.6	62
55-64	6058	3901	14.1	64.5	104	2597	14.2	42.9	104	1962	14.6	28.4	107	1038	14.3	17.1	105	279	10.5	3.2	55
65+	8507	4878	17.7	57.3	93	3368	18.4	39.6	96	1732	14.6	20.4	77	1072	14.8	12.6	77	271	10.5	3.2	55
AB	7615	5888	21.3	77.3	125	3437	18.7	45.1	110	3386	28.5	44.5	167	2063	28.4	27.1	151	193	7.4	2.5	44
C1	10169	6960	25.1	68.4	111	4522	24.6	44.5	108	3339	28.1	32.8	123	1872	25.8	18.4	113	503	19.4	4.9	85
C2	12237	7634	27.6	61.9	100	5331	29.0	43.2	105	2895	24.4	23.6	88	1872	25.1	15.4	95	966	37.2	7.8	135
D	7864	4372	15.6	55.6	90	3121	17.0	39.7	96	1468	12.4	18.7	70	972	13.4	12.4	76	637	24.6	8.1	139
E	6614	2758	10.0	41.7	67	1936	10.6	29.3	71	794	6.7	12.0	45	489	6.7	7.4	45	295	11.4	4.5	77
ABC1	17784	12847	46.5	72.2	117	7959	43.4	44.8	109	6725	56.6	37.8	142	3934	54.1	22.1	136	696	26.8	3.9	67
C2DE	20201	12006	43.5	59.4	96	8451	46.1	41.8	102	4363	36.7	21.6	81	2843	39.1	14.1	86	1603	61.8	7.9	135
ABC1 15-34	6381	4475	16.2	70.1	113	2558	13.9	40.1	97	2363	19.9	37.0	140	1455	20.0	22.8	140	299	11.5	4.7	81
35-54	6117	4720	17.1	77.2	125	3037	16.6	49.7	121	2363	19.9	38.6	145	1369	18.8	22.4	137	109	11.1	1.7	81
55+	5286	3652	13.2	69.1	112	2363	12.9	44.7	109	1780	15.0	33.7	126	1110	15.3	21.0	129	109	4.2	2.1	35
C2DE 15-34	10166	5331	19.3	52.4	85	3742	20.4	36.8	89	1906	16.0	18.7	70	1188	16.3	11.7	72	937	36.1	9.2	158
35-54	7381	4305	15.6	58.3	94	3045	16.5	41.3	100	1560	14.5	21.1	79	1045	14.4	14.2	87	579	22.3	7.8	125
55+	9269	5127	18.6	55.3	89	3600	19.6	38.8	94	1691	14.2	18.2	68	1100	15.1	11.9	73	382	14.7	4.1	71
GREATER LONDON	5580	3624	13.1	64.9	105	2083	11.4	37.3	91	1882	15.8	33.7	127	1059	14.6	19.0	116	429	16.6	7.7	132
SOUTH EAST/EAST ANGLIA	9981	6478	23.5	64.9	105	4254	23.2	42.6	104	2918	24.6	29.2	110	1690	23.3	16.9	104	622	24.0	6.2	107
SOUTH WEST	3397	1935	7.0	57.0	92	1247	6.7	36.7	89	896	7.5	26.4	99	507	7.0	14.9	91	159	6.1	4.7	81
WALES	2529	1486	5.4	58.7	95	928	5.1	36.7	89	671	5.6	26.5	100	435	6.0	17.2	106	168	6.5	6.6	114
EAST & WEST MIDLANDS	7329	4692	17.0	64.0	103	3484	19.0	47.5	115	1632	13.7	22.3	84	1040	14.3	14.2	87	473	18.2	6.4	111
NORTH WEST	5172	3222	11.7	62.3	101	2714	14.8	40.9	99	1051	8.8	25.6	96	924	12.7	17.9	110	269	10.3	4.6	89
YORKSHIRE & HUMBERSIDE	4110	2536	9.2	61.7	100	1780	9.5	43.3	105	1051	8.8	25.6	96	646	8.9	15.7	97	189	7.3	4.6	79
NORTH	4094	2391	8.7	58.4	94	1617	8.8	39.5	96	949	8.0	23.2	87	562	5.0	13.7	85	125	4.8	5.2	86
SCOTLAND	3950	2531	9.2	58.0	94	1640	8.9	41.4	100	949	8.3	23.4	87	604	8.3	11.9	73	159	6.1	4.1	67
H/D INCOME £20,000 OR MORE	3950	3164	11.5	80.1	129	1664	9.1	42.1	102	2098	17.7	53.1	199	1165	16.1	29.5	181	137	5.3	3.5	60
£15,000 - £19,999	4411	3406	12.3	77.2	125	2117	11.5	48.0	117	1773	14.9	40.2	151	1070	14.7	24.3	149	200	7.7	4.5	76
£11,000 - £14,999	6089	4395	15.9	72.2	117	3016	16.4	49.5	120	1861	15.6	30.6	115	1241	17.1	20.4	125	444	17.1	7.3	126
£9,000 - £10,999	4682	2927	10.6	62.5	101	2059	11.2	44.0	107	1164	9.8	24.9	94	721	9.9	15.2	94	343	13.2	7.3	126
£7,000 - £8,999	4170	2531	9.2	60.7	98	1769	9.6	42.4	103	965	8.1	23.1	87	604	8.3	14.5	89	252	9.7	6.0	104
£5,000 - £6,999	4272	2436	8.8	57.0	92	1697	9.2	39.7	96	942	7.9	22.0	83	604	8.3	14.1	87	241	9.3	5.6	97
£4,999 OR LESS	9514	4492	16.3	47.2	76	3014	16.4	33.7	82	1393	11.7	14.6	55	835	11.5	6.8	54	475	18.3	5.0	86
NOT STATED	7511	4259	15.4	56.7	92	2814	15.3	37.5	91	1688	14.2	22.5	84	999	13.7	13.3	82	502	18.3	6.7	115
OWN/BUYING HOME	30143	20522	74.3	68.1	110	13256	72.3	44.0	107	9604	80.8	31.9	120	5900	81.2	19.6	120	1594	61.4	5.3	91
RENT HOME	13308	6324	22.9	47.5	77	4600	25.1	34.6	84	1918	16.1	14.4	54	1156	15.9	8.7	53	941	36.3	7.1	122
SINGLE	10458	6116	22.1	58.5	94	3699	20.2	35.4	86	3090	26.0	29.5	111	1690	23.3	16.2	99	644	24.8	6.2	106
ENGAGED (INCLUDED IN SINGLE)	1153	638	2.3	55.4	89	400	2.2	34.7	84	207	2.7	29.5	103	222	3.1	19.3	118	83	3.2	7.2	124
MARRIED	28611	18522	67.1	65.0	105	12751	69.5	44.6	108	7679	64.4	26.8	101	4946	68.1	17.3	106	1743	67.2	6.1	105
SEPARATED/DIVORCED/WIDOWED	5530	2873	10.4	52.0	84	1896	10.3	34.3	83	1114	9.4	20.1	76	535	8.7	11.4	70	207	8.0	3.7	64
MARRIED UNDER 1 YEAR	707	459	1.7	64.9	105	298	1.6	42.2	103	220	1.8	31.1	117	164	2.3	23.2	142	32	1.2	4.5	77
1-4 YEARS	2552	1343	5.2	56.4	91	1072	4.8	41.9	102	693	5.8	27.5	99	422	5.7	15.1	93	138	5.3	5.2	93
5-9 YEARS	3225	1505	6.0	56.4	91	1476	7.7	45.7	110	693	5.8	24.5	92	422	13.3	15.1	91	264	10.2	8.1	141
10-19 YEARS	5226	4415	16.0	56.4	91	3239	17.7	50.2	122	1585	15.3	24.5	92	961	13.3	19.0	91	598	20.1	8.1	159
20 YEARS OR MORE	14998	9914	35.9	66.1	107	6611	36.0	50.1	107	4317	36.3	28.8	108	2856	39.3	19.0	117	675	26.0	3.2	77
NO CHILDREN IN HOUSEHOLD	22945	18109	65.6	62.6	101	11420	62.2	39.5	96	8492	71.5	29.1	110	5366	73.9	18.5	114	1087	41.9	3.8	65
CHILD(REN) UNDER 1 YEAR	1585	738	2.7	55.0	75	207	1.1	37.0	90	207	1.7	13.1	49	105	1.5	6.6	43	499	19.8	9.8	106
1-4 YEARS	5523	3039	11.0	55.0	89	2352	12.8	42.6	104	851	7.2	15.4	58	483	6.6	8.6	54	499	19.2	7.0	155
5-9 YEARS	5973	3780	13.7	63.3	102	2895	15.8	48.5	118	1225	10.3	20.5	77	694	9.6	11.6	71	640	24.7	10.7	184
10-15 YEARS	8480	5400	19.6	63.7	103	3826	20.9	45.1	110	2086	17.6	24.6	92	1135	15.6	13.4	82	907	35.0	10.7	184

	POPULATION '000	ALL HOLIDAYMAKERS				ALL HOLIDAYS IN U.K.				HOLIDAYS ABROAD				PACKAGE TOUR ABROAD				HOLIDAY CAMP			
		A '000	B down %	C across %	D index	A '000	B down %	C across %	D index	A '000	B down %	C across %	D index	A '000	B down %	C across %	D index	A '000	B down %	C across %	D index
DAILY EXPRESS	4316	3016	10.9	69.9	113	1997	10.9	46.3	112	1377	11.6	31.9	120	959	13.2	22.5	136	186	7.2	4.3	74
DAILY MAIL																					
THE SUN																					
THE STAR																					
TODAY																					
DAILY MIRROR																					
DAILY RECORD																					
MIRROR/RECORD																					
FINANCIAL TIMES																					
THE GUARDIAN																					
DAILY TELEGRAPH																					
THE TIMES																					
THE INDEPENDENT																					
MAIL ON SUNDAY																					
NEWS OF THE WORLD																					
SUNDAY EXPRESS																					
SUNDAY MAIL																					
SUNDAY MIRROR																					
SUNDAY PEOPLE																					
SUNDAY POST																					
THE OBSERVER																					
SUNDAY TELEGRAPH																					
THE SUNDAY TIMES																					
OBSERVER COLOUR MAGAZINE																					
SUNDAY TIMES MAGAZINE																					
TELEGRAPH SUNDAY MAGAZINE																					
SUNDAY EXPRESS MAGAZINE																					
SUNDAY (NEWS OF THE WORLD MAG)																					
YOU (MAIL ON SUNDAY MAGAZINE)																					
I.L.R - ONCE A WEEK OR MORE																					
HEAVY																					
MEDIUM																					
LIGHT																					
ITV)																					
HEAVY																					
HEAVY-MEDIUM																					
LIGHT																					
CHANNEL 4																					
HEAVY																					
MEDIUM																					
LIGHT																					
TV-AM 1 HOUR OR MORE A WEEK																					
LESS THAN 1 HOUR																					
ALL CINEMA																					
HEAVY																					
MEDIUM																					
LIGHT																					
THE STANDARD																					
EVENING MAIL (BIRMINGHAM)																					
EVENING TIMES (GLASGOW)																					
YORKSHIRE EVENING POST (LEEDS)																					
LIVERPOOL ECHO																					
MANCHESTER EVENING NEWS																					
EXPRESS & STAR(W'TON)/SHROP.STAR																					
REGIONAL MORNING																					
LOCAL WEEKLY (PAID FOR)																					
LOCAL WEEKLY (FREE)																					

13 *Sequence for success*

There is great similarity between the way that a practising manager addresses a problem, and the approach taken by a 'case study' student. This chapter identifies an excellent methodology for approaching a real or a case problem, and shows how to move step-by-step through a case. We shall, of course, use Hollins Holidays as our example. It is worth re-emphasizing that the process of handling a problem at work is very similar to that adopted to deal with a case study.

Time management
The promise you must make to yourself is not to hurry. There is a great temptation to rush forward. But the best way to succeed is to think first. Take your time.

Learn through doing
About ten years ago Russell identified that one moves through four stages when learning a skill:

1 Unconscious incompetence – where one is unaware of the needs of a particular task.
2 Conscious incompetence – where one is aware of one's inability to cope.
3 Conscious competence – where one can do the task, with conscious effort.
4 Unconscious competence – where the task is perfectly natural, and routine.

In learning to drive a car most people go through these four stages. So will you in learning how to handle a management problem – a case study.

It is very important that you work *with* the material given in this section of the book, that you experience *in practice* how a problem is broken open, and that you gain total confidence in your ability to handle the method. Once learned it is never forgotten, and you will find yourself using it when dealing with problems in everyday life.

Some words of warning

- Working this case study thoroughly is likely to take between 30 and 40 hours. It is necessary to make a commitment now to the level of involvement you are prepared to give.
- You will need to be very strong with yourself, especially if you are working alone. You *must* follow the method which we explain next.
- You will be tempted to move ahead too soon. We cannot over-emphasize the importance of completing the ground work with an open mind. You must get the facts out of the case *before* you do anything else, i.e. problem identification is crucial.
- You will have good and bad days. We all do. Capitalize on the good, do not be put off by the bad. Expect them, allow for them in your planning – then they will not come as a surprise and you will not be demoralized by them.
- Make a resolution NOW that when tempted to push on too soon you will instead

come back and re-read this section. Then make a judgement – are you really ready to move forward, or are you just a little bit bored at the effort of breaking information out of the data in the case?

Methodology

The key points are:

- Understand the 'Sequence' (see below) and what must be achieved at each stage before attempting to start work on 'Hollins'.
- When ready, follow the sequence shown below, and explained in the remainder of this chapter.
- Get 'Hollins Holidays' inside your head as quickly as possible. Get away from the printed case, do not even refer to it once you have completed your basic analysis.

It is very important that you work your own personal solution to the 'Hollins Holidays' case. Please do not peek ahead, and *whatever you do* stay away from our suggested answer in chapter 21.

There are eight steps to a successful answer: we call them The Sequence (figure 13.1).

Overview

Purpose

To give you a very fast understanding of the width of the case. It is a familiarization, an examination of the scenario in the round. There must be no detailed penetration, no working on any data, above all *no decisions*.

Method

1 Read the case *fast*. Skip read it, skim it through. Get from start to finish in about 10 minutes. You should *not* have pen or pencil anywhere near you at this time!
2 The case is divided into Narrative and Data. Narrative is the story, the description of the organization and of your role. Data contains the information, presented usually as Appendices although some data is usually tucked away inside the narrative.
3 Read carefully through the narrative. Examine each of the Appendices. Still without pen or pencil, and still without any attempt at judgement or decisions.

At this stage you will have a clear general knowledge about the broad area of the case. You will know, in general, what data is available to you. You will have the beginnings of a feel for the scenario. Think of this stage as your first day at a new job. It is all very new, and you are feeling your way around. You need certain signposts, some reference points. You are certainly not going to start telling the MD what changes to make!

4 Take a large sheet of paper, and pick up your pen. Read the case again, but this time extremely thoroughly. Examine every sentence, make a heading on your paper for each area that is important. (Each situation is different, the relative importance of each area must be determined.) Certainly you will have headings for the four main

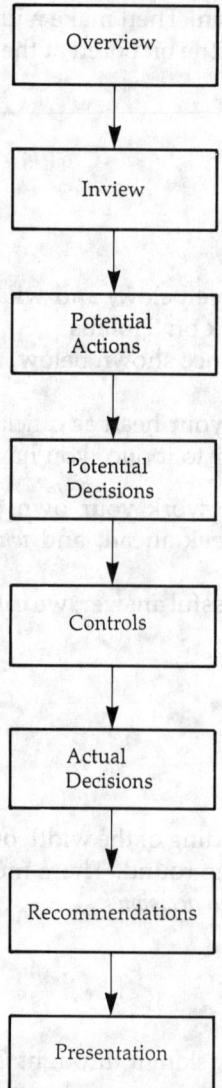

Figure 13.1 *The sequence*

functions – marketing, finance, production and personnel – but there will usually be need for major sub-sections within each. As you find a piece of significant information jot it down under the correct heading. Also indicate the source (e.g. line 16).

Do *not* work out any numbers. Simply indicate that they may be worth closer examination at the next stage.

5 You will be very tempted to examine data at this stage, to get involved with the Appendices. *Resist the temptation* (Only ever go into data analysis when you have clearly defined objectives, when there is something definite you need to know. *Never do it for its own sake.*) You will also be very tempted to start to form decisions, to see a way forward. Everybody is, always. If you succumb to this temptation you will then start to analyse data so that it confirms your prejudices, your biases, your opinions. Be warned: it must not happen. Only *you* can prevent it.

Question yourself: 'Why am I doing this?' If you have not got a good answer, reprimand yourself, and stop!

Overview result

You will know your role, and be clear on 'we' and 'they'. You will have a very clear understanding of the case. You will be ready to penetrate the detail of the situation.

Inview

Purpose

To give you a detailed understanding of the case and its constituent parts. This is the detailed fact finding part of your work. It is *not* judgemental, it is a straightforward extraction and simplification of the data presented to you. *No decisions* are made at this stage.

Method

1 Working from your analysis (on the large sheet of paper) set up a ring binder or lever arch file with indexed sections for each area that requires detailed study. You will work exclusively from this file, and it will become your prime reference, so be sure to manage it effectively.
2 Working from your Overview carry out a detailed investigation of aspects of the case. To take 'people' as an example you may find you need:

   2.1 A personnel profile on your role character.
   2.2 A schematic showing your consultancy structure.
   2.3 Personnel profiles on your consultancy colleagues.
   2.4 A hierarchical diagram of your client's company structure.
   2.5 A detailed personnel profile on each main client character.
   2.6 Job descriptions for each main client role.
   2.7 A breakdown of client wage and salary costs, by department.
   2.8 Staff turnover and stability ratios, by client department.

3 Appendices are sometimes red herrings. Be certain that you only analyse tables for a purpose.
4 Data can usually be cross-analysed. By working with two or more tables at the same time greater penetration, greater understanding, can be achieved.
5 Be certain to reference all work. You may need to justify your figures later and it is embarrassing to forget where your analysis came from.
6 Do not be afraid to seek help with analysis of data, but do be sure that you understand the analysis. *Work all the figures through for yourself*. It is essential that you understand how they work. Going to see the boss, or into an exam, with good data is essential, but there may be need to modify it slightly in the light of the questions that you are asked. You must be able to do this.
7 Be careful with the numerical data. Everybody makes mistakes, and you should not take numbers at face value.

8 By the end of the Inview all the information should be in your head and in your reference file. There should be no need ever to refer to the printed material again. Put it at the back of your reference file, in the unlikely event you have to go back to it.

Result

You will have a detailed understanding, in very great depth, and from the correct perspective. You will be working from your own papers, and not from the published case.

   This stage is the same as settling into a new job or consultancy project. It takes a while to be fully confident at work, but then you are equipped to answer a question from your own head, backed up by your reference material – your filing system.

Potential actions

Purpose

To identify *as many as possible* of the actions open to the subject of the case in order that each may be examined for practicality and tested against appropriate investment criteria.

Method

It is now that you can start to be creative, begin to act as a forward-thinking manager. All the hard ground work is now behind you.

1 In your reference file you will have a vast amount of information, but you will find that it is in your head also. The background information in your reference file will be used less and less as you build up your Action File.
2 Your Action File is where you build up contingency plans, fully worked through, so that no matter what questions you are asked you have material pre-prepared. This material will require little, if any, additional work when you write your report.
3 This part of the Sequence will be fun. You can identify actions that, provided they do not contradict any given material, are only limited by the breadth of your imagination.
4 Brainstorming techniques are good to use at this stage, and you can certainly involve other people.
5 You will find that common sense comes into play here. If the case has several Appendices covering the same area it is important that you provide for their use in your answer. It is extremely likely that, having produced the Appendices, your manager, or the examiner, will use them.
6 You will probably find up to a dozen potential actions, each of which will have a series of decision strata to work through. At this stage you are *identifying*, not working through.

Result

You have identified the areas about which you can be questioned.

Potential decisions/controls

Purpose

To establish strategic and tactical decision areas that are possible of Control. To ensure that Control mechanisms are in place, and/or that clear recommendations for their implementation are, or can, be made.

Method

1 Decisions that cannot be controlled are useless. Thus there is no point considering an increase in market share if no reliable information on the market exists. You would have to consider expressing your decisions in terms of volume targets, and you would have to be sure that a Management Information System (MIS) exists to report back efficiently on progress.
2 Control ensures that one knows results, in time for remedial action. It prevents one from drifting helplessly. Or, perhaps, steaming at full speed in the wrong direction!
3 The Decision Sequence is always the same:

   3.1 Mission statement – what business are we/you in?
   3.2 Policy statement – expressing specific intentions to achieve.
   3.3 Strategic objectives – written in clear objective/time format.
   3.4 Tactical objectives – follow from strategic, and break down the plan into small, manageable pieces. They are also *always* written in objective/time format.

4 Reasonable assumptions may be made at this stage. An example:

   A British firm in a case wants to go into export. It is large. It would be reasonable to assume that it has fluent speakers of European languages in its employ. It would not be reasonable to assume fluency in a language from the Far East.

5 As you identify the decision areas open you will be able to allocate levels of urgency, of practicality.

   5.1 Some things *must* be done, and quickly.
   5.2 Some can be done and are desirable.
   5.3 Some could be done, and are desirable.
   5.4 Some could be done, but are not desirable.
   5.5 Some *must not* be done.

6 In many cases you will find that a lack of information prevents a clear decision being taken. There are two alternatives:

6.1 Go for the decision, in the knowledge that the information is lacking, but clearly justify your decision/recommendation.

6.2 Recommend the correct type of marketing research, so that a decision can be taken at a specified time in the future.

Note that recommending marketing research in itself is of *no value*. The need is to identify the decision that needs to be taken, the constraint(s) that make it inadvisable without further information, the exact information needed, the time scale for research completion, and the research budget. In many cases there is need to write a research brief.

7 At this stage of the Sequence you are beginning to firm up on your thinking, and roughing out the detailed work that needs to be done next. Therefore you should be working to general criteria, not specific.

7.1 You are looking to *exclude* the options that are not viable – and to be able to justify your decision.

7.2 You are quantifying the probability of each course of action being successful.

7.3 You are measuring it against investment criteria.

7.4 You are getting your own personal perspective into the case.

Result

You own the case now. It is in your head, and the Action File has clear sections, each self-standing. You have an opinion on the best course(s) of action. All you need now is to tighten down on specific plans.

Actual decisions

Purpose

To take hard decisions on your alternative recommendations and to work them through in considerable detail so that you are fully prepared.

Method

You will have noted we have suggested that up to a dozen areas need work. This is essential because it is necessary to consider thoroughly all the options – it is unusual for senior managers to know exactly what they want – and one can never predict their supplementary questions. Examiners are not quite as unpredictable, but one still has to over-prepare.

You have to over-prepare. You will feel let down when you leave your manager, or the examination room, with over half of your preparatory work unused, but be ready for this. It is, after all, a lot better than getting caught out unprepared.

1 Actual decisions will come to you quite easily. You will know so much about the case you will be almost a part of it by now.
2 Decision *areas* must be clarified, and within them the full hierarchy of policy, strategy, tactics and control worked through and costed.
3 Decisions must be clear, specific, unambiguous. They must be expressed in terms of objective/time.
4 Decisions must be practical, realistic and within the remit of the questions asked.

Result

You will go into your manager, or the examination room, with all the information you need readily to hand, and well thought through.

Recommendations

Purpose

To express your decisions clearly, succinctly and without ambiguity.

Method

With your decisions made, you now only have to write them up into a form that is acceptable to management. They *must* be in the form of a report. There is no choice.

1 Prepare each of your decision areas as a Management Report. Be sure to use the same style throughout.
2 Use visuals as much as you reasonably can. If it is clearer to set out a segmentation analysis visually, then do so.
3 A *very important* word here about technique. Do not allow yourself to become so set in your thinking that you panic if the questions you are asked are not exactly as you had envisaged.

Result

You have pre-prepared and scripted answers to more questions than you can be asked. The style is the same, so you can make them into one long report, or four short ones, as required. You can relax, knowing that you have all it takes to answer anything the boss can ask.

Presentation

Purpose

To impress, and to communicate your recommendations clearly, succinctly and without ambiguity.

Method

Managers, and examiners, react favourably to well-presented material. Be sure that your report is crisp and tidy, and that you create an excellent first impression.

Result

Your work will be of value, and your personal achievement will be recognized.

What next?

A summary of the method to be used at each step of the Sequence is to be found at the beginning of each subsequent chapter, but do not hesitate to check back into this chapter if you need to be reminded of the detail.

Important note

Our suggested answers may recommend actions with which you do not agree. Do not see this as a problem. Your answers need to be personal statements of your own decisions. Read our answers as much for style, for approach, as for anything else. The test is, would a boss accept our answers as a competent management report? If so, we pass. If not, we fail.

Next step

You have already read through Hollins Holidays, and so have an idea of its content. It is now time to conduct an Overview.

14 *The Overview*

Before proceeding further you should have completed your own Overview of the case.

You should have the main points of the case extracted on to one sheet of paper and, more importantly, you should be confident that you can turn to information you need quickly. You should also have a feel for the case, for its strengths and its limitations. You will not have a detailed understanding, but you should know where you are going to start a more detailed examination.

You should have put an order of priority onto your work. It could be that there is material in the Appendices that you will not need.

When confident that you have progressed this far, compare our work with yours. Do not worry if it is not identical. Remember that you are working with your perceptions, your experience.

NOTE

Questions not equal	Notes
Instructions in exam	Notes
NO research outside case	Notes
CONFIDENTIAL	77

ROLE

I am Chris Knight	Brief
Executive responsibility	Notes
Control team	Notes
Direct & Act	Notes
Decide & Recommend	Notes
Best decision possible	89

TIME

January (no year)	1
Last project over December	13
On site – 27 months	97

ICCC

14 floors up (large?)	7
Status – Blue Folder – (a big firm, bureaucracy?)	15
Major gap – intend/exploit	79
Board decision	80

JAY

KM's Secretary	16
Late	102
Still late	117
DOESN'T APPEAR – IGNORE?	

OVERSEAS

Falling numbers? (check!)	48
US Tourists	61
Terrorists	61

CHRIS KNIGHT

Executive	Notes
Has team	Notes
Manages	Notes
5 yr senior	9
Last project ended	13
Compliments on	14
MD too	20
Best decisions possible	89
Shining opportunity	91
'CK project'	92
Firm proposals	94
100% on project	96
say if impractical . . . oh yes!	110

KIM MEDWAY

Senior to CK	10
Marketing Director	11
Complimentary/supportive	14
Firm/strict/clear	27
Pleased with CK	72

UK HOLIDAY MARKET

Package firms trouble	25
Changing face	32/39

Holiday camps	42/45
T. H. Forte	44
Developing British taste	53
New venture – Dutch	65/67
Butlins – water world (?) (check!)	68
Committed to report	74
Major gap	80
Secondary data available	115

NEW PROJECT/HOLLINS

Need to roll	74
Board decision	80
Decision specified***	84/86
No test market	88
Best decisions possible	89
Theme – sport/history	103/108
Specific: structure	112/114
operation	
segments	
targeting	
<u>preliminary proposal costed</u>	114

APPENDICES

A   2 December
   A/1 Background – value?
   A/2 F. E. Rates – value for UK holidays?
   A/3 VERY USEFUL – analyse

B   5 December – value?

C 7 December
   <u>FUNDAMENTAL</u> must provide basis of
   costs. But (?) nothing on Full Theme costs?

D 10 December
   Reliable researcher, valid results.
   D/1 Britain/England (?) important?
       Take out trends?
   D/2/3 'Holidays', why 4 nights?
       A basis for segmentation
   D/4 Geographic profile too detailed?
   D/5 POPULAR MONTHS

E Map of UK – use?

F 20 December
   Holiday camps – Only work through if
   these turn into potential segment – seems
   pretty full at the moment!

G 24 December – Center Parcs
   Newest in, may parallel. Must have gone
   same route as ICCC will. Study, especially
   the pricing structure

H TGI data from BMRB – reliable.
   Detailed segmentation, also media. Tie
   back to App. D? 4 nights obviously
   statistical basis in trade – (?) value to us –
   Center Parcs (App. G) on 3 day packages.

***

'. . . whether or not to enter the UK holiday market
with a series of holiday centres that will be custom
built to meet the perceived needs of a segment of the
public . . .'

Summary of impressions following Overview

1 This is about the UK holiday market, but no specific definition of a Hollins 'centre' is given. A task for me?
2 ICCC is, apparently, a very large firm – like British American Tobacco, perhaps. I will assume so. It is reasonable given the clues – status of folder, 14th floor, five years' seniority, a Head of NPD.
3 Reasonable for ICCC to be diversifying – Marlboro, Silk Cut, Dunhill, all are opening opportunities outside tobacco.
4 Chris Knight – *ME* – is senior, trusted, known to the MD. Therefore Chris's boss is very senior. A Board Member? Not important, per se, but the derived authority will be considerable.
5 Clear decisions have been taken. This is a feasibility study – in confidence of course (must remember to head the report with 'CONFIDENTIAL').
6 Secondary data has been researched; obviously my managers feel they have given me sufficient information for me to make a clear recommendation.
7 I can assume, therefore, that they know the likely costs, and I can proceed without worry on that score.
8 The brief is 'whether or not to enter'. So it is primarily a feasibility study.
9 It is an NPD operation – I must read up on NPD, market entry, etc. (That is not research into the case.)
10 Finally – is the case, in fact, about UK holidays? Or UK leisure?
   Is it for UK people? British? English?
   Tourists from overseas?
   There is obviously a lot of conceptual and definition work to do once I have broken out the detail from the Appendices.

15 *The Inview*

Reminder

This is the detailed, fact finding, part of the work. It is crucial – but time-consuming. You will be tempted to skip through. Please do not. Your examination success is dependent on the quality of the Inview.

Make no judgements at this stage. At all costs avoid even the smallest decision. You must stay objective and impartial through the Inview.

Work from your Overview and dig out every fact, every reasonable assumption, from the case. Cross reference data. Put tables into graph form (it is *much* easier to understand visual data).

Generate an Action File from your Inview. One section for each area, with subdivisions as needed. Reference all your work! This is the file you will work from in the examination room; it will be your information, much more detailed and useful than the examiner's data, more understandable than any analysis you can buy. Understanding is crucial to success in the examination.

Double check your work, but do not be surprised if case data turns out to be wrong. Misprints happen, and it has been known for an examiner deliberately to provide questionable data as a check on candidates' ability.

Work your Inview of Chris Knight and of ICCC. Then check against ours before progressing with the remainder of your Inview.

Your complete Inview should differ in degree from ours. Your perceptions of the case will be different, your assumptions will be coloured by your own personality. This is how it should be. One reason case study examinations are valid is that from identical cases a range of candidates come up with a range of answers. You should submit your own individual response to the examiners. Your Inview is the start of the process of individualizing the case.

Hint: It can be very helpful to label your files prominently with your case name and authority, e.g.

My name is Chris Knight.
I recommend not decide

Chris Knight

Source: Scenario.

Analysis

As we noted in the Overview, we have been given the role of Chris Knight. As a full time employee of ICCC our report must be written in the first person singular (or plural if writing on behalf of the NPD team).

The first lines of the text reveal that we are a senior person in the organization ('on reaching the corner desk, earned by five years' seniority'; 'Chris grasped the blue folder that was, in ICCC, a mark of status') and highly thought of ('since his team had wrapped up their latest project in the middle of December, Kim had been very complimentary'). This view is further reinforced in Line 20, '. . . on that job you put to bed last month. The Managing Director was most pleased.'

Line 28 demonstrates that we are also ambitious: 'here was an obvious opportunity to make the step up that was so necessary to career development'.

The conversation that we have with Kim Medway reveals a considerable amount of additional information about our job at ICCC. While we have a high level of ability at New Product Development, our knowledge of the UK holiday market is comparable to any reasonably aware (British) person. (*Note:* Need to revise New Product Development from text(s).)

Our enthusiasm for the task is unquestionable, as demonstrated on Line 91: 'Gosh yes, thought Chris. What an opportunity to shine. With the MD taking a personal interest in the project – the Chris Knight project – this was an opportunity not to be taken at less than full commitment . . .' Furthermore, as Line 96 also shows, we have no excuse for failing to excel: 'From now on you are 100 per cent on this project . . .' We obviously have a high ego, supported by a record of success. It is certain therefore that we will write a very decisive report and that our commitment to it will be evident.

An additional useful insight into our standing in the company can be gleaned from Lines 9/16. It is noted in the narrative that Kim Medway is our boss. Kim is probably a Board member (note section 'ICCC') and we appear to have a fairly good working relationship. At least we are on first name terms! More seriously, Kim Medway holds us in high regard: 'Kim smiled, Chris was obviously the person for the job.'

One area of possible conflict is raised in the penultimate paragraph of the text. Kim Medway has apparently given us *carte blanche* as far as our report is concerned. However, he has made the comment 'No doubt the Board would not be put out if you felt that its ideas had no future'. . . It may prove very difficult at the decision/recommendation stage to bring ourselves to recommend that ICCC not proceed. The Board is most important, and our normal reaction if told to 'Jump!', would be to ask 'How high?' We should, however, be prepared to cope with this dilemma if it arises.

We must remember that at our level of seniority we will be producing a report that addresses strategic issues. The time horizon for our recommendations is measured in years. However, we must also consider each tactical point carefully since strategy can only be achieved through tactical management. We do not have to solve tactics – just be sure that what we recommend strategically is capable of tactical achievement.

In Line 76 we are told 'everything from here on is totally confidential'. . . We would only be made aware of such matters if our level of responsibility were appropriate.

We are empowered to recommend, not decide.

Finally, we can draw up a brief Curriculum Vitae which provides a succinct statement of our character.

CURRICULUM VITAE
Name: Chris Knight
Superior: Marketing Director (Board member).
Subordinates: New Products Development Project Team.
Comment: Chris Knight is highly thought of by the Board including the MD. Chris is experienced in assessing New Projects and has recently produced a particularly impressive report.

ICCC

Source: Scenario, Appendices A–E.

Analysis

Our employer is quickly outlined in Lines 5/6 of the case. It is the International Cigarette and Cigar Corporation (ICCC). We are informed that it is located in London. It could be that it occupies all 14 floors (or more) that we had to walk up on the unpleasant Monday morning in January. We cannot tell from the case but further details tend to suggest that it is a large organization – perhaps similar to British Tobacco. Examples of this are the fact that it has been trading for more than 20 years and owns dormant companies (Lines 80/83). We know that it has a Group Economic Research Department from Appendices A and B and this further supports the view that it is a large corporate. The very use of the term 'Group' and the in-house resource of an Economic Research Department are associated with large organizations. Furthermore, the Internal memorandum from Lan Dagent (Appendix B) suggests that there is a property department/division and there is also a research librarian (Appendices D and E).

Having established that we are employed by a major company, we can now confidently assume that financial support will be available internally to carry out the project if it is recommended that ICCC proceeds with the Hollins Holidays concept.

We have already produced an inview analysis on ourselves – Chris Knight.

The other characters are Kim Medway – a Main Board director (note Line 79: 'We, that is the Board of ICCC . . .), the Managing Director, other Board members, Lan Dagent and Jay – Kim Medway's secretary (Line 16). Although it is unlikely that Jay will have any further involvement Lan Dagent could appear again in the exam paper. At this stage, however, as already stated, the best assumption that we can make is that Lan Dagent is located in a Property Department/Division of ICCC.

Summarizing the information in the case in visual form is usually very helpful. Unfortunately we have very little hard data about ICCC, as figures 15.1 and 15.2 demonstrate.

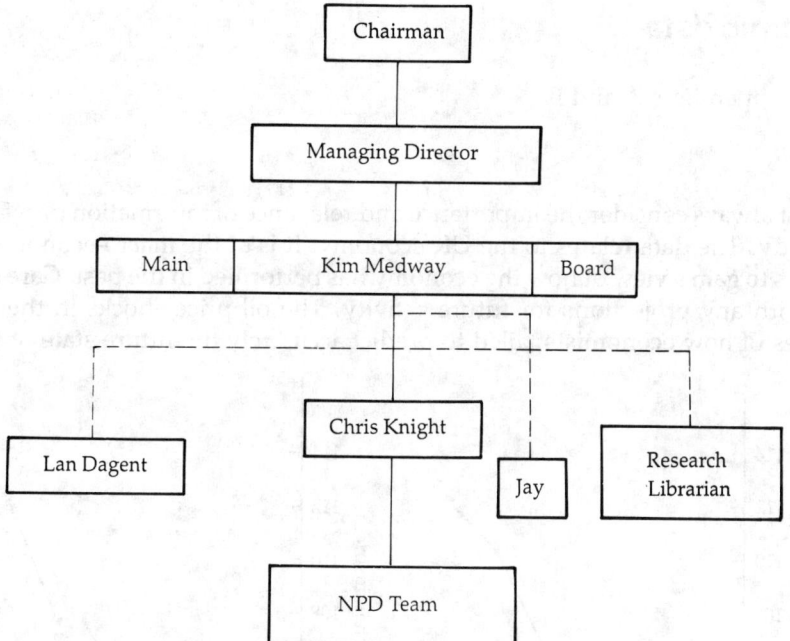

Figure 15.1 *ICCC structure*

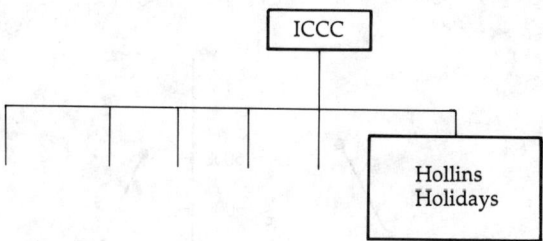

Figure 15.2

Economic data

Source: Appendices A and B.

Analysis

We must always consider the importance and relevance of information provided in the case study. The data relates to the UK economy. It is at the macro-economic level. It allows us to gain a view of how the economy has performed in the past. Care should be taken with any projections for future activity. The oil price shocks in the 1970s are examples of how economists failed to predict accurately the future state of the world

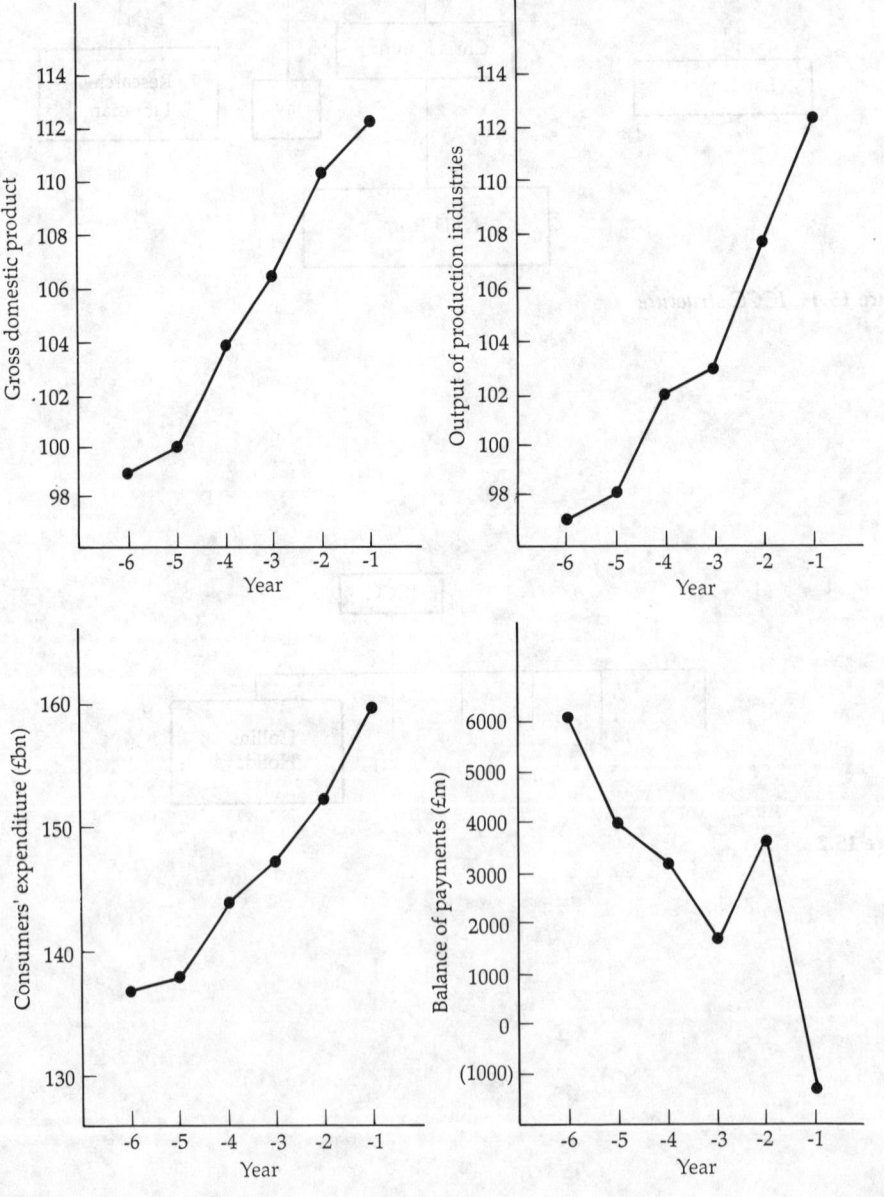

Figure 15.3   *Economic indicators 1*

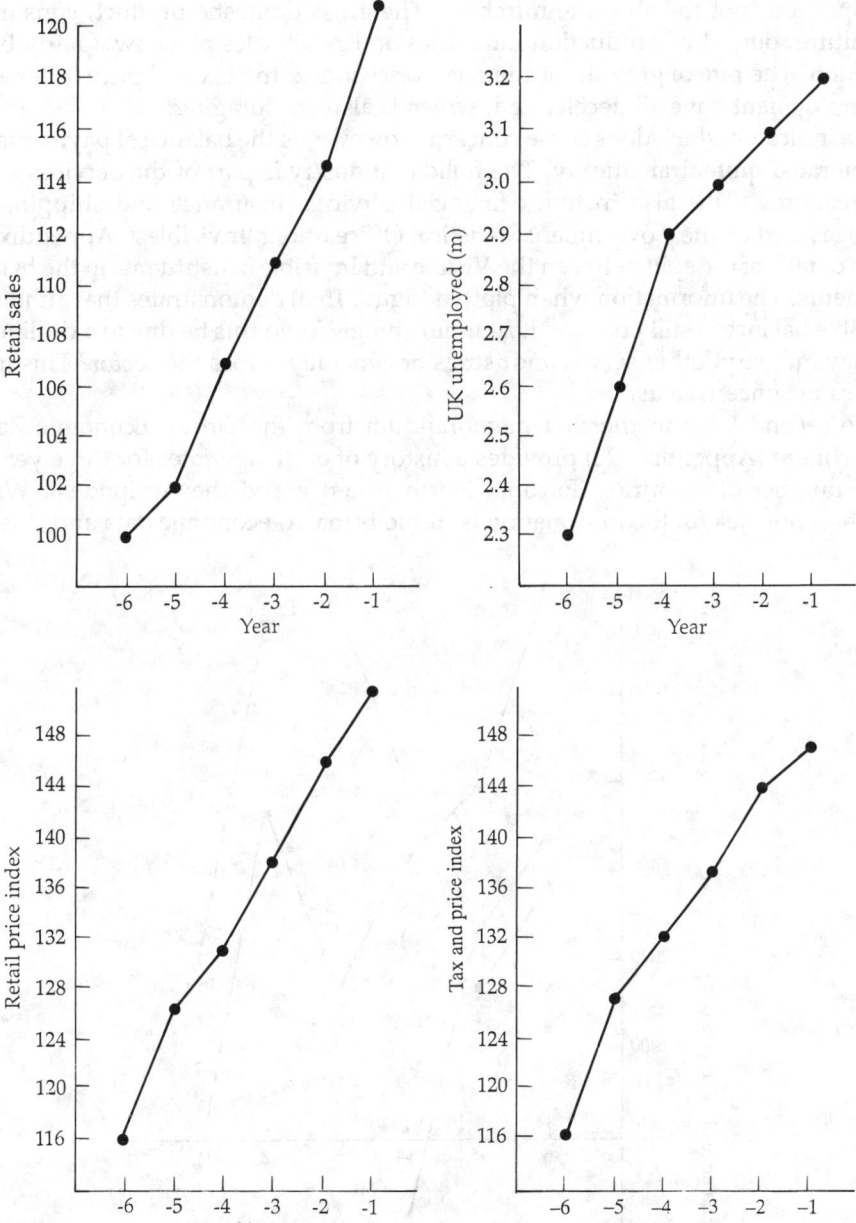

Figure 15.4 *Economic indicators 2*

economy. Nevertheless, Appendices A and B (note that Appendix B is only a more detailed statement of information already shown in Appendix A) permit us to gain an appreciation of the environment in which we are working. The holiday centre concept will operate over a period of many years and its profitability will be subject to the vagaries of the UK economic performance.

At this stage (the Inview) the best form of analysis for Appendix A/1 (Economic Indications) is to represent the information pictorially (figures 15.3 and 15.4). The diagrams are able to provide us with a visual analysis of the data. It is the pattern that is important, not the absolute numbers. The gross domestic product, consumer expenditure, output of production industries and retail sales all show a fairly buoyant situation. The rate of growth for the retail price index, the tax and price index and UK unemployment have all decelerated, which is also encouraging.

The indicator which does cause concern, however, is the balance of payments. It has deteriorated quite dramatically. The holiday industry is part of the Services sector of the economy. This also includes financial services, insurance and shipping. They are measured by the Government Statistical Office under 'Invisibles'. Appendix C provides details of the split between the Visible and Invisible constituents in the balance of payments. The information when plotted (figure 15.5) demonstrates that although the invisible balance is still positive, it is diminishing. Could this be due to a decline in the holiday industry, other service industries or generally across the sector? This must be an area of concern to us.

The second table in the first memorandum from the Group Economic Research Department (Appendix A/2) provides a history of exchange rates for three years for a large number of countries (Europe, North America and the Antipodes). We must question how useful the information is. It too is macro-economic data and, therefore,

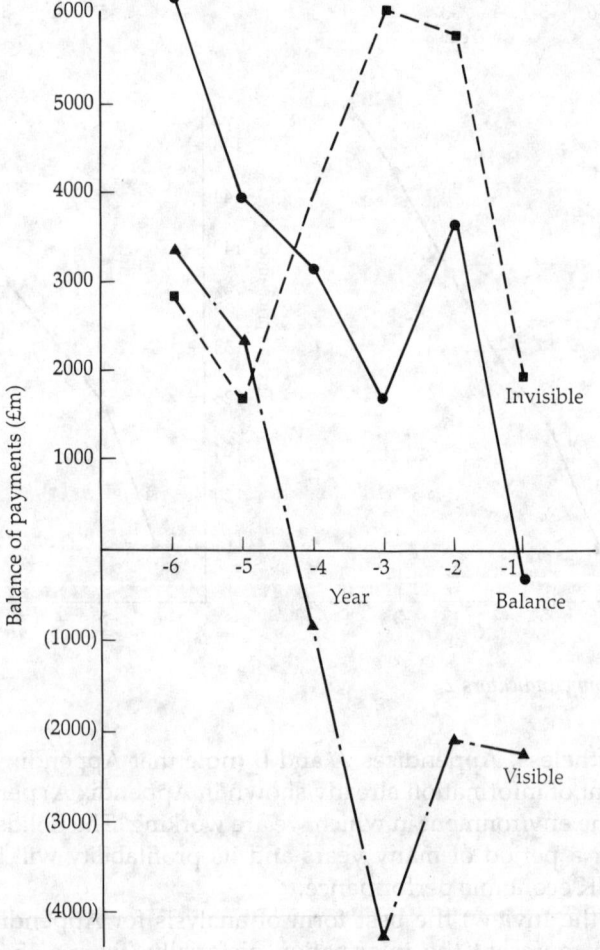

Figure 15.5   *Balance of payments*

further expands our knowledge of the environment within which we are operating. Perhaps this is its only value?

To obtain a feel for what it tells us, we should establish the relative change in the value of sterling compared to the other currencies. Table 15.1 provides an index value for the pound in each of the past three years. Values less than 100 show that the pound has fallen, those greater than 100 reveal a stronger pound. When our domestic currency is stronger the exchange rate encourages overseas travel. When the pound is losing value foreigners are more likely to visit the UK since their currency will have a proportionally higher value in sterling. A UK holiday will appear cheap, or at least cheaper. Thus a holiday provider looking to attract tourists is to a great extent affected by the rate of exchange, over which he can have no control.

Table 15.1: Relative Value of Sterling

Country	Currency	Index Year −3	Index Year −2	Index Year −1
Australia	Dollar	100	151	154
Austria	Schilling	100	97	79
Belgium	Franc	100	99	82
Canada	Dollar	100	131	129
Cyprus	Pound	100	107	99
Denmark	Krone	100	99	83
France	Franc	100	97	85
Germany	Mark	100	97	79
Greece	Drachma	100	143	136
Irish Republic	Punt	100	99	90
Italy	Lira	100	108	89
Malta	Pound	100	108	94
Netherlands	Guilder	100	97	79
New Zealand	Dollar	100	118	114
Norway	Krone	100	104	103
Portugal	Escudo	100	116	109
Spain	Peseta	100	110	96
Switzerland	Franc	100	97	81
USA	Dollar	100	124	124
Total		1900	2102	1905
Divided by number of readings (19)		100	111	100

Indexing the change in value of sterling produces some intriguing patterns. The overall weighted index also reveals an interesting result between December of Year −3 and December Year −1 (100/100). However, this is probably a red herring. It is human nature to add up a column of numbers (and in this case take an average). The relative importance of each currency has been assumed to be equal – a questionable statistical decision.

More importantly, if we look at regions of the world we may be able to provide some segmental views. Sterling has gained value against the North American (US and

Canadian) and the Antipodean (Australian and New Zealand) dollars. This suggests that there is a lower probability of the UK increasing its attractiveness as a holiday destination for nationals of these countries. However, apart from Greece, Portugal (two popular destinations for UK holiday makers) and Norway, sterling has lost value against the currencies of European countries. We should consider such markets for targeting when potential decisions are being drawn up.

The analysis of foreign exchange rates appears to have produced some very useful thoughts on future segmentation of target markets. However, a word of warning. Foreign exchange markets are very fickle in the short term. While in the medium to long term the economic performance of a country does express itself in the exchange rate of its currency, day movements in the value of a currency can be very dramatic. (This is known as the Fisher effect: interest rates, inflation rates and foreign exchange rates fall into equilibrium in the long term.)

Values can change by large amounts (25 per cent or more) in just a few days (or hours). Such movements could quickly make the cost of a foreign holiday (in this case to the UK) totally out of the question. The opposite effect is of course to cause Britons to change their plans for overseas holidays and switch to taking a vacation within the UK.

There is a tendency nowadays for the media to magnify even small changes and for this to cause non-financial specialists (lay people) to change their plans – often with no reason. For example, a move of 5c on the US dollar affects a UK holidaymaker only marginally:

Price of holiday $800 @ $1.60 = £500
                        @ $1.55 = £516

Add the enjoyment value of the US holiday into the equation and the extra £16 can be seen to be well spent: i.e. price should not be the only decision criterion. (But this has often to be expressed very clearly in promoting the holiday.)

The table showing a comparison of interest costs (Appendix A/3) is expressed in local currency. To gain any appreciation from it the values should be compared against a common denominator. We shall use the December Year −1 rates of exchange for sterling (table 15.2). What do we glean from this information? Perhaps we could attempt to calculate the cost of a week's holiday in each country (e.g. seven nights in a

Table 15.2: Comparison of International Costs (Year −1 prices)

Country	Currency	Hotel room	Meal	Bottle of wine
Australia	Dollar	20.79	11.55	1.39
Austria	Schilling	34.95	18.02	2.46
France	Franc	44.97	13.20	0.63
Greece	Drachma	11.82	4.92	0.74
Italy	Lira	20.00	8.00	1.50
Norway	Krone	46.08	25.35	5.99
Spain	Peseta	8.75	3.09	1.54
Switzerland	Franc	59.55	18.48	12.32
UK	Pound	40.00	10.00	6.00
USA	Dollar	27.92	8.38	6.28

hotel room, two meals and one bottle of wine per day). How do we then build up additional costs such as travel within the country, other local costs of living, spending on gifts etc.? If we are looking at foreign holidays air fares would have to be included. We would begin to move out of the realm of reasonable assumption into that of pure guesswork.

A qualitative view should suffice. The UK appears to be middle of the range as far as costs are concerned. The relative cheapness of Greece, Spain and Italy provides one reason why these destinations are popular with UK holidaymakers, but guaranteed sun and sand must be attractive too. As far as visitors from other European countries would be concerned the costs are similar. They are cheaper if later on we do decide to target the USA or Australia as potential markets for customers to the Hollins Holidays centres.

We now have a good understanding of our economic environment.

Finance

Source: Scenario, Appendices C and D.

Analysis

There are two distinct sets of information contained within the case. Appendix C provides a detailed report from Lan Dagent on the costs for building and operating while part of Appendix D provides a source of information as an aid to determining likely levels of revenue.

Initially we can consider the cost side of the equation. If we produce an analysis of the costs to build a centre for either 250, 500 or 1000 holidaymakers it will make us fully conversant with the figures in the case study and also produce the method for costing a centre of any size. By also choosing two different regions, i.e. the South East and Wales, the technique for assessing costs in various locations will also be determined.

We will have to make assumptions about the area of land required for the holiday centre, the size of the accommodation units, the number of recreational facilities and other ancillary items. These must be reasonable and no doubt we will each have slightly (but in the same ball park) different views.

Let us consider first the capital expenditure (Appendix C) to set up the various centres. Table 15.3 begins the analysis. We can see that the cost of land in the South East is by far the most expensive item. This, later in the analysis, could lead us to choose an area where land is cheaper, e.g. Wales. Economics of scale begin to operate when the size of the holiday centre is large enough to cater for 500 to 1000 visitors.

There have been a number of reasonable assumptions to build up a view of how the capital expenditure might be incurred. At this stage it is important that we consider the result intuitively. Would we not agree that a range in costs from £3.750 mn to £26.1 mn has a reasonable feel about it? If we had come up with a range of £100 K to £100 mn there would have been raised eyebrows. However, our figures do tie in closely and are supported by Appendix F, where rivals' investment is quoted.

The analysis in table 15.3 can be used to draw up a provisional balance sheet for Hollins Holidays at the beginning of its trading. We can produce as many examples as

Table 15.3: Capital Expenditure

Item	South East England			Wales		
	250	500	1000	250	500	1000
Area of land required (sq miles)	1/4	1/2	2/3	1/4	1/2	2/3
Area of land required (acres)	160	320	427	160	320	427
Cost per acre (£)	50 000	50 000	50 000	15 000	15 000	15 000
Cost of land required	8 000 000	16 000 000	21 350 000	2 400 000	4 800 000	6 405 000
Accommodation per person (sq yd)	35	35	35	35	35	35
Total accommodation space	2 100	4 200	8 400	2 100	4 200	8 400
Dining area including kitchens (sq yd)	400	800	1 200	400	800	1 200
Reception and relaxation areas	500	1 000	1 500	500	1 000	1 500
Total building requirements (sq yd)	3 000	6 000	11 100	3 000	6 000	11 100
Building costs (per sq yd)	340	340	340	340	340	340
Total building costs	1 020 000	2 040 000	3 774 000	1 020 000	2 040 000	3 774 000
Initial decorations @ £30 sq.yd	90 000	180 000	333 000	90 000	180 000	333 000
Landscaping @ £1500 per acre	240 000	480 000	640 500	240 000	480 000	640 500
Total capital expenditure (£)	9 350 000	1 870 000	2 609 750	3 750 000	7 500 000	11 152 500
Cost per holidaymaker (£)	37 400	37 400	26.1	15 000	15 000	11 153

Hollins Holidays

Centre for 1000 visitors in South East England

Balance Sheet as at day zero of trading

	£	£
Fixed Assets: Land		21 350 000
Buildings		3 774 000
		25 124 000
Current Assets: Landscaping	640 500	
Decorations	333 000	
	973 500	
Current Liabilities:	0	
Net Current Assets		973 500
Total Assets		26 097 500
Financed by:		
Intercompany Loan/Share Capital from ICCC		26 097 500
Total Liabilities		26 097 500

Figure 15.6   *Forecast balance sheet for Hollins Holidays*

we wish. One should suffice at this stage to familiarize ourselves with the approach (see figure 15.6.)

A similar analysis of the data in Appendix C can be made for the revenue (profit and loss) account; albeit only for expenditure items at this stage. We are again looking at two hypothetical locations, each accommodating three different volumes of holidaymakers. Our workings are contained within table 15.4.

We can make two assumptions to expand upon the material continued within the case. First, a ratio of staff to guests of one to 20 for cleaning, supervision etc. would seem reasonable; plus a general management team of 12 people (say on an average annual salary of £10,000). Secondly ICCC would expect a return of about 18 per cent per annum on its investment. This is a fair commercial norm of ROCE for a new, relatively high risk venture.

From table 15.4 we can draw up a specimen profit and loss account (figure 15.7). For he moment we may as well assume that Hollins Holidays operates at break-even level. The target level of profit – if one is required that more than covers the interest/dividend payments to ICCC – will be determined later in the case study analysis.

Omitted from the expenditure analysis is the cost of equipping the holiday centres. The brief is that they should have a theme, and this has to be provided for over and above the basic costs of site and buildings etc. (see Lines 105/108 'we could set up one as

Table 15.4: Revenue Expenditure

Item	South East England			Wales		
	250	500	1000	250	500	1000
Total building requirements (sq. yd)	3 000	6 000	11 000	3 000	6 000	11 100
Rates (per sq.yd of building per year)	10	10	10	7	7	7
Rates per year (£)	30 000	60 000	111 000	21 000	42 000	77 700
Decorations per sq. yd building (30/2)	45 000†	90 000	166 500	45 000	90 000	166 500
Power per guest per year *	52 000	104 000	208 000	52 000	104 000	208 000
Food per guest per year *	390 000	780 000	1 560 000	390 000	780 000	1 560 000
	517 000	1 034 000	2 045 000	508 000	1 016 000	2 012 200
No. of staff	25	37	62	25	37	62
Salaries @ £10,000 per person/year*	250 000	370 000	620 000	250 000	370 000	620 000
ROCE @ 18% per annum	1 683 000	3 366 000	4 697 550	675 000	1 350 000	2 007 450
TOTAL ANNUAL COST	**24 500 000**	**4 770 000**	**7 363 050**	**1 433 000**	**2 736 000**	**4 639 650**
Annual cost per holidaymaker/ week*	**186.46**	**183.46**	**141.60**	**110.23**	**105.23**	**89.22**

The figures marked with an asterisk * assume that occupancy levels will be 100 per cent for 52 weeks a year. They will have to be altered once we have determined utilization during the Decision and Recommendation stages.
† Calculated as 30/2 × 3000.

Norman, another as Tudor, another as Victorian, and so on' and 'Alternatively we could go for Bat and Ball, Sea and Surf etc.'). If they do become viable concepts, the costs of decor, costumes and entertainment in the case of the history concept or equipment and supervision for sports complexes can be considered as marginal in the context of this initial feasibility study.

Before moving on to analyse the information concerning potential revenue, it would be a good idea to consider how the work done on the financial data in Appendix C complies with the approach recommended earlier and to reflect again on the reasonableness of the assumptions that have been made.

At the Inview stage, we are told to analyse the data in the case and to refrain from making recommendations and/or to attempt to support any initial plans which we may (subconsciously?) feel are appropriate. We have not moved outside these criteria. Our

Hollins Holidays

Centre for 1000 visitors in South East England

Profit and Loss Statement for a specimen year

Sales	7 363 050
Cost of Sales	2 665 500
Profit Before Interest and Tax	4 607 550
Interest (*)	4 607 550
Profit Before Tax	0
Tax on Profits	0
	0
Dividend (*)	0
Retained Profits	0

* We are assuming that the company is financed entirely by debt. During the recommendation stage we may decide to recommend that the company be capitalized in a more conventional manner. The interest charge would fall and the dividend payments (probably) rise. This would be a further adjustment to the Profit and Loss statement.

Figure 15.7 *Forecast profit and loss statement for Year One for Hollins Holidays*

work has been to analyse the available data and at the same time develop processing techniques.

Our assumptions have been based upon our own views on how the concept operates. There is no additional information in the case regarding the resources needed for holiday centres and so we have filled out the partly painted picture. The validity of our work will be confirmed or contradicted when we have obtained a better picture of consumer expenditure from Appendix D.

Working through the case, the first time we come across data likely to reveal consumer expenditure on holidays is in Appendix D/1, the table headed 'Volume and Value of Tourism'. The information is valid as it is taken from the BTS–Y. Our research librarian has been very busy, but we should tuck away the thought that there is much additional data that we can go to if our initial feasibility study is positive. (Of course we, as candidates for the examination, cannot access it. But we could, as Chris Knight, recommend that it be accessed. A full secondary data search would at some time prove necessary. For the moment we must be content with the data that has been presented to us.)

Using the information in Appendix D/1, in table 15.5 we have calculated the average length of a holiday in Britain/UK and also England (a sub-set). The results in table 15.6 provide us with holiday costs. The top half of table 15.6 shows the average expenditure

Table 15.5: Average length of holiday

Year	Tourism to Britain/UK		Tourism to England	
	Average length of holiday (days)		Average length of holiday (days)	
	British	Foreign	British	Foreign
−11	3.79	14.50	3.79	12.75
−10	4.69	14.88	4.51	13.13
−9	4.70	12.90	4.48	12.56
−8	4.50	12.18	4.31	11.70
−7	4.50	12.42	4.29	11.91
−6	4.45	11.46	4.26	10.75
−5	4.45	11.92	4.28	11.33
−4	4.23	12.17	4.10	11.73
−3	4.13	11.25	3.99	12.00
−2	4.11	11.33	3.96	10.91
−1	4.16	11.23	3.95	11.55
	Average expenditure per night (£)		Average expenditure per night (£)	
	British	Foreign	British	Foreign
−11	2.29	6.25	2.50	6.62
−10	3.36	7.56	3.31	7.86
−9	3.91	9.30	3.95	9.73
−8	4.40	13.06	4.43	13.46
−7	4.82	15.60	4.76	16.22
−6	5.85	16.61	5.93	17.44
−5	7.24	17.90	7.29	18.57
−4	8.27	20.03	8.10	20.74
−3	8.85	21.85	8.86	22.50
−2	8.91	22.98	9.00	23.75
−1	9.82	24.83	9.89	25.98

on a holiday. It is a reasonable assumption to use the average expenditure figure per night to estimate an average spend per week (seven nights). It may be useful during the potential decisions stage to know this as holidays tend to be scheduled in multiples of a week. We are also able to compare the results with our estimated costs in table 15.4. The expenditure ranges from £68.74 per week (British holidaymakers) to £181.86 per week (foreign holidaymakers). The required income from the examples in table 15.4 ranges from £89.22 to £188.46 per week. We are certainly in the right 'Ball Park'!

Table 15.7 and figure 15.8 show the growth in expenditure on holidays in real terms (by adjusting money prices to Year −7 value). The graphs in figure 15.8 show that in real terms there has been little increase in spending by the British. However, foreign holidaymakers appear to have shown a general rate of increase since Year −6. In view of the absolute (actual pounds) levels of spending by foreign tourists, and the growth in real terms, we may later use this information to consider where our target markets lie.

The final area of detailed financial analysis arises in Appendices F and G. The two memoranda from the research librarian provide us with a useful collection of financial

Table 15.6: Holiday costs

| Year | Tourism Britain/UK | | Tourism to England | |
| | Average expenditure on holiday | | Average expenditure on holiday | |
	British (£)	Foreign (£)	British (£)	Foreign (£)
−11	8.68	90.63	9.48	84.41
−10	15.76	112.49	14.93	103.20
−9	18.38	119.97	17.70	122.21
−8	19.80	159.07	19.09	157.48
−7	21.69	193.07	20.42	193.18
−6	26.03	190.35	25.26	187.48
−5	32.22	213.37	31.20	210.40
−4	34.98	243.77	33.21	243.28
−3	36.55	245.81	35.35	270.00
−2	36.62	260.36	35.64	259.11
−1	40.85	278.84	39.07	300.07

Average expenditure on seven day holiday

Year	British (£)	Foreign (£)	British (£)	Foreign (£)
−11	16.03	43.75	17.50	46.34
−10	23.52	52.02	23.17	55.02
−9	27.37	65.10	27.65	68.11
−8	30.80	91.42	31.01	94.22
−7	33.74	109.20	33.32	113.54
−6	40.95	116.27	41.51	122.08
−5	50.68	125.30	51.03	129.99
−4	57.89	140.21	56.70	145.18
−3	61.95	152.95	62.02	157.50
−2	62.37	160.85	63.00	166.25
−1	68.74	173.81	69.23	181.86

Table 15.7: Expenditure on holidays

| Year | Retail price index | Tourism to Britain/UK | | Tourism to England | |
| | | Average expenditure on holiday | | Average expenditure on holiday | |
		British (£)	Foreign (£)	British (£)	Foreign (£)
−7	100	21.69	193.75	20.42	193.48
−6	116	22.44	164.09	21.78	161.62
−5	126	25.57	169.34	24.76	166.98
−4	131	26.70	186.08	25.35	185.71
−3	138	26.49	178.12	25.62	195.65
−2	146	24.81	178.33	24.41	177.47
−1	152	26.88	183.45	25.70	197.41

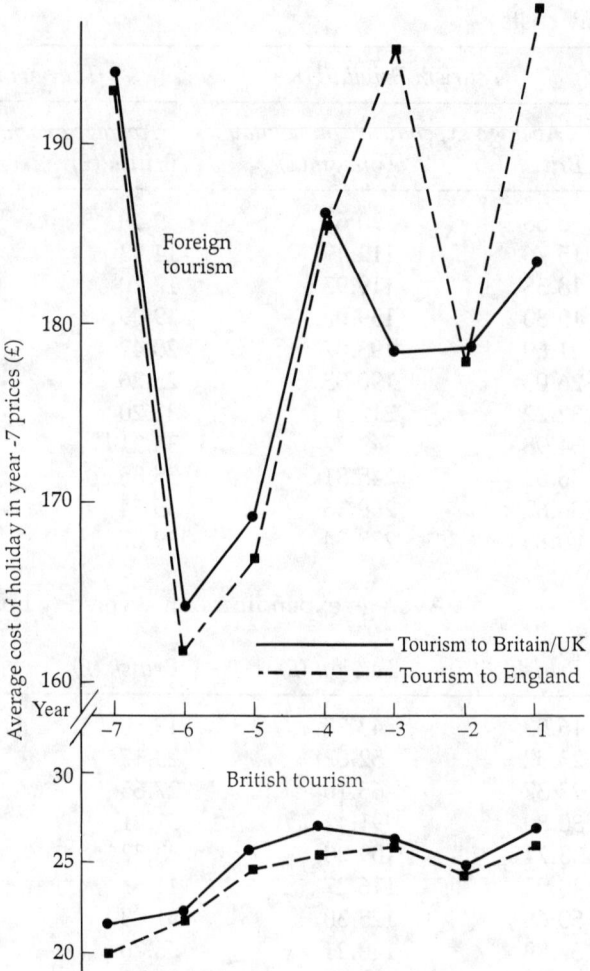

Figure 15.8   *Average cost of holiday in Year −7 prices*

Table 15.8: The competition – financial data

Company	Investment	Turnover	Profits	Costs high season per week	Costs low season per week	No. of centres	No. of holiday-makers/centre	Enter-tainment
Butlins	£10m per centre	£60m	8.33%	?	?	10	5 000–11 000	Free
Pontins	£30 m total	?	?	?	?	25	250–4 000	?
Ladbrokes	£2m per year	?	?	?	?	17	250 approx −5 000	?
Warners	£7m in Year −3	?	?	?	?	10	500–600	?
Center Parcs	?	?	?	£52 max See table	£125 max See table	1	600	Extra
General	?	?	?	£125	£150	?	?	?

data. The best way of breaking down the information is to produce a table to provide absolute and comparative (wherever possible) figures. At this stage little else can be done with the data but it will provide us with a very valuable reference sheet when potential actions are formulated and a quick comparison with other holiday companies' expenditure, income and size is required. Table 15.8 provides us with the model we need.

Competition

Source: Scenario, Appendices E, F and G.

Analysis

The first passing reference to the potential competition arises in Lines 42/44. We (Chris Knight) remark upon the perceived difficulties that holiday camps are experiencing: 'Holiday Camps, I think, have suffered. The Costa del Sol must have been a nightmare for Billy Butlin and Fred Pontin . . . although I believe they have opened up over there.' We have revealed that we believe that the holiday camp market is in problems even before we have been made aware of the Hollins Holidays concept.

Fairly quickly thereafter, our view changes slightly. After a little more thought the new developments in the market place come to mind. 'There is a Dutch operation now open in the UK . . . I can't recall the details, but I believe they operate specialist sporting villages and have opened one in Sherwood Forest . . . and . . . haven't Butlins been very successful with a Water World (or something) down in the West Country?' Our increased optimism continues: 'it could be that there is a new trend in vacations, just beginning . . .'

ICCC believes that extreme care must be taken over the competition. Kim Medway tells us that 'everything from here on is totally confidential'.

Although there is very little else in the text for us to cite specifically, there is certainly a general impression that entering the UK holiday centre market is a very serious opportunity as far as ICCC is concerned. It is not a new product and, therefore, the competition will be fierce as is usually the case in the mature stage of a product life cycle.

We do not come across any further information on the competition until Appendices F and G, the two memoranda from the group's research librarian.

Table 15.9 provides us with a very useful summary of the competition which can be referred to whenever we need such information. It can be read in conjunction with table 15.8. It will show that valuable secondary data is missing, but we can do nothing about that.

We have little information on the location of existing holiday centres, although from Appendix E we can see that Butlins are strategically placed throughout Great Britain. We also have the Center Parcs site marked. We know that Ladbrokes operates as far north as Yorkshire. It is a reasonable assumption that the other competitors also provide centres within easy reach of their customers.

The quality of the centres appears to be improving constantly, with the Center Parcs concept being at the forefront. It is also interesting to note that they all promote sport (this is implied by the Pontins holiday centres, although not explicitly stated). There is no mention of a historical theme by any of the competition.

Table 15.9: The competition – accommodation and facilities

Company	Accommodation	Facilities	Owner
Butlins	Half-board chalets Self-catering suites De-luxe caravans 'accommodation is the holiday ingredient that holidaymakers are most likely to talk about'	Self-contained centres Free entertainment, including funfairs, cinemas, cabaret, sports, late night discos. One centre is a £multi-million subtropical water centre	The Rank Organization since 1972
Pontins	A private bathroom is now the minimum . . . full-board customers expect, and get, tea making facilities	Keeping up with the expectations of the consumer	Bass since 1980
Ladbrokes	Chalets and caravans (Yorkshire to Cornwall)	Fun parks BMX cycle tracks	Ladbrokes
Warners	Facilities you would expect from a top class hotel. (Mainly on the South Coast.)	Futuristic sports complex that includes a gym of exclusive health club standards, a sauna and a jacuzzi (Upmarket, more Cs than Ds)	Grand Metropolitan since 1981
Center Parcs	Bungalow Village (villas) in Sherwood Forest near Nottingham Occupancy in Holland, and reportedly in the UK is 95% Villas are equipped to high standard with central heating, wall-to-wall carpeting, colour TV with teletext and two video channels, and open fire and a patio Price includes use of the villa and all of its services, cot, playpen, high chair, playground Bookings are Friday to Friday; Friday to Monday, and Monday to Friday	Almost every imaginable facility: country club, sports club, health farm, sub-tropical swimming paradise (in a dome) which contains 22 different features from wild water rapids to a solarium Outdoor sports: 18 Indoor sports: 13 Health & beauty: 4 Shops & services: 15 Conference centre 450 acres of woodland	Sporthuis Centrum Recreatie of Holland

Another common factor is that all the UK holiday centre companies are owned by large corporations. The fact that Sporthuis Centrum Recreatie operates nine holiday villages in Belgium and Holland, attracting 1.5 million visitors each year, would suggest that even if it is a separate company it is reasonably substantial.

We are considering entering a market where the competition are big league players. Our competitors are not small operators who might be forced out quickly by such techniques as price-cutting or massive investment in new ideas causing the existing centres to become obsolete. They have the capital resource of large groups to match the backing that Hollins Holidays enjoys as part of the ICCC group. They also have market experience, a most valuable asset which Hollins will have to buy-in since market entry will be a diversification for ICCC. Thus any plans to enter this market must be very carefully laid, and entry must be a determined effort over a long time scale.

The possibility of market entry through takeover should not be ignored – but can probably be discounted since (1) it is not part of our brief and (2) Kim Medway (and the MD) can be presumed to have taken this under consideration. They have, after all, gathered a lot of secondary data, normally the job of junior staff! (NB: This further reinforces the fact that our bosses take this project very seriously.)

The market

Source: Scenario, Appendices D, F and H.

Analysis

We are quickly directed in general terms to the probable target market on Line 23 when Kim Medway asks 'What do you know about the UK holiday market?'. Despite our immediate comments about the package holiday firms, Kim Medway continues on Line 27 'Not enough, . . . dig a bit deeper.' It is evident that we will be expected to become somewhat of an expert on the market within which we may operate in the future – a vital exercise for any marketer.

The remainder of the text in Lines 24 to 26 and also that in Lines 32 to 45 of the case provides a very comprehensive analysis of our general awareness. We believe that there has been a major shift in holiday patterns. Tours abroad have increased at the expense of the domestic holiday providers, including those offering holiday camps (Butlins, Pontins etc.). More recently, however, we feel that the trend of taking holidays abroad may have slowed down or even turned round. The increase in overseas holidaymakers to the UK also sounds a more optimistic note. Obviously other big operators have seen a market opportunity, and one at least (Center Parcs) appears to be working at high capacity.

If our early views are substantiated . . . 'it could be that there is a new trend in vacations just beginning', then we may have an opportunity to gain a stake in a growing market rather than attempting to carve out a share in a mature or declining market environment.

It is interesting and important, to note on Line 79 that only after obtaining our (reasonably bullish) views on the market potential does Kim Medway reveal that 'the Board of ICCC are convinced that there is a major gap in the UK holiday market. A gap that we intend to exploit.' It is questionable whether we should have been given the project if we had come up with a view in conflict with that of the Board. As it is we are pretty firmly committed, and it is getting harder and harder as we progress with this analysis to see how we could possibly make a case for non-entry to this market.

The final comments from Kim Medway sum up precisely the question that must be answered in the analysis of the market. . . 'The decision that must be made is whether or not to enter the UK market with a series of holiday centres that will be custom built to meet the perceived needs of a segment of the public. We cannot afford to test market.' This is not an easy situation!

We can now move forward to extract pertinent information from the data in the appendices. The detailed numerical data on the market is provided in Appendices D and H. We have already undertaken the analysis of Appendix D/1 in the section on finance above and can, therefore, proceed to consider the other parts of this appendix. There is little further analytical work that can be undertaken on Appendix D/2. The columns of figures can be added up to assist our understanding of the information. The totals of the first two sets of figures (i.e. the sum of holidays in Great Britain, Ireland and abroad), and also the sum of one, two and three holiday-takers are not equal nor do they tie exactly into the figure for showing how many people take a holiday. It must be assumed that rounding the individual figures has caused this. Nevertheless, a significant trend can be established. The decrease in holidays taken in the UK has been from 52 per cent in Year −10 down to 40 per cent in Year −1. On the other hand, holidays taken abroad have risen from 13 per cent to 23 per cent during the same period.

The table for the profile of British holiday-/non-holiday-takers in Year −1 (Appendix D/2.2) also reveals some important factors. Although people over 65 years of age represent the largest sample (20 per cent) they take the fewest holidays abroad (9 per cent). In the socio-economic groupings, ABs are the smallest population (17 per cent). However, they take the largest number of holidays abroad (36 per cent).

The third set of figures showing the home locality of holiday-takers reveals a concentration in the South East. Coupled with those in the London area, they represent a major proportion of a possible target market. We should recall these key observations when we produce statements of potential actions and also the final examination answer.

Appendix D/3 also requires no further detailed analytical work but does provide some key pieces of information. The first table (Appendix D/3.1) shows that holidays of four nights or more in Britain have fallen by about 12 per cent whereas those taken abroad have more than doubled. The overall trend has been an increase in holidays taken of approximately 9 per cent. There is, perhaps, a problem with the use of this data. It specifically excludes holidays of three nights or less, and so takes no account of long-weekend breaks. There is no evidence that any market exists for short breaks, except that Center Parcs is catering for combinations of three, four and seven night stays (Appendix G). They are experienced, and also the newest concept in the UK. They will have taken very careful note of the market, and if they feel three, four and seven is a viable offering perhaps we ought to take this as expert opinion that should not be ignored?

The record table in Appendix D/3.2 also provides some very useful key statistics. The expenditure on holidays in Britain, in money terms, has increased by just over double. However, the expenditure on holidays abroad has increased by more than 500 per cent. The combined increase is almost 350 per cent. Once again there are startling indicators showing the dramatic rise in holidays taken abroad versus the decline in those taken in the UK.

Looking at Appendix D/4, only the first table is really relevant. It can be seen that the South West of England is by far the most popular location.

Appendix D/5.1 can best be represented graphically (figure 15.9). It is very interesting to note that there is a much more dramatic peak in the summer for holidays taken in Britain than for those taken abroad. Also, the tails on the distribution (an average) show a greater proportion of winter holidays abroad.

Useful information is contained within Appendix D/5.2, in particular, the fact that holiday camps account for only 5 per cent of holidays in the UK and 1 per cent of those taken overseas. As far as the modes of transport and type of holiday arrangement (Year −1) are concerned, it is important to note that 70 per cent of transport is by car (Appendix D/5.3). Also, while 62 per cent of holidays taken abroad are package holidays only 12 per cent are structured in this way in the UK.

From Appendix D we have only highlighted the key statistics. While it is always possible to present information in a different form (graphically, in proportional terms, fractionally, in percentages etc.) until we have established some potential strategies, hours of work could be invested to provide no further assistance.

Although Appendix F has been analysed in detail already, one particular comment should be noted: 'People spend two weeks in Majorca with Thomson and then a week in Devon with Ladbroke'. Is there an important clue here?

Our final analysis in the Inview will be Appendix H – the Target Group Index. As we decided for the analysis of Appendix D, until we know what we are trying to identify, we cannot re-work the information very much without spending hours of number-crunching which may in the end still not provide any further help. However, once we have produced a possible strategy for the type of centre and hence consumer, the size of that target market can be established *vis-à-vis* the rest of the population. The habits and characteristics of the target markets can then accurately be established to allow it to be accessed as efficiently as possible.

Target Group Index

This is a reliable and respected survey, carried out by the British Market Research Bureau. An example page, Vodka/Demographics (figure 15.10), illustrates the methodology used to present the results of the survey. This methodology is consistent throughout the TGI, and so it applies to the two tables in our Appendix H.

The data in the example tells us for the period covered:

9.496 million adults are users of vodka. 1.540 million are heavy users.

For the Heavy Users:
Column A   352,000 are adults aged 25–34.
Column B   these represent 22.9 per cent of the heavy user segment (352/[588 + 352 + 260 + 163 + 115 + 61]).
Column C   4.6 per cent of adults aged 25–34 are heavy users of vodka ([352/2477] × 32.1%).
Column D   The index for heavy users, 25–34 is 128 (28 per cent above the average for all adults: [4.6%/3.6%] × 100 = 128).

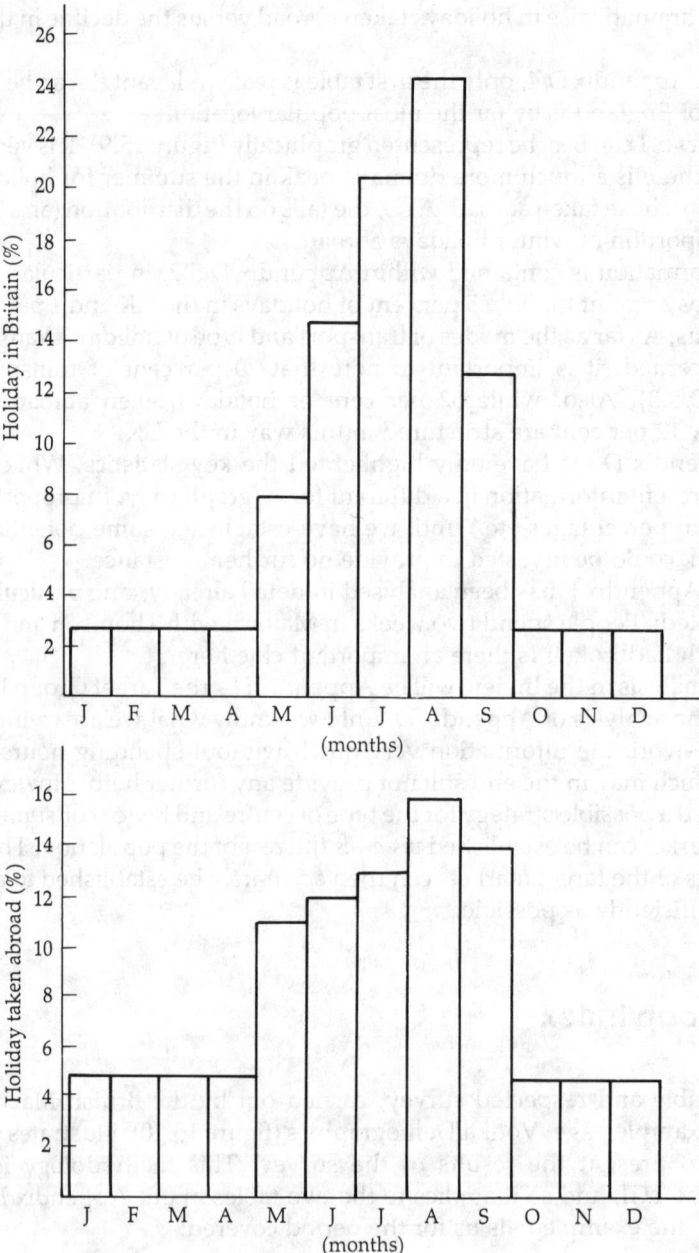

Figure 15.9   *Month in which holiday started (Year −1)*

The quick way into the TGI is via Column D, but beware! Do check the absolute values. How many people make up the segment with the high index? Percentages alone are of little value.

The TGI also provides data on the media reaching users of the product – it is not included here for vodka, but it is in Appendix H of the case. It is read in exactly the same way. Note the word 'reaching'. Given a precise market target one can specify media with a considerable degree of confidence.

VODKA

Note: this is a dense statistical Target Group Index table (rotated on the page). Best-effort reading of the data follows. Columns for each user group are: A ('000 down), B (across %), C (%), D (index).

	ALL USERS A	B	C	D	HEAVY USERS A	B	C	D	MEDIUM USERS A	B	C	D	LIGHT USERS A	B	C	D	NON USERS A	B	C	D
ALL ADULTS	*496	100.0	22.0	100	1540	100.0	3.6	100	3295	100.0	7.6	100	4661	100.0	10.8	100				
MEN	*480	47.2	21.6	98	699	45.4	3.4	95	1570	47.6	7.6	99	2211	47.4	10.7	99				
WOMEN	5017	52.8	22.3	102	841	54.6	3.7	105	1726	52.4	7.7	101	2450	52.6	10.9	105				
15-24	2964	31.2	34.3	156	588	38.2	6.8	191	1209	36.7	14.0	183	1167	25.0	13.5	12				
25-34	2477	26.1	32.1	146	352	22.9	4.6	128	785	23.8	10.2	133	1340	28.7	17.4	16				
35-44	*674	17.6	25.3	115					576	17.5	8.7	114	839	18.0	12.7	14				
45-54	*124	11.8	18.5	84	163	10.6	2.7	76	342	10.4	5.6	74	619	13.3	10.2	9				
55-64	725	7.6	11.9	54	115	7.5	1.9	53	241	7.3	3.9	52	369	7.9	6.0	9				
65 OR OVER	533	5.6	6.6	30	61	4.0	0.8	21	144	4.4	1.8	23	328	7.0	4.1	3				
AB	*459	15.4	20.9	95	158	10.3	2.3	66	506	15.4	7.3	95	794	17.0	11.5	10				
C1	*254	23.2	22.9	104	517	24.7	3.8	108	742	22.4	7.9	98	1601	34.5	11.5	11				
C2	*250	30.2	23.7	108	517	24.7	3.8	108	1147	34.8	8.4	110	1541	18.0	10.4	9				
D	*881	19.8	23.1	105	380	24.7	4.3	131	656	19.9	8.1	106	844	18.1	6.3	6				
E	643	6.8	14.1	65	104	6.8	2.3	65	244	7.4	5.4	71	295	6.3	6.6	6				
ABC1	*722	39.2	22.1	100	539	35.0	3.4	90	1248	37.9	7.7	97	1935	41.5	11.5	11				
C2D	5131	54.0	23.5	107	897	58.3	4.1	115	1804	54.7	8.3	108	2431	52.1	11.1	10				
ABC1: 15-34	2044	21.5	22.0	101	307	19.9	4.9	138	755	22.9	12.1	159	982	21.1	15.8	11				
35-64	*182	12.4	20.7	94	160	10.4	3.0	84	355	10.8	6.7	87	667	14.3	6.1	5				
55 OR OVER	496	5.2	9.3	42	72	4.6	1.3	38	139	4.2	2.6	34	286	6.1	3.2	5				
C2DE: 15-34	5396	35.8	33.5	153	633	41.1	6.3	175	1238	37.6	12.2	160	1525	32.7	15.1	14				
35-54	*616	17.0	22.0	100	263	17.1	3.6	100	563	17.1	7.7	100	790	17.0	10.8	10				
65 OR OVER	762	8.0	8.6	39	105	6.8	1.2	33	246	7.5	2.8	36	411	8.8	4.6	4				
GREATER LONDON	*383	14.6	25.2	115	327	21.3	6.0	167	474	14.4	8.6	113	581	12.5	10.6	9				
SOUTH EAST/EAST ANGLIA	2091	22.0	21.9	100	324	21.0	4.0	95	673	20.4	7.1	93	1094	23.5	11.5	10				
SOUTH WEST	600	6.3	21.9	81	66	4.3	2.0	55	194	5.9	5.8	76	340	7.3	10.1	9				
WALES	*510	5.4	21.6	98	71	4.6	1.8	51	162	4.9	6.8	90								
WEST AND EAST MIDLANDS	*004	14.1	19.0	97	129	4.8	1.4	89	378	11.5	7.2	94								
NORTH WEST	702	10.4	18.4	84	146	9.5	1.8	98												
YORKSHIRE & HUMBERSIDE	548	5.8	18.4	84	80	3.2	2.3	86	207	6.3	5.4	71								
NORTH	*316	13.9	32.1	148	347	22.6	8.6	241	208	6.3	5.4	110								
SCOTLAND	335	13.9	32.6	148					524	15.9	13.0	170								
LONDON	2685	28.3	23.9	109	509	33.1	4.5	127	897	27.2	8.0	104					4109	12.2	78.7	101
SOUTH	*109	11.7	21.3	97	178	11.6	3.4	96	334	10.1	6.4	84					2983	8.9	79.2	101
EAST OF ENGLAND	785	8.3	20.8	95	125	6.1	3.3	93	258	7.8	6.8	90					1237	3.7	82.3	106
SOUTH WEST	266	2.8	17.7	80	31	2.0	2.1	58	78	2.4	5.2	68					1439	13.2	79.3	102
WALES AND WEST	*132	10.2	20.7	94	156	6.0	1.8	57	363	11.0	6.5	85								
MIDLANDS	*738	18.3	19.6	89	188	11.6	2.0	57									7141	21.2	80.4	103
NORTH WEST	*276	12.1	19.6	89	92	6.0	1.5	42									5222	15.5	80.4	103
YORKSHIRE	*952	11.8	18.2	83	104	6.8	2.3	63									5035	14.9	81.8	105
NORTH EAST	*152	10.0	20.7	94	294	18.8	8.0	246									3647	10.8	79.3	102
CENTRAL SCOTLAND	*132	11.9	33.7	153	92	6.0	8.7	244									2227	6.6	66.3	85
NORTH EAST SCOTLAND	335	3.5	31.7	144													721	2.1	68.3	87
H/D INCOME £12,000 OR MORE	*348	14.2	28.1	128	210	13.6	4.4	123					443	9.5	14.7	137	3452	10.2	71.9	92
£10,000 - £11,999	*885	9.3	26.5	121	123	8.0	3.7	103					912	19.6	13.0	120	2454	7.3	73.5	95
£ 8,000 - £ 9,999	*810	11.3	26.0	118	183	6.1	4.4	124									3048	9.0	74.0	95
£ 7,000 - £ 7,999	*722	18.1	24.6	112	132	8.4	4.4	123									2174	6.5	72.4	93
£ 5,000 - £ 6,999	*179	12.4	24.5	111	225	18.2	3.9	111									5319	15.8	75.5	97
£ 3,000 - £ 4,999	*179	12.4	19.9	91	225	14.8	2.2	61					530	9.9	8.9	83	5217	15.4	80.1	103
£ 2,000 - £ 4,999	*896	9.4	14.7	67	134	8.7	2.2	61					463	15.1	8.0	74	7293	21.6	82.3	106
£ 2,000 OR LESS	*566	16.5	17.7	80	253	16.5	2.9	80					705	15.1	8.0	74				
NOT STATED																				
WHICH READERS	757	8.0	25.2	115	76	4.9	2.5	71					430	9.2	14.3	133	2249	6.7	74.8	96
YELLOW PAGES	*887	40.9	26.9	122	663	43.0	4.6	129					1824	39.1	12.6	117	10574	31.4	73.1	94
ALCO. DRINKS MORE THAN ONCE A WEEK	*649	49.0	29.1	132	966	62.8	6.0	170					1987	42.6	12.4	115	11342	33.7	70.9	91
ONCE A WEEK OR LESS	*848	51.0	19.8	90	573	37.2	2.3	66					2675	57.4	10.9	101	19554	58.1	80.2	103

DEMOGRAPHICS — **PRODUCT TABLE**

Explanatory notes (annotation boxes):

Column A .000's
The projected number of people in thousands who are users in that subgroup. Thus 352,000 adults aged 25-34 are heavy users of vodka.

Column B. Down
The percentage of all heavy users who are aged 25-34. The percentages in each demographic subgroup add up to 100% vertically (except TV overlap, presence of children).

Column C. Across
The percentage of all 25-34-year-olds (or whatever group is listed on the table side headings) who are heavy users.

Column D. Index
An index based on the percentage in column C: 4.6% of adults aged 25-34 are heavy users. This is 28% above the average for all adults (3.6%), thus giving an index of 128.

BMRB 1982 This report is the property of BMRB Ltd. Any unauthorised reproduction or use of reproductions is forbidden.

Figure 15.10 *Target Group Index – explanatory notes*

Should one need to, it is possible to read information straight off the TGI sheet. Thus you will be able to, for example, select the three most important media that you would recommend. (For holiday-takers it would seem from index column D that the *Telegraph Sunday Magazine* has the edge. Indices: 122, all holidaymakers; 112, holidays UK; 151, holidays abroad – here second to *The Sunday Times*. The absolute numbers look good too: 1.647m, 1.007m, 0.876m).

Finally, note that although the TGI data here and in the case is expressed in socio-economic groups it is available in conjunction with ACORN. The much smaller groupings into which ACORN divide the populace give a very tight control on segmentation policy, and enable market and media profiles to be matched very closely. (In other words, each publication knows the ACORN profile of its readership. This can be matched against the profile of a target segment. Thus the most effective media is selected, and overspill is reduced to a minimum.)

16 *Potential Actions*

Reminder

This is where you brainstorm to provide the basis for your contingency plans. It should be *fun* because there is no working through data, no analysis. This is where you start to be creative.

To remind you: Brainstorming works best over a period of about 20 minutes. Do *not* be restrictive. Do *not* use any judgement. Just get down every idea, every possibility, that is triggered from your mind. Do not worry if the same idea comes up several times. The trick is to relax and let your subconscious take over. Trust your mind – you know a tremendous amount about this case by now, and your mind will have made many connections without you being aware of them. The idea is to let them out – *now*.

Your brainstorm will be muddled and untidy. It will repeat itself, it will *not* be a logical list. Fine. That is how it should be. You will be able to tidy up your brainstorm – clean out the obvious non-possibles – and present the result in a considered form. When your brainstorm is complete, and tidy, compare it with ours in figure 16.1.

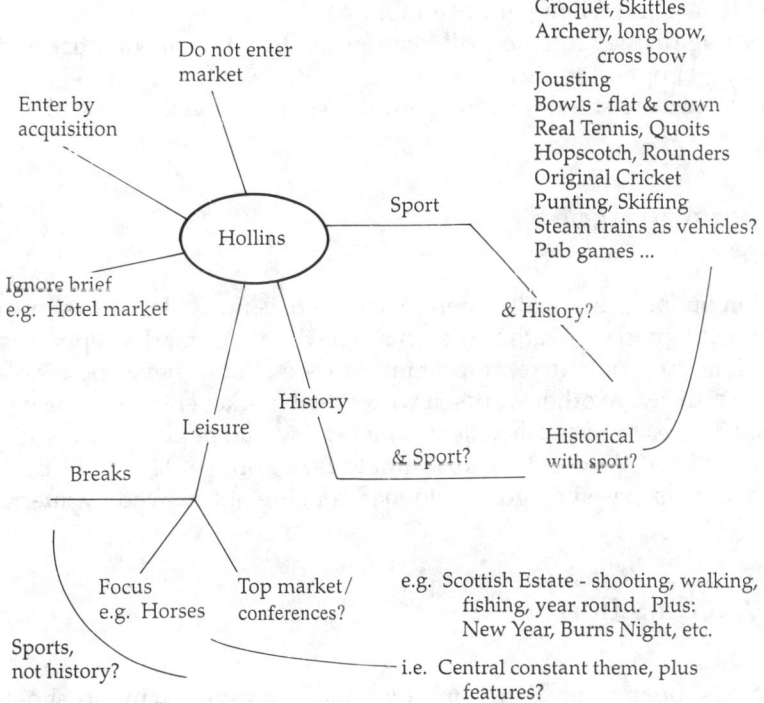

Figure 16.1 *Brainstorm of potentials*

17 *Decisions and Controls*

Reminder

Your objective now is to establish potential decision areas, and to ascertain what Controls are possible.

The Decision Sequence is always the same:

- Mission – What business are we in?
- Policy – Expressing specific intentions to achieve.
- Strategy – In clear objective/time format.
- Tactics – The breakdown into small, manageable pieces, also expressed in objective/time format.

The task now is to ascertain for each of the areas in the brainstorm how practical it appears to be, and whether it is capable of Control. Remember, control is unlikely to be possible if clear objectives cannot be established. Note that an area where Control is not possible is not a 'no-go area', but it automatically becomes a higher risk area since there will be no way to know results in time for remedial action.

Reasonable assumptions must be clarified at this stage. There would be need to make these clear to an examiner or a manager, and you certainly *must* know when you are working with fact and when with assumption.

From this stage of the Sequence will come an identification of potential, and of risk . . . thus a ranking of opportunities.

Remember, you are still not taking hard decisions, but you soon will be.

Do not enter market

This decision option is not really open to us. There is no evidence to show that ICCC cannot enter the market – rather it seems that there are market opportunities. The Board's feelings are, of course, important; but we should never be dissuaded from reporting objectively. In other words, if we felt that market entry was the wrong policy *and could produce good evidence to support our belief* it would be correct to recommend the Board not to proceed. An organization cannot survive on 'Yes Men'. The best managers take clear decisions, based on good evidence, and are not swayed by internal politics.

Enter by acquisition

This option is open, but there are two main reasons why it should not be recommended:

1 Our role is in NPD and we have been briefed to investigate how to enter through Hollins. 'A Board level decision has been made to activate a company that we have owned for many years . . .'.
2 Much preliminary work has been carried out by Kim Medway, who has taken the unusual step of commissioning secondary data searches without calling in any staff of our seniority. It is not unreasonable to deduce, therefore, that the aspects of entry by acquisition have been taken into account by the ICCC Corporate Finance Team, or perhaps by the Financial Director with Kim Medway.

We should not meddle, and we do not have sufficient facts anyway.

Ignore brief

A very dangerous action! To ignore, amend or redirect a brief is to show a degree of arrogance that must be supported by 100 per cent success. Even then the individual concerned may become a marked person – and long term career progression will be damaged.

Again, in this case there is little need to ignore or amend the brief. It would seem that opportunity does exist, and it is always easier to do what one is told.

Note

These first three potential actions are almost always present, as is one other – Do Nothing. They should always be considered, and carefully. If they are discarded it is necessary to do so only upon consideration, and one must be able to explain why each has not been explored.

The Do Nothing option is not open to us in this case, but it almost always is. Many businesses suffer through management's inability to leave well alone; yet the only reason to disturb an operating system is to improve or replace it with something better. Change for its own sake is not beneficial.

Market entry

'The decision that must be made is whether or not to enter the UK market with a series of holiday centres that will be custom built to meet the perceived needs of a segment of the public' (Kim Medway). This must surely be a major question in any examination? It is the focus of the whole brief. Certainly we must be prepared to become involved with product segmentation, but first we must know whether it is feasible. We have done a lot of work on this, and the figures seem to indicate very clearly that our costings would allow us to enter, and to be competitive.

Given that we can reprise the figures from the Inview, we have to put together a framework of a report that presents a positive view and which makes clear recommendations. Efficiency and effectiveness must be built in from the start – no point having a superior product, with excellent marketing, if the potential consumers are treated badly when they try to book! There will be a lot of detailed thinking to do to ensure we cover all the major points, and we must be careful not to go below strategic level.

Sport

Clearly this is an area in which there is already major competition. This need not deter us, but why get into head-to-head competition if it is not essential? Is there a market segment interested in sports that is not yet catered for? If so, is it large enough to justify the investment? (We know we need 500 guests for most weeks of the year.)

What sort of sports packages are on offer at present? It would seem that they are non-serious, i.e. holidays with sports available. If this is so, is there a market for the serious sportsperson? We know from general reading that Tennis Ranches exist, usually associated with big name tennis players. Is this a market for Hollins? On the basis of 500 guests, probably not, but one could re-work the figures around this concept if one wanted.

One would then be defining one's target market very closely – How many couples share a serious interest in the same sport? In different sports? Which sports would fit in with the British climate, and/or what costs would be involved for indoor accommodation.

Given very tight market segmentation one should have good control over promotion . . . but accessing serious sportspeople from amongst the general population is likely to be very different. (Remember, a segment only exists if it can be Measured, is Substantial, and if Access of both promotion and product is possible.) Probably a case can be made for sports, but it seems a tough way into the market.

History

This is a big unknown. It seems very attractive in concept – one can imagine all guests changing into fancy dress at the gates and living the life of a Tudor noble (say) for a week. But the difficulties of achieving the transformation could be horrendous: think how large the wardrobe would have to be! Yet it would be wrong to have someone in Bermuda shorts and a floral tee-shirt jousting or sitting down to a Victorian afternoon tea.

It would certainly provide a unique entry to the market, given that the creativity could be managed. For this a very good agency would be needed – perhaps the services of people expert in film or stage effects? Certainly professional costumiers would be needed, and the staff would have to include people expert in garment repair and renovation.

This option would open up the potential for attracting overseas visitors in a very big way. One could envisage tying up with an exclusive travel agent in each major overseas market, and for them to sell all-inclusive packages. This would have the major benefit of securing party bookings, and responsibility for promotion could be delegated.

There would be need for a very detailed primary research activity, and one would require a brief to be prepared, in outline at least. Control would be a simple matter of linking an MIS on to the operational objectives.

History and Sport

Is it possible to get the best of both options? Sport has been played through the ages, so why not a historical theme with the sports that associate with it?

This has a more relaxed feel about it, and allows for a family to stay together, or split up as they choose. One could be learning the polka, while others were playing skittles, croquet, or riding on a steam train. All ages could be catered for, or specific packages tailored to match tight market segments.

Leisure breaks

Judging from Center Parc's package it seems that three, four and seven night stays make sense. (Using our common knowledge we are aware that people do go away for long weekends.) It also makes logical sense, and hence appeals to our desire for efficiency.

We have no research on less than four night holidays. (A serious omission that we must rectify – or at least be prepared to recommend be rectified.) There is no way in which we could be cost-effective if open only at weekends, but the leisure break market plus, perhaps, business conferences to fill mid-week nights could make a very useful addition to our main business. Again we have the opportunity to tie up with overseas travel agents. They could sell short stays, in their own right or as part of a larger holiday.

We must remember the Ladbroke quote: 'people spend two weeks in Majorca with Thomson and then a week in Devon with Ladbroke'. The extra week's holiday, additional to the main break, must surely be targeted.

Note

We are beginning to see a shape to our segmentation, whatever form our package finally takes – and we know it to be feasible.

It is also apparent that Control is possible because we can see that tight segmentation decisions can be taken.

Top market/conferences

There is no evidence to support recommendations concerning this market area, although it is general knowledge that top people go on holiday, and that business conferences are held. Perhaps the best we can do with this idea is to use it, if appropriate, to supplement whichever product offering we (ICCC) decide upon?

We should not forget it, but we must be careful how we use it at this stage.

Focus (e.g. horses)

First this idea segmented the product very tightly indeed – into simply horses, and the offering of exclusively equine activities. But then it triggered the thought that the theme could be wider, e.g. a Scottish Experience. Centred upon a Scottish Estate one could offer a variety of activities throughout the year: shooting, walking, fishing. But one could also focus on specifics that would be very attractive – Hogmanay, Burns Night, St Andrew's Day, etc.

This concept readily transfers to any of the other areas, and is good in that it provides a series of opportunities to promote; hits potential new guests from a variety of directions; and encourages re-booking. An MIS system would be essential to ensure that the data base that was built was exploited, and not simply for selling holidays either! The opportunity to direct market Hollins clients should not be missed.

Summary

From the brainstorm, and the supplementary work set out above, one has begun to see a way through to the examiner or manager.

- He or she is surely going to want an answer to the feasibility question.
- He or she knows we do not have enough research to determine theme, and so is likely to ask us what more we want.
- Product logistics are reasonably clear: we know our preferred size, and we have identified and clarified the need for efficiency and effectiveness.
- We have identified a variety of possible ways into the market, upon which we cannot *decide* but upon which we ought to have clear opinions.
- We have identified a variety of potential markets to target, again we cannot *decide*, but should have clear opinions.
- We can propose some good ideas about making our offering (whatever it is) attractive to overseas visitors, to weekend and mid-week guests, to the selected target market.
- We are in NPD not in an operational role. Therefore it is reasonably certain that we shall not be asked about detailed operational matters. We may, of course, be asked about NPD itself.

It is now necessary to prepare to answer the questions that could be put in the examination or asked by our manager.

18 Decisions and Recommendations

Reminder

At this stage of the Sequence students need to take hard decisions on their alternative recommendations and to work them through in considerable detail so that they are fully prepared for the examination. They do not know which questions will be asked, but they have up to a dozen alternatives. They will be pretty certain of one, have a strong hunch about two, the third and fourth will be harder to pre-select.

They have to over-prepare. Better to go into the examination with good answers to more questions than needed than to go in with weak answers to fewer.

Clarify decision areas, and within them work out the full hierarchy of Mission, Policy, Strategy, Tactics and Control. In this case you must have a thorough understanding of NPD. Almost certainly there will be a question on the feasibility of the venture, and a time plan to see the project through to completion on schedule would be useful to have on hand.

Decisions must be clear, specific, unambiguous. They must be expressed in terms of objective/time. Decisions must be practical, realistic and (in the examination room) within the remit of the questions asked.

By working your decisions through away from the stress of the exam room you have time to 'proof read', to check. You also have a fund of material that can be adjusted in the light of the questions asked. Far better to adjust material you know thoroughly than to write it from raw data under the pressure of the exam.

It is important that you work your exam answer plans for yourself. Therefore we have worked through only one, as an example. (You will, of course, find a complete answer to the examination question paper when you arrive at chapter 20.)

Time plan

It is important to have a clear idea of the time scale for any new product launch. It is common practice to utilize Network Planning, especially when one has computer back-up. But the computer cannot produce the network without the programmer inputting data.

As a basis for the detailed network a simple time plan is an excellent starting point. At first this should be general, covering the main areas, as a test that the activity is feasible in time. Only if it appears to be feasible should one progress to detailed planning.

We leave it to you to progress your own time plan, in whatever format you are most comfortable; but remember that you will have to transpose it by hand in the examination room, so you cannot have anything too complicated.

Be exciting

It is always very useful, if not vital, to have the framework for one or two highly creative concepts available to form examination answers if the opportunity exists to excite the examiners. Apart from producing the more obvious responses, an original idea will ensure that your answer paper attracts the examiner's attention.

It should not be used at all cost. The question paper may not have an appropriate section to allow its introduction. However, if it does allow such a response it will give you a significant advantage over your peers.

Also, and very importantly, if you have worked through several creative ideas you will truly have command of the data and of the case in its entirety. The Isle of Hollins is a creative idea, written up fully.

The Isle of Hollins

1 Mission
  We are providing up-market people with exclusive facilities in which to work and relax, in complete security, whether on business or vacation.
2 Policy
  To provide a working and leisure facility which will attract an exclusive clientele from the most rich and powerful across the world.
  To ensure that the very best staff are engaged, and retained.
  To adopt a pricing policy commensurate with that operated by the world's best five star hotels.
3 Strategy
  To locate and purchase a suitable island off the coast of Cornwall within eight months.
  To landscape it in accord with architect's plans within 24 months.
  To open it to market test by ICCC personnel only within 27 months.
  To take first non-ICCC guests in month 36.
4 Tactical Overview
  4.1 Security – will be state of the art, both active and passive. All transactions on the island will be charged. No cash will change hands.
  4.2 Communication – systems will be state of the art including the use of satellites.
  4.3 Standards – conference, support facilities and accommodation will be to standards demanded by Boards of Directors of multinational organizations.
  4.4 Leisure – activities will be mainly associated with exclusive sports.
  4.5 Travel – consumers will be encouraged to use their own transport (e.g. boats, light aircraft and helicopters), although there will be a hydrofoil service between the island and the mainland at least three times each day.
  4.6 The Product
    • 200 apartments which each include a double bedroom, reception room and bathroom.
    • Fully equipped conference centre.
    • Health centre (jacuzzi, sauna, beauty salon, etc).
    • Indoor sports, including squash, tennis, a gym, an Olympic size swimming pool and a golf simulator.

- Outdoor sports, including all-weather tennis courts, clay pigeon shooting and polo.
- Full programme of indoor games and pastimes – from bridge to Trivial Pursuit.
- Water sports, including powerboat racing, surfing, parascending, water skiing, scuba diving, sea fishing and sailing out of the marina.
- Six restaurants – English, French, Far Eastern, Italian, Mexican and Fish.
- Six bars – a mixture from character public houses to sumptuous hotel style lounges.
- Evening entertainment, including casino, night club and theatre.

4.7 Personnel – key members of staff, i.e. the general manager and departmental heads, will be head-hunted and in post within 12 months. Pay will be generous, and a stock bonus scheme will operate.

4.8 Promotion – will be lavish, and very highly targeted.

An international creative agency will be engaged as soon as the general manager is in post.

Note that the PR task will be as much to prevent bad publicity/exploitation as to enhance the positive image.

Highly targeted promotion: No national media, no broad-based mail shots.

4.9 Outline programme for operation:

Month 1   – Project initiation.
Month 9   – Personnel selection starts.
Month 12   – Creative agency appointed.
Month 27   – Site fully prepared, trial usage by ICCC only.
Month 28/34 – Improvements and modifications.
Month 34   – Promotion. Highly targeted. Highly creative.
Month 36   – First non-ICCC guests arrive.
Month 48   – Review performance for possible change of emphasis.
Month 69   – Payback period.

5 Finance based upon:

(a) Staff 200.
(b) Accommodation units 200.
(c) Building as described above.

5.1 Capital Expenditure:

Island	£5 000 000	
Buildings	£10 000 000	
Equipping facilities	£5 000 000	
Security measures	£4 000 000	
Marina	£10 000 000	
Total		£34 000 000

5.2 Revenue Expenditure:

Salaries	£2 000 000	
Power	£2 000 000	
Food and drink	£8 000 000	
Maintenance	£8 000 000	
Marketing	£3 000 000	
Total		£23 000 000

5.3 Revenue:
   Accommodation:
   300 people × 365 days × £300 × 75% occupancy   £24 637 500
   Daily spending:
   300 people × 365 days × £50 × 75% occupancy   £4 106 250
                                                 £28 743 750
   Surplus: (Income − Expenditure)   £5 743 750

Note: These are working figures only: it is not realistic to expect to achieve such a high occupancy in Year 1. On the other hand, the daily expenditure is expected to be considerably higher than that forecast.

Payback Period:
34,000,000/(28,743,750 − 23,000,000) = 5.91 years = 69 months.

6 Points for consideration:
   6.1 Local community: There will be very little benefit to any mainland community – possibly up to 100 miles away. No assistance by way of government grants.
   6.2 Staffing: Potential problems with an island operation. However, there will be sufficient 'on-island' accommodation for staff and access to mainland three times each day. Salaries will be set to attract and motivate staff of high calibre.
   6.3 Political/security: The island will be vulnerable to terrorist attacks. The media impact would be enormous given the uniqueness of the island and the status of its guests. A high level of electronic and physical security measures will be required.

Note

Control does not have to be spelled out precisely, but it does have to exist! In the above example you will have seen that very clear objectives are set, against which it is possible to measure achievement. We are saying 'this is our plan, act upon it'. We are also saying, by implication as we are managers 'if it goes slightly wrong we shall not be surprised, and can correct; if it goes very wrong we expect to be disciplined'. Managers earn their money through the quality of their decisions – and the effectiveness of their controls.

This is a strategic document, therefore the objectives (and controls) are wide. If it were approved in principle there would be need to flesh it out in considerably more detail, and very specific objectives written. As one progresses into more detail so the control becomes easier to apply, and easier to express.

19 *For management students*

Everything we have said about management problems in real life applies equally to students when working on Case Studies. The difference is that you are working to an examiner, who is simulating the role of a senior manager.

The best way to handle a case is to forget all about it being a scenario. To you it is real, a living and breathing entity with which you are involved. You may be a consultant expecting to charge a fee for your services, you may be on salary and expecting to enhance your promotional prospects. Live the scenario. That way your material will be written with conviction. It will exude a vivacity, it will convince the examiner that you are worthy of a pass.

Hints and tips

Play the game by the examiner's rules

Read the instructions that come with the case study very carefully. Understand them! Typically they will read something like this:

> The examiners will be marking your scripts on the basis of questions put to you in the examination room. Questions may not carry equal marks.
>
> The marks available for each question will be clearly indicated and candidates are advised to allocate their time accordingly.
>
> Your role is specified in the Candidate's Brief. As a person with executive responsibility in the company you are required to carry out the instructions of your superior(s) and direct and control the operations of members of your team. Above all, you are required to take action. Examiners will award marks to students who take decisions and make firm recommendations. Marks will not be awarded merely for analysis of the case, which should have been completed as part of your preparation for the examination.
>
> Acquaint yourself thoroughly with the Case Study and be prepared to follow closely the instructions given you in your examination paper.
>
> Candidates who ignore the above comments are likely to lose marks.

This, of course, exactly parallels the requirements of managers in post. They have to take decisions, make recommendations, take action, give senior management what they ask for and carry out instructions in a responsible fashion.

Prepare to pass by following the Sequence

The method of securing a pass is covered in detail in this section. It has secured passes for hundreds of students. It works. But *you* must understand it, *you* must contribute.

There is need for you to work on your examination case, there is need for you to work on the case in this book. Unless you are willing to give the effort needed there is nothing anybody can do for you. A case study examination cannot be passed by cramming at the last moment; *you* have to know the facts yourself, *you* have to be thoroughly familiar with them. We explain how to achieve this with the minimum of effort – but effort there must be.

You will have about four weeks with the examination case. For the first two weeks – yes, two weeks – you should be analysing the material, 'breaking the case'. Do not be tempted to move forward any quicker.

Our approach may appear simplistic, and at first you may not appear to be achieving as much as you would like. Postgraduate students often comment when we first meet that we are simplistic in our approach. Always they come to realize that we are not. The detail is vital, the big issues are easy. (In a classroom we can show students, by asking questions; here we can only ask you to read on – and learn.)

Pre-worked analyses

Students are offered a number of very reputable and a lot of dubious analyses of each examination case as it is issued. They are tempting and they appear to take a lot of the workload off the student. Our advice is do without them if you can; but, if you decide to invest, follow these rules:

1 Seek advice before ordering, if you can.
2 Use the analysis only to add perspective to your work. Do not even open the envelope it comes in until *your* analysis is 95 per cent complete.
3 *Never* repeat any bought analytical material in your answer – dozens (hundreds) of others will, and the examiner is very far from stupid!
4 Any analysis must have been put together in a hurry since the case is not issued early. Therefore there will be errors and omissions – not through inability, simply through the pressure of time. Be warned!

Properly used, an analysis can be psychologically supporting. It is great to discover that you have more in your analysis, overall; that your opinion stands, that there are one or two angles you did not see that you ought to check up upon. But you should not need, and must not rely upon, someone else's work.

Do please use analyses from *anyone* (a tutor, a friend, a vendor) as merely viewpoints on a common problem, opinions that you will accept or challenge as you decide.

Examiner's purpose

The examiner is concerned to know that you can do four things:

1 make decisions based upon a situation presented to you;
2 make clear recommendations for action;
3 present your recommendations in a properly constructed management report;
4 complete your report within the time allowed (usually 3 hours).

To achieve these four things you have to be master of the situation, and be in control of your time.

Candidate's secret of success

A candidate who is clear and logical in his or her thinking must pass a case study examination. The only question for you is 'How good a pass will I get?'
    You must pass. Why?

1 You will be working with the data in the case, and normally not permitted to research outside it. Thus your task is set out for you from the beginning.
2 You are allowed to make any assumptions that are reasonable to supplement the limited data in the case.
3 The case will be about management, and management works to the future. As there is no certainty about the future your report will be judged on its credibility, it will not be put to the test of the real market.
4 You will be presenting an individual report, it will not contain any data identical to other students. (Similar is OK, identical is worthless.)
5 You will be planning your time to achieve maximum impact in the examination.
6 Finally – and importantly – there will be a lot of students competing with you who will not be well prepared, who will use bought material, who will write an essay and not a report . . . who are definitely going to fail.

Thus your material is going to look good, a lot better than most that the examiner sees.
    Examiners are human; they are the consumers you are selling to. Therefore sort out your selling points, present your material in an effective package, ensure that you are offering what the consumer wants. Many examiners mark up or down from first impression. It really cannot be helped, it becomes instinctive. So on first sight the reaction to a paper is either positive – 'How good is this going to be?' – or negative – 'How bad will this be?'. It is very hard to give a pass mark to a paper that does not impress from the start. The best hope is that it will go into the 'marginal' pile for a second opinion later. *Your* paper will, of course, impress. It will market itself. You must make certain that it does.

Outside help

You need outside help. Perhaps you will be able to work with other students, but even if so, you need outside help – someone who has intelligence and can be used to bounce ideas off. Someone with common sense who will ask you 'Why?' Why? is the question. You should be asking 'Why?' constantly: about the case, about aspects of the case, about yourself (Why are you stopping work at 9.30 in the evening? Would an extra 30 minutes be of help? Why not stay with it?).
    When you get to the point of having provisional plans you can test them against other people's views. It does not matter that they do not know the case, you can give them enough background very quickly. Something like:

I'm thinking of introducing a new soft drink into the grocery market and must get fast distribution. How would you react, as a grocery chain store manager, if I . . . How would you react as a housewife, if I . . .

When a group of students work a case each should come up with his or her own individual recommendations. It is a question of perspective, and of judgement. The examiner is looking for a personal response in the examination room. Be sure you give it to him.

When you receive your case

1 Read the instructions very carefully – do not assume that they are the same as those issued previously (the examiner may have changed). Be sure you thoroughly understand what is required of you, and what are the limiting criteria (e.g. can you research outside the case?).
2 Be certain you know your role. Who are you? Are you a consultant, looking into the firm from outside? Are you an employee of the organization? What will be the behavioural effects of your role? Are you to *decide*, or to *recommend*?
3 It is no bad thing to endorse your file, and all your papers, with the name you have been given. You *must* be clear who are 'we' and who are 'they'. You *must* use 'we' and 'they' correctly from the very first. (Note: it may be 'I' and 'them', be clear.)

Do not ignore the apparently trivial

We found at the Overview stage in one case that a member of the sales force had the same name as the chairman of the company. We jotted it down as interesting, but probably irrelevant. Much later we discovered that the company was vulnerable to takeover and had to choose between accepting or fighting. Those candidates who made the reasonable assumption that the salesman was in the family, and being groomed for directorship, opted to fight. Those who took it that the name was pure coincidence opted for acceptance.

There was nothing else in the case upon which to base the final decision to accept or fight, both responses could be argued with equal validity. But a decision was necessary, and a reasonable assumption helped it to be made.

Prepare for the unexpected

In one case some very suspect statistics were presented. In the examination a question asked for detailed critique of the tables and the methodology. Many candidates were totally unprepared for this. They had assumed that because the data was in the case they (the candidates) must be wrong in not being able to work with the tables.

You set up your pass in your Action File

Examiners are limited in what they can ask. It is perfectly possible to be prepared ahead of the examination. For example, one case, about a large country house being converted into some form of hotel/training centre, was supported by a mass of segmentation data about Further Education provision in the area. Any candidates wanting to position the hotel up-market still had to be thoroughly conversant with the appendices. They were in role as consultants, and therefore had to follow their client's lead or resign their consultancy. Their client had not realized that he could not work up- and down-market at the same time from the same venue. The exam paper could have been open – 'Recommend the best course of action' – or closed – 'Recommend action to secure a minimum of 100 days usage of the establishment by Further Education'. In an open example the candidate can offer his or her own best solution. In the closed he or she has to meet client requirement whatever he or she personally feels. A consultant can, of course, resign if he or she disagrees with the client. But then the client will not pay.

The question paper

Normally there are four questions on an examination paper, and you can be confident that you will have identified the three of them that carry the greatest marks (90 per cent, usually). Therefore the three are more than enough to get your pass. The fourth question, we find, comes up out of nowhere – sometimes we forecast it, usually not. It is put in, we believe, to sort out the distinction candidates. If you are lucky you will have forecast all four questions. We have never failed to forecast three by the Recommendations stage in the Sequence.

Individual perspective

Whether you work alone, or in a group, it is necessary to have your own individual perspective on the case. (Remember the examiner is looking for a personal response in the examination room.) Use your own personal management skills, trust in your own judgement, see the case through your own eyes.

You will have inevitably applied your own value judgements as you broke the case open, and you will have been restraining yourself from making decisions. When you are free of the Overview and can make decisions you will find that every decision will have an impact on every other. Thus even a minor decision variation from that of a friend with whom you have worked will set off a chain reaction throughout your answer that will have an effect on every other decision that you have to make. Therefore every answer read by the examiner should differ in detail from every other. Only in that way can the examiner be certain that it is your own unaided work that is submitted.

Don't panic!

Easy to say, hard to do. But by working through your decision areas in great detail in a stress-free area you put yourself in a commanding position. When written up into Recommendations you will be able simply to copy parts of your Action File straight into the answer book.

But be careful. Do not copy blindly. Use your material wisely. You *must* answer the question set. We have seen very good candidates struggle because they were determined to impose their pre-thinking onto the answer paper. It is an easy trap to fall into. For example, a case concerning a German lift manufacturer had a question about export from Germany. Candidates panicked. Only after the exam did they realize that the principle of export from Germany is the same as from anywhere else. Specialist staff are needed, a line of credit must be secured, customs and shipping documentation completed etc. Similarly, in a case involving the entry of Spain into the EC we had decided that the harmonizing of Spanish law with EC and British law was too difficult and specialized for the CIM Diploma. It was. But the examiner asked *how to promote the benefits of Spanish law* in the UK. A simple marketing question, not a law question at all, yet a lot of candidates panicked.

The major problem is that panic on one question affects the whole of the rest of the examination paper. Confidence is damaged (or destroyed). The solution is obvious – go in well prepared, read carefully through the questions, check you understand them. You will be able to pass from three answers, and you must pick up some marks from the fourth – providing you make an attempt to answer it.

Points to remember

- Line numbers are not normally printed by publishers of case studies – but it is time well spent to add them for yourself. They have been added for you in 'Hollins Hollidays'.
- Follow the instructions given out with the case, and in the examination room: e.g. if it says that no research outside the case is allowed *do not do any*. Candidates from across the world must not be disadvantaged by those living in or near to the area(s) where the case is set.
- Knowing little (or nothing) about the industry is not a problem; all you need will be in the case. If you do know about the industry there is still no problem; the examiner is experienced, and there is a vast difference between the report style of a candidate who knows because he is thoroughly experienced, and of one who has done a hasty job of research.
- Get into role. In a case about the music industry, candidates were given the role of a consultant. Some detail was given of the consultancy, but not much. Very many candidates missed the importance of role – and were shocked in the exam room to be asked for clear decisions about the objectives of *the consultancy*. They were also asked to recommend action to their client.
- Remember that in a case study examination one is being tested across the full width and depth of the syllabus and particularly to demonstrate self-confidence. A candidate is expected to be able to handle any aspect of the syllabus. This means the whole of each of the certificate and diploma syllabuses.
- You will probably need to top up your knowledge in some areas. This is perfectly OK. The embargo on research outside the case refers only to research into the market

area covered by the case. Top up, but only as needed, and only to the amount required.

- Not answering the questions the examiner sets is the equivalent of resigning a consultancy. Remember, he or she is in charge, not you.
- A reasonable assumption can be implied through its use in an answer. More usually it will be stated clearly so that the examiner can take it into account when marking.

Style

Always write a management report.

1 Work in black ink that will not smudge. Use a contrasting colour only sparingly to highlight, e.g. by underlining. *Never* use red ink – this is the examiner's colour.
2 Very neatly put all your details on the outside of the answer book while waiting for the examination to begin.
3 Start your answer on the first facing right-hand page. Leave the inside cover blank. Always write from reality. If you are a consultant then take the time to head the first page with the name of the consultancy. Address your report. Date it.
4 *Never* go in with very clever logos etc. They are so far over the top that their effect is more likely to be damaging than enhancing.
5 Start each section of your answer on a fresh page, even if only one or two lines have been used on the last sheet.
6 Rough work *must* be handed in. Put yours at the back of the answer book, not at the front. Despite being a professional, the examiner is going to be more impressed with a first page of report than of rough work.
7 Ensure that your first three pages are as well written and laid out as you can possibly make them. Take time. After that you will naturally relax, but by then the examiner is also relaxed into finding out just how good your answer is. He or she is looking for content by then; your presentation skills are established.
8 Use white space. Do not cramp your material. Do not write into the examiner's margins.
9 If you use additional sheets make certain they are numbered in sequence, and that they carry your candidate number.
10 At the end of the examination read through and make any obvious corrections, but neatly. Tippex etc. should only be used for minor touching-up. If you have to change a word, a phrase or a sentence, neatly rule it through so the original can be read, and put your correction in place above it.
11 A well-presented answer book can make all the difference if you are marginal for Distinction or (heaven forbid) for Pass.

Content is vital, but presentation is crucial

20 *Management requirements*

THIS CHAPTER CONTAINS AN EXAMINATION PAPER FOR HOLLINS HOLIDAYS.

YOU SHOULD ONLY OPEN IT WHEN FULLY PREPARED FOR A MOCK EXAMINATION.

1 You should be in a quiet area, free from interruptions.
2 You should have *three hours* free from interruptions.
3 You should have either an alarm set for three hours, or made some other arrangement so you are notified when time is up.
4 You should have all you need for a professional examination.

You should complete your paper,
even if you run over time

Make a note when the alarm sounds
so you can judge how
effective is your time management

EXAMINATION PAPER

HOLLINS HOLIDAYS   Time Allowed: 3 hours

This paper requires you to make a reasoned and practical evaluation of the problems and opportunities you have identified from previously circulated case material.

From your analysis you are required to make a report, as directed on the following page.

Graphing sheets and ledger paper are available from the invigilators, together with continuation sheets, if required. These must be identified with your candidate number and fastened securely into the back of your answer book for collection at the end of the examination.

Candidates are permitted to use silent, battery or solar powered calculators on approval of the invigilating staff.

Examiners can only consider work personally undertaken in the examination room. Nothing previously completed, nor any reference data you have introduced to the examination room, should be included in your answer book.

ICCC

INTERNAL MEMORANDUM

FROM: Kim Medway   DATE: 28 January
TO: Chris Knight
CONFIDENTIAL

I realize that you have not had sufficient data upon which to make a firm
recommendation on theme but, nevertheless, I would like this day your report on the
following:

1   Feasibility of the venture, as outlined in our meeting (i.e. viability, size of site,
    location(s), payback, etc.)

(40 marks)

2   A recommended time plan/programme showing each stage from now until the first
    'centre' is handed over to operational management. (Assume Board approval is
    given on 1st February.)

(30 marks)

3   Your primary data research brief in order that theme may be selected.

(20 marks)

4   In view of your success in NPD I would welcome your recommendations on the
    practical constraints of managing a new product development team.

(10 marks)

.../ENDS

21 *Report on Hollins Holidays*

Expect differences between your answers and ours. Providing your answers are decisive, crisp and clear, and that they answer the questions asked, you will be all right on the day.

Do not be put out because you cannot use all the material you have prepared. It is better by far to have too much good material than not enough.

Question 1

ICCC

INTERNAL MEMORANDUM

FROM: Chris Knight
TO: Kim Medway
CONFIDENTIAL   DATE: 28 January

In response to your memo of today's date I submit my report on progress to date.

1   Feasibility – Review

Headed by myself, the New Product Development Team has undertaken a complete review of the concept of UK holiday centres and the probability of success in entering the holiday market through our dormant company, Hollins Holidays.

We have analysed the macro-environment within which we will have to operate and the level of existing and potential competition. The market for the holiday centre concept has been considered in detail, in its own right, and also in the context of current holiday patterns. A thorough appraisal of the financial considerations has also been carried out.

I am pleased to state that we concur with the view of the Board in that an opportunity does exist to enter the market for holiday centres. Our rationale follows.

2   Background

The 1980s saw a significant improvement in the strength of the UK economy. The increased wealth in the economy has led to higher disposable incomes and an increase in the expenditure on leisure – of which holidays are a constituent. British citizens are able to spend more on holidays.

The relative value of sterling against the currencies of the USA, Canada, Australia and New Zealand has increased. It is, therefore, less likely to make Britain a more attractive destination for nationals of these countries. However, apart from Greece,

Portugal and Norway, sterling has depreciated against Continental currencies and we can therefore see a potential additional target market. The relative physical closeness of these countries is an additional benefit.

There is a problem in that the pattern of holiday destinations has changed. There has been a well established trend over many years for UK citizens increasingly to head for overseas holiday destinations. However, the total spent on UK holidays has continued to rise. This is due to increasing numbers of overseas visitors and also people taking second and even third holidays.

3 Policy

The company should enter the holiday market through Hollins Holidays as the vehicle company. It should aim to provide holidays of good quality at the middle-to-upper end of the market. It's unique selling point should be an offering based upon a combination of history with sport such that customers are encouraged to revisit a different centre to experience another historical period.

Visitors to a Hollins Holiday should be offered the interest of a historical setting, with the excitement of sports appropriate to the theme.

4 Strategy

4.1 The first holiday centre should be open within 30 months, and payback period should be 6 years.

4.2 A second and third centre should be opened in each of the years following market entry.

4.3 Prime target should be the B/C1 UK citizens in Greater London and the South East. Secondary target – visitors to the UK from Continental Europe.

4.4 Themes – each centre should have as its focus a different historical period, sports and pastimes should relate to the period, but not at the exclusion of popular modern day activities. These should, however, be customized to the period as far as possible.

4.5 Target markets

4.5.1 Socio-economic groups B/C1, with concentration upon the area of Greater London and the South East. This represents a dense population in a concentrated area and would be an ideal initial target market. We have a considerable amount of secondary data (in particular Target Group Indices) which would allow us to identify with a high-degree of accuracy the appropriate media to use to access the potential UK consumer, but there is considerable detailed work to be done in order to define a viable market segment within the amorphous whole that is B/C1. At this stage we are simply content that sufficient market exists and that it can be accessed both by media and by channels of distribution.

4.5.2 Continental targeting is more difficult, but given that sufficient market exists within the UK we have a viable venture. There is then the opportunity also to target high spending visitors to the UK. They are visiting for a purpose, and one suspects that our cultural heritage must be of significance. Thus the Unique Selling Points of an Historical Theme will be especially attractive to non-British visitors.

We have insufficient data on overseas visitors for this to be other than conjecture at this stage. It is felt, strongly, that the opportunity exists, however, and that when we move to primary research it should be examined most carefully.

4.6 Marketing research

The only way to increase our level of confidence is by primary research, which we feel is justified. My brief for theme selection is set out as Section 3 of this report.

5 Competition

There are five main competitors. They are Butlins (Rank Organization), Pontins (Bass), Ladbrokes, Warners (Grand Metropolitan) and Center Parcs (Sporthuis Centrum Recreatie of Holland). They are all major organizations. In view of the backing of ICCC, Hollins Holidays can succeed. The market is dominated too much by large corporates for small companies to enter under their own resources.

All the competitors offer holiday centres based on a sporting theme. The cost of a holiday is in the range of £200 per week. Many include all facilities free of charge including food.

It is unlikely that any of the competitors will pull out of the market and we must be aware that there may be very fierce competition – through pricing and the level of promotional activity. We shall, however, have the unique proposition of a linked historical/sporting theme.

6 Summary

It has been established, by looking at the competition, that a market does exist for holiday centres based on a sporting theme. To adopt this concept would give us a higher degree of confidence that demand exists than if we adopt historical themes. However, as we have already stated, the market is very competitive, and five major competitors are already in place.

A centre providing a different type of holiday (eg. Tudor, Elizabethan, Victorian environments) would be a higher risk than a sporting centre, but there would appear to be potential demand from discerning members of our suggested market target. We would have a unique selling proposition, and could secure a clear identity in the marketplace.

Our marketing would have to be extremely carefully planned and carried through, and the risk factor is certainly higher than for a sports theme. We feel, however, that there is a risk in entering the already crowded sports market and that we could not guarantee success, nor a high rate of return, given the competition.

7 Location and size

It appears possible to enter the holiday market successfully on a sports or historical/sports theme. Whichever approach we adopt, I would recommend that we locate our first centre in the South West of England. It is the most popular destination in the UK and easily reached by members of our target market.

The centre should accommodate approximately 500 people. This size allows costings to be set at an acceptable level and is not too large – bearing in mind the type of person we would be seeking to attract (B/C1) We should aim to bring in holidaymakers in the Summer for their main holiday and also people taking second holidays in the winter.

8   Revenue Maximization

To maximize return we should adopt the pattern set by Center Parcs for our booking periods: i.e. periods of seven, four or three days or combinations thereof.

9   Financing

Based upon the criteria set out above and the information supplied by Lan Dagent, the following detailed costings have been prepared:

Location	South West England
Area of Land Required	320 acres
Buildings Required	6 000 square yards
No. of staff	37
Land @ £40,000 per acre	£12 800 000
Buildings @ £340 per sq. yd	£ 2 040 000
Decorations @ £30 per sq. yd	£ 180 000
Landscaping @ £1500 per acre	£ 480 000
Capital Expenditure per site	£15 500 000
Rates @ £10 per sq. yd	£ 60 000
Decorations @ £30/2 per year per sq. yd	£ 90 000
*Power per guest per year	£ 104 000
*Food per guest per year	£ 78 000
Salaries @ £10,000 per person per year	£ 370 000
ROCE @ 18% per annum	£ 2 700 000
Total Annual Costs	£ 3 492 000
* *Annual Cost per holiday maker*	£ 134.31

Figures assume 100% occupancy 52 weeks per year

10   Payback

Assuming that 18 per cent per annum is the company's target rate of return on capital employed, this represents an amount of £2,700,000 each year.

$$\text{The Payback Period} = \frac{15\,500\,000}{2\,700\,000} = 5.56 \text{ years}$$

I would suggest that this is an acceptable time scale. One could reasonably expect a holiday centre to operate for 10–15 years and we are comfortably predicting a payback in less than half its operating life.

Based upon full occupancy, the cost for a holiday is £134.31 per week. We have already stated that the market price is in the region of £200.00 per week. The buffer value of £65.69 provides a significant degree of leeway for increasing margins and/or lower levels of occupancy and/or differential seasonal pricing strategies.

Our price should reflect the quality we are offering and thus serve as an indicator to potential customers. Given that we go for an up-market operation with carefully planned USPs we are confident that a premium price can be charged, and that the payback period is comfortably within ICCC criteria.

— — O — —

The above represents a succinct appraisal of our very detailed examination of the data pack which you handed over to me a few days ago.

My view is that the project has a greater chance of succeeding than it does of failing. Without the benefit of primary data I would put the probability of success at a 75 per cent confidence level.

I shall be pleased to furnish any further information you may require to support our findings.

Question 2

1   General

As part of our analysis of the concept for entering the holiday market we considered the timescale which you mentioned to me earlier this month, namely 30 months to build the centre(s) and have it (them) available for taking holidaymakers. As we are now almost at the end of January, I assume that two years from this coming June remains the deadline.

Please find detailed below the key tasks which must be undertaken.

Key Tasks

Event	Event	Timescale (months)	Preceding event
(i)	Obtain board approval	1	–
(ii)	Prepare proposal	1	(i)
(iii)	Produce specifications	3	(ii)
(iv)	Invite tenders	3	(iii)
(v)	Award contracts	2	(iv)
(vi)	Construction Phase I	6	(v)
(vii)	Construction Phase II	6	(vi)
(viii)	Decorations Phase I	2	(vi)
(ix)	Decorations Phase II	1	(vii) + (viii)
(x)	Recruit and train staff	2	(v)
(xi)	Final preparations	1	(ix) + (x)
(xii)	Marketing promotion	5	(v)
(xiii)	Open Holiday Centre(s)	1	(xi) + (xii)
	Total	34	

As you can see, the total time for the project would be 34 months if one took each event in sequence. However, we can see that several events can take place simultaneously. We have therefore adopted Network Analysis as the planning and control technique to allow us to optimize the scheduling of work.

Please find our prepared schedule as Appendix to this report.

2   Conclusion

By use of Network Analysis it has been established that the overall time scale can be reduced to 25 months. This provides a 5 month float over the target time scale.

Staff recruitment shows an 11 month float but personnel are not really needed until the holiday centre is in its final preparation stage and so there is an ample discretionary period within which recruitment can be commenced. The marketing/promotion can start as early as month 10 and end as late as month 24. However, careful planning for its timing is crucial to maximize its effectiveness.

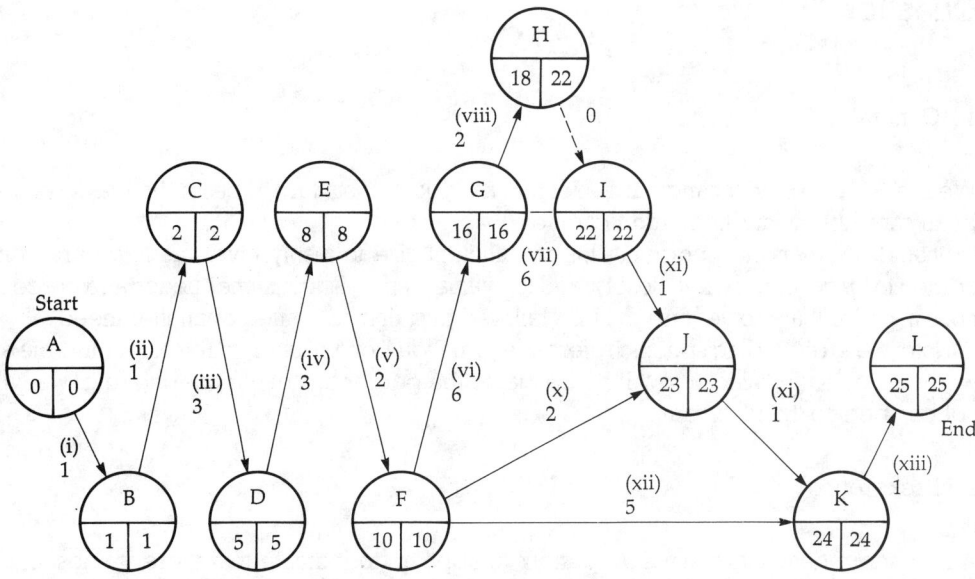

CRITICAL PATH IS A – B – C – D – E – F – G – I – J – K – L

Figure 21.1   *Network Analysis*

Question 3

1 General

We are interested in testing our belief that a market exists for UK based holidays/leisure breaks for upper/middle-market clientele.

Should the market opportunity be of sufficient size to justify investment we are concerned to target our market closely, and to evaluate specific consumer needs and perceptions in order that the venture may be tailored to satisfy identified quantified need.

Note: we are avoiding specific reference to 'holiday' or 'leisure break' etc. at this time as we believe that terminology will be crucial to the perception of our offering (e.g. we will not be opening 'holiday camps').

2 Background

A secondary data search (see Appendix *) appears to indicate that there is substantial coverage of down-market holiday centres (e.g. Butlins) and that holidays with children are provided for in plenty.

It further appears that there is a growing tendency for up-market consumers to take second and third holidays/leisure breaks in addition to the main holiday which will be taken overseas.

It also seems that there is a sufficiently large potential demand from the B/C1 S/E groups, and that this is only just beginning to be provided for (e.g. Center Parcs and some 4/5 star hotels).

*Appendices: Note to examiner: these not included, but would be

- appendices from the case, as issued;
- my development of the initial data, including the cross referencing etc.;
- competitive literature that I would have collected, as routine, had I not been instructed to refrain.

There is, we believe, an oppportunity to enter this market with a carefully planned package that is well conceived and properly funded.

3 Market Segment

We believe:
- 3.1 that our prime target consumers will be couples from social groups B/C1 aged between 25 and 50, married and/or enjoying a stable relationship. They will want to take a break without children, and will be able to make arrangements for their children while they are away. They will have a high level of disposable income, and expect 4 star hotel standard as the normal minimum;
- 3.2 that they will respond to a package offering short breaks, three, four or seven days (exactly as Center Parcs);
- 3.3 that the package will need to be tailored to a theme, or series/ combination of themes from which will come our USPs.

4   Research requirement

4.1   Immediate
Within a 95% confidence level:
4.1.1   Identification and quantification of the segment described in (3) above. We would expect to see ACORN classifications replacing the S/E broad band segmentation used to date.
4.1.2   Identification and quantification of the current use and anticipated need for 'supplementary' holidays/leisure breaks in the UK by the segment(s) identified in (4.1.1).
4.2   Supplemental (and dependent upon the results of (4.1)):
4.2.1   Identification of the individual, series or combination of theme(s) to which the segment will respond.
4.2.2   Identification and quantification of potential market of visitors to the UK from the continent who would respond favourably to the theme(s) identified in (4.2.1).

5   Timescale

Proposal   required two weeks from today.
Stage 4.1   report required within six weeks from proposal acceptance.
Stage 4.2   report required within five months of our authority to proceed following (4.1).

6   Proposal

Your proposal for the conduct of this research should include: specification of the research you propose; methods to be used; sample design; data to be collected; the security protection that will be in force; a clear indication of cost, broken down for each stage.

7   Supplementary Data

Provided as Appendices to this brief are: the secondary data from which we have drawn our provisional conclusions, a range of literature from the marketplace.

8   Contact

Management of this initiative is the responsibility of the undersigned, to whom all enquiries and/or requests for supplementary briefing etc., should be directed.

Chris Knight
New Product Development

Question 4

I am using the term 'line manager' to indicate one who is managing a product or function anywhere in ICCC except in NPD.

I do not see that management, as such, is any different in NPD. It is the achievement of results through people. The differences are ones of degree, and I feel that a time in NPD is of great help in the development of an individual.

Specifically:

1 Personnel

1.1 I would suggest a need for specific training, and support, especially in the early days of taking over as an NPD Manager. Team building when one is working across a range of disciplines (accounts, production, design, marketing etc.) is not easy.

1.2 Recruitment is never easy – there is need for staff to have a width of perception, for minds that welcome new concepts and that are capable of well-channelled imagination. For people who are self-starters, yet can develop synergy in a team.

I know of no psychological tests that are of help (perhaps none exist?). Therefore there is sometimes need to return a new team member to whence he or she came, without damage to ego, career, departmental relationships or damage to the NPD team. Not easy!

1.3 Best source of NPD staff is from ICCC operating departments – they know the company, the system . . . but they also bring their perceptions of what is possible (See 1.2 above.)

I believe that a team is healthier for one member who is recruited from outside ICCC – but not from NPD elsewhere.

2 Relationships

2.1 Relations upwards are crucial – it is sometimes extremely hard to get a precise objective, expressed clearly, from top management. Understandable – they are very busy. But the NPD manager often (always?) has to reformulate a brief and take it back for approval. He or she must then allow the superior to take credit for the whole brief. A lot of tact, and discrete self-effacement needed!

2.2 Other departments can be jealous of NPD, and the high status that it acquires through its highly confidential projects and its access to top management. This sometimes reveals itself in petty ways, designed to be obstructive while appearing to be quite justified. (Am I getting paranoid? It can be a problem for NPD I am coming to believe.)

2.3 External agencies are usually fine to work with – but there can be problems when using an agency already working for a line manager (e.g. research for NPD and for current product marketing, where the marketing manager may feel shut out – snubbed – especially if the agency expect him to know, and he naturally does not). This is a delicate area, calling for very careful briefing and tactful handling.

3   Budget

No problems here that a line manager does not have. There is usually not enough, and one has to fight one's corner.

4   Disengagement

When it comes time to turn the NPD over to line management there can be problems in getting staff to disengage. Temptation is to want to stay with the product, and to 'mother' it (to the point of 'smotheration') long after it rightfully belongs to line management.

5   Credit

There can be a problem in defining clear objectives against which to measure success. It is probably not the successful launch, certainly not the mature product. But where, exactly, does one take credit for success – and walk away satisfied?

6   Idea generation

Successful trawling for new ideas cannot be confined to NPD alone. Yet the development of ideas is confidential to NPD. There must be feedback to ideas generators, in the fullness of time; and this must be managed.

7   Idea management

Clear responsibility must be assigned, with authority delegated – no difference here to a 'normal' line manager.

8   Decisive capacity

The ability to establish criteria, and to measure against them for a series of go/no-go decisions is crucial. This has to be taught, in the majority of cases; but it is a lesson of inestimable value when the individual returns to line management.

9   Overall

The role of NPD is unique, shrouded in secrecy, yet dependent upon the goodwill and support of line management. Members of the NPD team should see their secondment as career progression, and developmental.

It is for the NPD manager carefully to select, train, monitor, motivate. In this he or she is no different from a line manager. The variation is one of degree, of emphasis, rather than of managerial quality.

Chris Knight
New Product Development

APPENDICES: ROUGH WORK

Question 1

Feasibility of venture
Review – team – macro-environment – agree with Board Background – sterling value
– holiday patterns

Policy – Hollins – B/C1, UK Citizens Strategy – 3 months – awareness – control

Tactics – B/C1, London & S. East – Continent of Europe

Competition – five, £200 p.w.

Product – Holiday v Historical themes, S.W. England

Finance – S.W., 320 acres, 6,000 sq. yds of buildings – – Payback period

Summary – 75% confidence

Board Issues – commitment – 3 year time horizon – ability to recruit staff?

Question 2

Approval given 1st February !!!!

Network analysis

    – events time scale
    – proceeding event(s)
    – critical path

Conclusion – reduced time scale
         – identify activities which have slack

Tutorial note

The potential for a Network should have been noted, and a schematic prepared in advance. In the examination room it is then only necessary to amend the time scale (if necessary) and add actual dates (again if necessary). The Network shown as part of this answer could not have been produced in the examination room – but it could have been copied from notes straight into the answer book.

Question 3

Who is responsible – ME!

No preconceptions – not 'camp'

Secondary search – down market (Butlins, etc.), camps, water, children.

Children (drag?) – parents leave behind.

B/C1 up-market ... but need for tighter definition (ACORN).

Center Parcs package – use case appendix.

USP – role for research ... first discover segment, prevent continuance without approval.

Time scale – 2, 6, 16 weeks? Perhaps 20?

Proposal – level of confidence – cost – time – method – validity - security, sample, questionnaire (?)

Our work to agency? YES

Question 4

KOTLER – Marketing Management, Analysis, Planning & Control 5th edition, pp 313/315.

Personnel – recruitment, selection, training, support, dismissal, source?

Relationships – upwards, downwards, sideways. – co-operation/jealousy

Agencies – relationship – with other line depts too?

People – a career path, in and out? Show I see it as progressive, I want to move on and out and up.

Budget – as any other line manager?

Contact with senior management – privileged info? Jealousy again.

Getting out/away, disengaging? and giving credit?

Ideas – management, giving up, generating, scapping, go/no go ...

[DECISIONS DECISIVE CAPACITY AND ACTION!]

Similar but different. Not unique, not special. A stepping stone (but a valuable/important one).

Index